CIMA EXAMINATION TEXT

Foundation Level

Paper 2

Management Accounting Fundamentals

ISBN 1 84390 091 2

British Library Cataloguing-in-Publication data

A catalogue record for this book is available from the British Library.

We are grateful to the Chartered Institute of Management Accountants for permission to reproduce past examination questions. The solutions have been prepared by The Financial Training Company.

Published by

> The Financial Training Company
> 22J Wincombe Business Park
> Shaftesbury
> Dorset
> SP7 9QJ

All rights reserved. No part of this publication may be reproduced, stored in a retrieval system, or transmitted, in any form or by any means, electronic, mechanical, photocopying, recording or otherwise, without the prior written permission of The Financial Training Company.

© The Financial Training Company 2002

Contents

	Page
How to use this examination text	v
Syllabus	vii
Mathematical tables and formulae	xi
Meaning of CIMA's examination requirements	xii
Objective test questions	xiii

Chapter

		Page
1	Introduction to cost and management accounting	1
2	Accounting for materials	11
3	Accounting for labour	31
4	Accounting for overheads using absorption costing	39
5	Absorption and marginal costing	63
6	Job, batch and contract costing	73
7	Service costing	87
8	Process costing	93
9	Cost bookkeeping	113
10	Introduction to decision making and the limiting factor decision	133
11	Cost volume profit analysis	153
12	Budgeting	167
13	Budgetary control	189
14	Standards and standard setting	199
15	Variance analysis	205
16	Solutions to practice questions	227
Index		299

How to use this examination text

Objective

The aim of this Examination Text is a simple one: to give you the best possible chance of achieving the pass mark when you attempt the CIMA Management Accounting Fundamentals examination. To do this, we follow three main principles:

- The texts cover **all** areas of the syllabus with sufficient depth to ensure that you are fully prepared. However, we use our knowledge and experience to home in on the key syllabus areas and give these areas extra attention.

- We use our extensive experience of teaching CIMA students to assess how much the majority of students can assimilate. We do not make the mistake of overloading you with material that you will find worthless in the examination room.

- We believe that the best way to prepare for an examination is by practice. We intersperse explanatory text with frequent examples for you to try your hand at. Full solutions are provided in all cases.

Using the Examination Text

Each chapter begins with a section headed 'Exam focus'. This reflects our key objective: we are interested above all in your examination success.

We set out CIMA's own Learning Outcomes and the main structural divisions into which the chapter is organised. This gives you a clear picture of what you should be aiming to achieve as you work through the text, and guidance on the steps to follow on the way.

The main body of each chapter consists of very full explanation of all syllabus areas. We concentrate on clear explanations of what really matters. We emphasise drills — standardised approaches that you can follow for typical questions. Never again need you ask: 'Where do I begin?'

Each chapter includes practice questions. These are graded: earlier questions involve material from the earlier sections of the chapter, while in later questions we progress to include more complex examples, including exam-standard questions. To get the best from the text you should make a serious attempt to tackle all the practice questions. Only then should you refer to our suggested solutions, which are contained in the final chapter of the text.

Each chapter ends by summarising the main points that you should have digested as you worked your way through.

Key features

The text is written in an interactive style:

- key terms and concepts are clearly defined

- 'pitfalls' and 'examination tips' help you avoid commonly made mistakes and help you focus on what is required to perform well in your examination

- frequent practice examples throughout the chapters ensure that what you have learnt is regularly reinforced

Icons

Throughout the text we use symbols to highlight the elements referred to above.

 Key facts

 Examination tips and techniques

 Pitfalls

 Practice questions

Syllabus

Syllabus overview

Management Accounting is an introduction to management accounting for students with limited knowledge or no knowledge of this subject. While this paper focuses on the application of fundamental methods and techniques, students are also expected to have an understanding of when and when not to use them. Students must also appreciate the contribution made by information technology to management accounting.

Aims

This syllabus aims to test the student's ability to:

- Explain the basic concepts and processes used to determine product and service costs.

- Explain absorption cost, marginal cost, opportunity cost, notional cost and relevant cost concepts.

- Apply C-V-P analysis and interpret the results.

- Apply a range of costing and accounting systems.

- Explain the role of budgets and standard costing within organisations.

- Prepare and interpret budgets, standard costs and variance statements.

Assessment

The examination will be a computer based examination.

All the questions will be objective test questions.

Learning outcomes and syllabus content

	Chapter where covered in this textbook
2(i) Cost determination – 30%	
Learning outcomes	
On completion of their studies students should be able to:	
♦ Explain why organisations use costing systems	1
♦ Explain raw material accounting and control procedures	2
♦ Explain and calculate re-order quantity, re-order level, maximum stock, minimum stock and economic order quantity	2
♦ Explain FIFO, LIFO and weighted average stock valuation methods	2
♦ Explain labour accounting and control procedures	3
♦ Discuss and calculate factory incentive schemes for individuals and groups	3
♦ Explain absorption costing	4
♦ Prepare cost statements for allocation and apportionment of overheads including reciprocal service departments	4

	Chapter where covered in this textbook
♦ Calculate and discuss overhead absorption rates	4
♦ Calculate under/over recovery of overheads	4
♦ Calculate product costs under absorption and marginal costing	5
♦ Compare and contrast absorption and marginal costing	5

Syllabus content

♦ Classification of costs	1
♦ Materials: accounting and control procedures	2
♦ Labour: accounting and control procedures	3
♦ Factory incentive schemes for individuals and groups	4
♦ Overhead costs: allocation, apportionment, re-apportionment and absorption of overhead costs. NB the repeated distribution method only will be used for reciprocal service department costs	4
♦ Absorption costing	5
♦ Marginal costing	5
♦ Materials: re-order quantity, re-order level, maximum stock, minimum stock, economic order quantity	2

2(ii) Standard costing – 15%

Learning outcomes

On completion of their studies students should be able to:

♦ Explain the principles of standard costing	14
♦ Prepare the standard cost for a product/service	14
♦ Calculate and interpret variances for sales, materials; labour; variable overheads and fixed overheads	15
♦ Prepare a report reconciling budget gross profit/contribution with actual profit	15

Syllabus content

♦ Principles of standard costing	14
♦ Preparation of standard costs under absorption and marginal costing	14
♦ Variances: materials: total, price and usage; labour: total, rate and efficiency, variable overhead: total expenditure and efficiency; fixed overhead: total, expenditure and volume (absorption costing); fixed overhead: expenditure (marginal costing); sales: total sales margin variance	15

2(iii) Costing and accounting systems – 20%

Learning outcomes

On completion of their studies students should be able to:

♦ Compare and contrast job, batch, contract and process costing systems	6, 8
♦ Prepare ledger accounts for job, batch, contract (in accordance with SSAP 9) and process costing systems. NB the average cost method will only be used for process costing and students must be able to calculate normal losses and abnormal loss/gains and deal with opening and closing stocks	6, 8
♦ Prepare and contrast cost statements for service and manufacturing organisations	7

	Chapter where covered in this textbook
♦ Prepare profit and loss accounts from the same data under absorption and marginal costing and reconcile and explain the differences in reported profits	5
♦ Prepare accounting entries for an integrated accounting system using standard costs	9, 15
♦ Explain the difference between integrated and interlocking accounting systems	9

Syllabus content

♦ Job, batch, contract and process costing	6, 8
♦ Cost accounting statements for services and service industries	7
♦ Marginal and absorption costing profit and loss accounts	5
♦ Accounting entries for an integrated accounting system	9, 15
♦ Interlocking accounting	9

2(iv) Marginal costing and decision making – 15%

Learning outcomes

On completion of their studies students should be able to:

♦ Identify relevant costs and revenues	10
♦ Identify cost behaviour	1
♦ Explain the contribution concept	5
♦ Calculate and interpret the break even point, profit target, margin of safety and profit volume ratio for a single product	11
♦ Prepare break even charts and profit/volume graphs for a single product	11
♦ Calculate the profit-maximising sales mix for a company with a single resource constraint which has total freedom on action	10
♦ Discuss C-V-P analysis	11

Syllabus content

♦ Relevant cost concepts, including sunk costs, committed costs and opportunity costs	10
♦ Fixed, variable and semi-variable costs	1, 10
♦ Contribution concept	5
♦ Break even charts, profit volume graphs, break even point, profit target, margin of safety, contribution/sales ratio	11
♦ Limiting factor analysis	10

2(v) Budgeting – 20%

Learning outcomes

On completion of their studies students should be able to:

♦ Explain why organisations prepare budgets	12
♦ Explain how organisations prepare budgets	12
♦ Explain the use of IT in the budget process	12
♦ Prepare functional budgets, profit and loss account, balance sheet and a simple cash budget	12
♦ Calculate simple cost estimates using high-low method and line of best fit	13

	Chapter where covered in this textbook
♦ Prepare simple reports showing actual and budgeted results	13
♦ Explain the differences between fixed and flexible budgets	13
♦ Prepare a fixed and flexible budget	13
♦ Calculate expenditure, volume and total budget variances	13

Syllabus content

♦ Budget theory	12
♦ Budget preparation	12
♦ IT and budgeting	12
♦ Cost estimation and estimating techniques	13
♦ Reporting of actual against budget	13
♦ Fixed and flexible budgeting	13

MATHEMATICAL TABLES AND FORMULAE

INVENTORY CONTROL

EOQ basic model $\sqrt{\dfrac{2C_O D}{C_H}}$

where:	C_O = cost of placing an order

C_H = stockcarrying cost

D = annual demand

Meaning of CIMA's examination requirements

CIMA use precise words in the requirements of their questions. In the schedule below we reproduce the precise meanings of these words from the CIMA syllabus. You must learn these definitions and make sure that in the exam you do precisely what CIMA requires you to do.

Learning objective	Verbs used	Definition
1 Knowledge What you are expected to know	List	Make a list of
	State	Express, fully or clearly, the details of/facts of
	Define	Give the exact meaning of
2 Comprehension What you are expected to understand	Describe	Communicate the key features of
	Distinguish	Highlight the differences between
	Explain	Make clear or intelligible/state the meaning of
	Identify	Recognise, establish or select after consideration
	Illustrate	Use an example to describe or explain something
3 Application Can you apply your knowledge?	Apply	To put to practical use
	Calculate/compute	To ascertain or reckon mathematically
	Demonstrate	To prove with certainty or to exhibit by practical means
	Prepare	To make or get ready for use
	Reconcile	To make or prove consistent/compatible
	Solve	Find an answer to
	Tabulate	Arrange in a table
4 Analysis Can you analyse the detail of what you have learned?	Analyse	Examine in detail the structure of
	Categorise	Place into a defined class or division
	Compare and contrast	Show the similarities and/or differences between
	Construct	To build up or compile
	Discuss	To examine in detail by argument
	Interpret	To translate into intelligible or familiar terms
	Produce	To create or bring into existence
5 Evaluation Can you use your learning to evaluate, make decisions or recommendations?	Advise	To counsel, inform or notify
	Evaluate	To appraise or assess the value of
	Recommend	To advise on a course of action

Objective test questions

There are several forms of objective test questions.

(a) Multiple choice questions. These are explained in more detail below.

(b) Single number entry questions. These are calculation questions similar to those found in this book but, rather than producing the entire answer, you will simply be required to produce a single number to be entered in the answer. The questions may require more than one number to be entered in the appropriate place.

(c) True or false questions.

(d) Identifying key features of a diagram.

This list is not exhaustive and you should read relevant CIMA notices for further details.

Multiple choice questions

A multiple choice question will comprise a question with four possible answers. For example,

1   What is the world's tallest mountain?

    A   Ben Nevis

    B   K2

    C   Mount Everest

    D   Mount Snowdon

You have to select the correct answer (which in the above example is of course C).

In the examination, however, the incorrect answers, called distractors, may be quite plausible and are sometimes designed if not exactly to mislead you, they may nevertheless be the result of fairly common mistakes.

The following is a suggested technique for answering these questions, but as you practise for the examination you have to work out a method which suits you.

Step 1

Read all the questions, but not necessarily the answers. Select the ones which you think are the most straightforward and do them first.

Step 2

For more awkward questions, some people prefer to work the question without reference to the answers which increases your confidence if your answer then matches one of the options. However some people prefer to view the question with the four answers as this may assist them in formulating their answer.

This is a matter of personal preference and you should perhaps practise each to see which you find most effective.

Step 3

If your answer does not match one of the options you must:

(a) Re-read the question carefully to make sure you have not missed some important point.

(b) Re-work your solution eliminating any mistakes.

(c) Beware the plausible distractors but do not become paranoid. The examiner is not trying to trip you up and the answer should be a straightforward calculation from the question.

CHAPTER 1

Introduction to cost and management accounting

EXAM FOCUS

This chapter introduces several terms which you must learn since it lays the foundation for much of what follows. You may be asked to define and give examples of this terminology in the examination. It is imperative that you understand the nature of fixed and variable costs and give examples if asked in the examination. The high low method of identifying fixed and variable elements of semi-variable costs always features in the examination and you must be totally confident in this calculation.

LEARNING OUTCOMES

This chapter covers the following Learning Outcomes of the CIMA Syllabus.

> Explain why organisations use costing systems
>
> Identify cost behaviour

In order to cover these Learning Outcomes the following topics are included.

> Identify the internal and external users of accounting information
>
> Distinguish between cost and management accounting and financial accounting
>
> Examine the role of the cost and management accountant in providing information to management for decision-making, planning and control
>
> Define the meaning of cost
>
> Identify the different ways in which cost and sales revenues can be classified:

- By nature
- By direct and indirect
- By function
- By cost behaviour

> Define terminology commonly used in cost and management accounting:

- Cost Unit
- Cost Centre
- Profit Centre

1 Internal and external users of accounting information

Accounting information is communicated to people who have an interest in the organisation. The following list are some of those people:

- Managers
- Shareholders
- Potential investors
- Employees
- Creditors
- Government

Accounting information is also provided for decision-making purposes.

The above users can be divided into **internal** and **external** parties. Accounting can also be divided into internal and external aspects ie external being financial accounts and internal being cost and management accounts.

2 Cost and management v financial accounting

Accountants have to provide information to very diverse groups (see above list). The specific needs of each determine whether these can best be served by the financial accounting or the management accounting function of the business organisation. Financial accounting may be the branch of accounting with which you will have most contact. The main differences between financial accounting and management accounting are:

(a) financial accounting provides information to users who are external to the business, whereas management accounting is usually concerned with internal users of accounting information such as the managers of the business;

(b) financial accounting draws up financial statements, the formats of which are governed by law and accounting standards for limited companies, whereas management accounting reports can be in any format which suits the user and may differ considerably from one company to another;

(c) financial accounting reports on past transactions, but management accounting records historic transactions, compares actual figures to budget figures and hence makes predictions for the future.

3 The role of the cost and management accountant

3.1 The role of the cost accountant

The main role of the cost accountant is to provide information to management. He/she is responsible for collecting and recording historical costs, analysing actual results against targets and using historical information to predict future costs.

3.2 The role of the management accountant

The management accountant is more senior than the cost accountant – his/her role involves presenting and interpreting information for management. They also have an advisory role to management assisting them in:

- **Planning** – long and short term objectives of the company
- **Organising** – co-ordinating staff to ensure the objectives are achieved
- **Controlling** the actual performance against the plan, identifying deviations and taking corrective action where necessary
- **Communicating** plans and results
- **Motivating** staff to achieve plans by including them in the planning process

4 The meaning of cost

The users of accounting information may wish to know the cost of something eg a product or service. Cost accounting is concerned with the calculation of this cost for use in a variety of ways. If, for example, we were asked to cost an item of furniture eg a table, we would consider the following cost items:

Example – table

Materials: screws
             frame
             wood

Labour: rate paid × number of hours taken

Overheads: Rent, rates, depreciation etc

Once the above production cost is established for our table we would then add an amount to cover selling, distribution and administration to arrive at total cost. In order to establish the selling price for our table we would then add a percentage mark-up. The percentage mark-up would then represent the profit element.

5 Cost classification

5.1 Introduction

There are many different types of cost. Classification involves forming logical, useful groups of costs. By doing this it makes it easier to understand, use and communicate to others.

The type of classification depends on the purpose to which the information will be put.

There are four main classification groups:

- By nature of the cost
- By direct/indirect cost
- By function
- By behaviour of the cost

5.2 Classification by nature

This involves grouping costs according to their type:

Material   - Cost of materials directly or indirectly used in production

Labour   - Cost of labour directly or indirectly used in production

Expenses   - Costs which are neither materials or labour directly or indirectly used in production

5.3 Classification by direct/indirect cost

This involves grouping costs according to their relationship with production ie:

Direct cost

Direct costs are those which can be related specifically to a cost unit. They are normally identified under three headings:

(a) *Direct materials* – the cost of materials entering into and becoming constituent elements of a product or service. The term "materials" covers raw materials (like the quantity of raw cotton used to produce a length of thread), components (like those used in assembling a television set) and finished products (like the quantity of paper used in printing a book).

(b) *Direct labour* – the cost of remuneration for working time applied directly to a product or service, such as the manual assembly time for the television set or the time spent in carrying out a property conveyancing by a solicitor.

(c) *Direct expenses* – other costs which are incurred for a specific product or service. Typical examples would be the hire of earth-moving equipment for a particular public works contract, or the cost of work sub-contracted to a third party.

The total of all direct costs is sometimes referred to as the **prime cost** of the product or activity concerned.

Indirect costs

All other costs, whether materials, wages or expenses, are termed indirect costs or "overheads".

They will normally be identified with cost centres, where they can be controlled by the managers responsible. The costs of management at all levels and of the provision of administrative services will fall into this category.

It may also include certain items which enter into a product but could not be identified with particular cost units without analytical effort disproportionate to any improvement in the accuracy of the product cost. A possible example is the relatively minor cost of screws, fixings and fastenings used in an assembly operation. The cost of such items, although classified as indirect, would be "variable" with the quantity of output achieved.

5.4 Classification by function

A manufacturing organisation is usually split into three broad functions:

- Production – cost of converting the raw materials into finished goods
- Administration – cost of managing the organisation
- Selling and distribution – cost of securing orders and despatching goods

Most costs will fall into these three categories.

The distinction between production and other costs is essential for stock valuation purposes, as we shall see.

5.5 Classification by cost behaviour

This involves grouping costs on the basis of their reaction to changes in activity.

Costs which change with activity are known as **variable costs.**

Costs which remain constant regardless of changes in activity are known as **fixed costs** (which may be **stepped**).

Costs which react to changes in activity but contain an element that doesn't are known as **semi-variable costs**.

We now consider these in more detail:

(a) *Variable cost*

A cost which varies with a measure of activity eg direct materials.

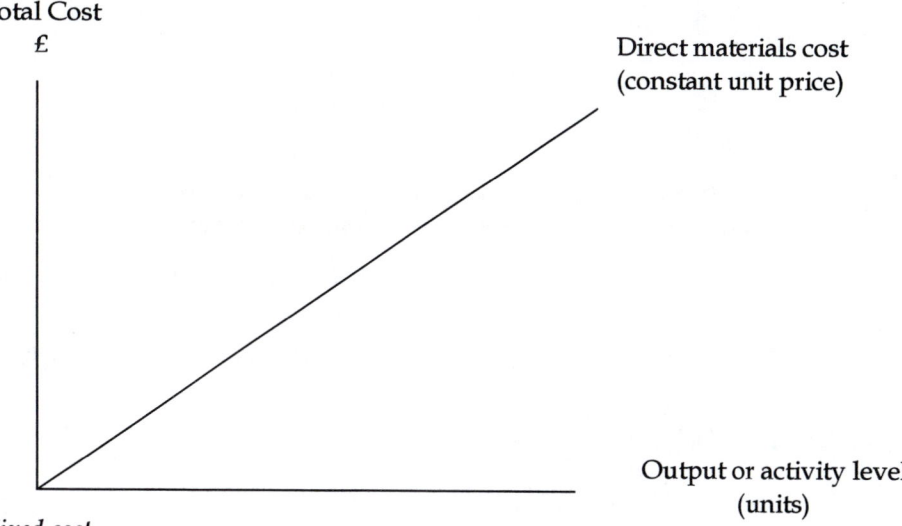

(b) *Fixed cost*

This is a cost which is incurred for an accounting period, and which within certain output or turnover limits, tends to be unaffected by fluctuations in the levels of activity eg rent.

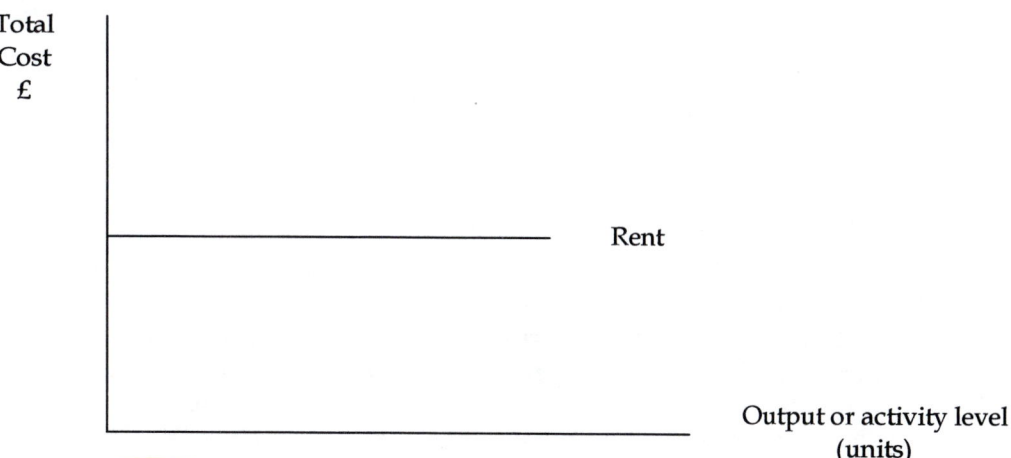

(c) *Semi-variable cost*

This is a cost which contains both fixed and variable components and which is thus partly affected by a change in the level of activity. Two examples are shown below:

(i) Salesmen's remuneration with added commission from a certain level of activity.

(ii) Electricity charges comprising fixed standing charge and variable unit charge.

5

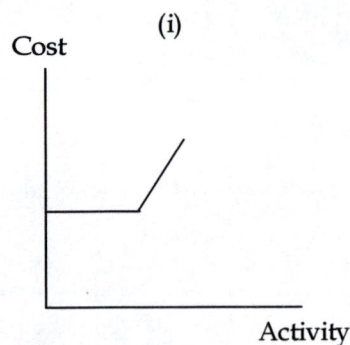
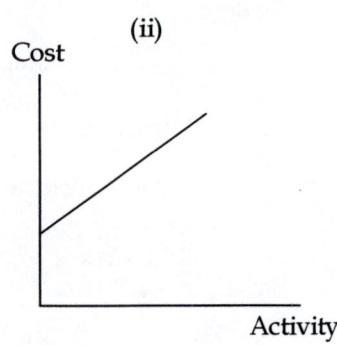

(d) *Stepped fixed cost*

A stepped fixed cost is where the fixed cost increases to a different level when certain levels of activity are reached. Two examples are shown below:

(i) Canteen cost where additional assistants are required as increases in activity result in larger numbers of factory personnel.

(ii) Rent of premises, additional accommodation eventually being required.

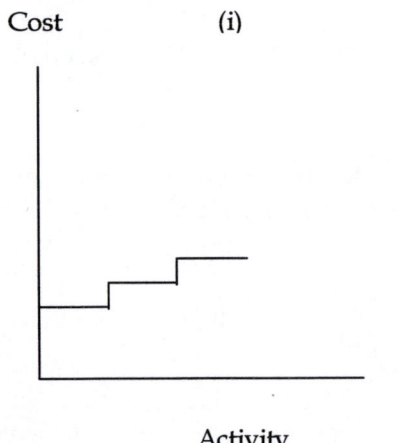
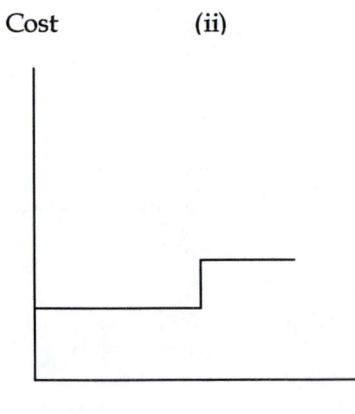

5.6 Splitting semi-variable costs

Where fixed and variable costs are known with reasonable accuracy total and unit costs may be predicted. Where semi-variable costs are present the situation is complicated and, in order to keep the model simple, the semi-variable costs are dealt with by splitting their fixed and variable portions and adding them to the other fixed and variable costs respectively. In order to split the semi-variable cost into fixed and variable components we use the high low method. This is an extremely important technique for your examination.

5.7 High Low Method - Example

Consider the following data:

Units produced per week	200	300	400	500	600	700	800
Total cost per week (£)	3,500	4,000	5,200	6,800	7,500	8,900	9,100

This method simply takes the highest and lowest numbers of units produced (activity levels) and bases the approximation on these.

Calculate the:

(a) variable cost per unit
(b) total fixed costs.

5.8 Solution

(a) Variable costs

increase in output between highest and lowest values = 800 – 200	600 units
increase in total costs = £9,100 – 3,500	£5,600

Assuming this increase is purely due to the additional variable cost attributable (at a constant rate per unit) to the extra 600 units:

variable cost per unit = $\dfrac{£5,600}{600}$ — £9.33

(b) Fixed costs

These are calculated as a balancing figure, as follows:

(i)
	£
Variable cost of 200 units = 200 × £9.33	1,866
Total cost of 200 units	3,500
Therefore, fixed cost	1,634

(ii) The answer would be the same if we considered 800 units

	£
Variable cost of 800 units = 800 × £9.33	7,464
Total cost of 800 units	9,100
Therefore, fixed cost	1,636

(Note that there is a small rounding error because the variable cost per unit is £9.33 recurring.)

5.9 Linear assumption of cost behaviour is allowed

The accountant is normally quite happy to assume that the cost function of a firm is linear even when this is not quite true. He argues that, while it may well be true that the function is not represented by a straight line on a graph, the activity range being considered is narrow enough to ensure that any loss of mathematical accuracy is not material to his calculations.

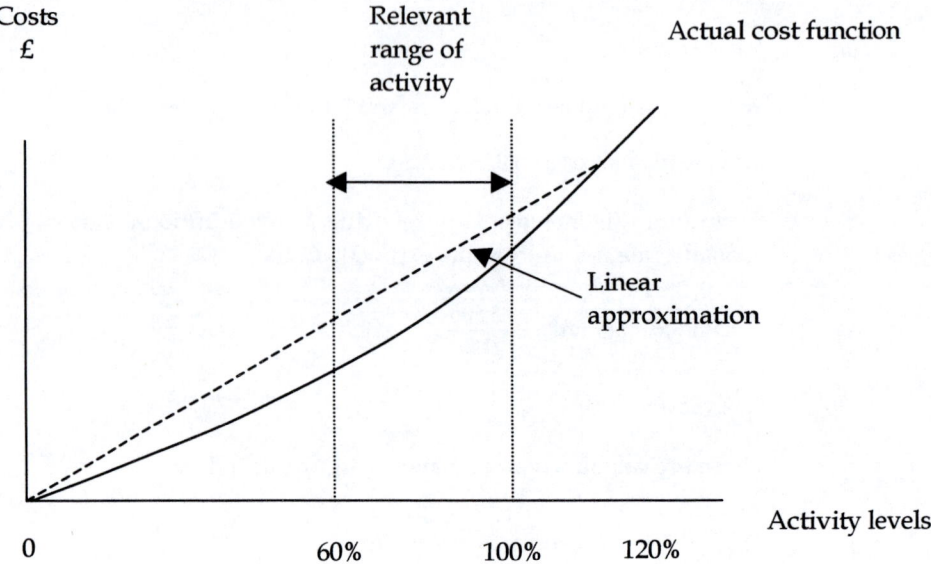

While the error taken between activity levels 0% and 120% may be quite large, a line drawn on the basis of the range of activity 60% to 100% shows a relatively close fit to the function curve. We can thus use our computed fixed and variable costs over this **'relevant range of activity'**.

For examination purposes it may be assumed that costs are linear unless the contrary is made clear. Practically, the assumption of linearity is still prevalent and acceptable – so long as the assumption is recognised – but as computers become more widely used it is likely that curvilinear cost behaviour will be recognised and used for prediction purposes; the benefits no longer being outweighed by the cost of calculation.

6 Terminology

The following terms will frequently occur in both the examination paper and within this text. It is important that you equip yourself with these terms:

6.1 Cost unit

A cost unit is defined as:

> "A unit of product or service in relation to which costs are ascertained."

6.2 Cost centre

A cost centre is defined as:

> "A production or service location, function, activity or item of equipment for which costs are accumulated."

6.3 Profit centre

A profit centre is defined as:

> "A part of a business accountable for both cost and revenues."

Chapter 1 Introduction to cost and management accounting

7   Summary

You should now be able to:

- Identify the internal and external users of accounting information
- Distinguish between management accounting, cost accounting and financial accounting
- Examine the role of the cost and management accountant in providing information to management for decision-making, planning and control
- Define the meaning of cost
- Identify the different ways in which cost can be classified
- Define terminology commonly used in cost and management accounting

Multiple choice questions *(The answers are in the final chapter of this book)*

1   Which of the following best describes a fixed cost? A cost which:

    A   represents a fixed proportion of total costs

    B   remains at the same level up to a particular level of output

    C   has a direct relationship with output

    D   remains at the same level when output increases

2   A business's telephone bill should normally be classified into which one of the following categories?

    A   Fixed cost

    B   Stepped fixed cost

    C   Semi-variable cost

    D   Variable cost

3   The total production cost for making 20,000 units was £21,000 and the total production cost for making 50,000 was £34,000. Once production exceeds 25,000 units, additional fixed costs of £4,000 are incurred. The full production cost per unit for making 30,000 units is:

    A   £0.30

    B   £0.68

    C   £0.84

    D   £0.93

4 The following data has been collected for four cost types:

W, X, Y, Z - at two activity levels:

Cost type	Cost @ 100 units £	Cost @ 140 units £
W	8,000	10,560
X	5,000	5,000
Y	6,500	9,100
Z	6,700	8,580

Where V = variable, SV = semi-variable and F = fixed, assuming linearity, the four cost types W, X, Y and Z are respectively:

	W	X	Y	Z
A	V	F	SV	V
B	SV	F	V	SV
C	V	F	V	V
D	SV	F	SV	SV

CHAPTER 2

Accounting for materials

EXAM FOCUS

This chapter introduces the principles of accounting for material. You must be able to explain the material accounting and control procedures as this could form a written question in the exam. Examination questions on stock control and valuation are common. You should ensure that you have understood the practical aspects of purchasing and controlling stocks of raw materials. The techniques described in this chapter also apply to other types of stock, such as finished goods.

LEARNING OUTCOMES

This chapter covers the following Learning Outcomes of the CIMA Syllabus.

> Explain raw material accounting and control procedures
>
> Explain and calculate re-order quantity, re-order level, maximum stock, minimum stock and economic order quantity
>
> Explain FIFO, LIFO and weighted average stock valuation methods
>
> Calculate stock, cost of sales and gross profit under LIFO, FIFO and weighted average

In order to cover these Learning Outcomes the following topics are included.

> Distinguish between direct and indirect materials
>
> Detail the documentation flow for the control and recording of materials
>
> Distinguish between periodic and continuous stocktaking
>
> Calculate stock control levels
>
> Calculating the EOQ using the formula and tabulation method
>
> Identify and calculate three alternative methods used for valuing material issues from stores to production and their subsequent effect on stock values.
>
> Compare and contrast the effect of LIFO, FIFO and weighted average methods on the cost of sales and gross profit of an organisation.

1 The distinction between direct and indirect materials

According to the nature of the activities carried on by a business, materials may be found in any of the following forms:

(a) Raw materials which are to be used in making a product: for example, flour and sugar used by a biscuit maker (direct material cost);

(b) Components for assembly into a finished product. The traditional type of clock or watch, for example, is produced by screwing or riveting together various shafts, gearwheels, levers and springs (direct material cost);

(c) Items which are used proportionately to the quantity or volume of a manufactured product, but which because of their small value are identified for costing purposes with the cost centres where they are used rather than with the cost units to which they relate. Examples may include nuts, bolts, rivets, screws, nails, paint. They may be referred to as 'consumables' (indirect material cost);

(d) 'Indirect materials' which are procured for use in one or more departments of the business. These can include stationery, drawing office supplies, cleaning materials, and fuel and lubricants for machines or motor vehicles (indirect material cost).

2 Documentation flow for the control and recording of materials

The four main documents used in accounting for purchases are:

- *a purchase requisition*, which is a request addressed to the buying officer or purchase manager by the person requesting materials (either the storekeeper or a departmental manager) asking him to obtain particular quantities of specified items;
- *a purchase order*, which is the official request from the company to a supplier, asking him to provide the goods required;
- *a goods received note*, (GRN) which is the company's record of what is actually received from the supplier;
- *the supplier's invoice* ('purchase invoice') which shows the charge made to the company and on which payments to the supplier are based.

This full set of documents will not necessarily be found in every case. The purchase requisition, for example, is only needed if there is a central buying office. It would not be necessary if managers requiring materials had authority to go out and buy them. A purchase order is sometimes omitted, particularly when supplies are needed urgently and are ordered by telephone or purchased out of petty cash. This is undesirable, and there should be a confirmatory order in every case for the following reasons:

(a) the order is evidence of the type of quality of the goods required and often of the purpose for which they are to be used;

(b) the order is the supplier's assurance that he has a valid claim against the company (this reason would not apply to cash purchases);

(c) by enforcing the use of official order forms, the company may make it more difficult for employees to make private purchases in the company's name.

3 Purchases accounting

3.1 Procedure

- When the supplier's invoice is received, its contents are checked with the copies of the purchase order, the goods received note and, where applicable, the inspection note. The quantities, prices, discounts, etc. shown are also checked, usually by the purchasing department.
- The invoice is sent to the accounts department for extensions, totals and deductions to be verified.

- The invoice (after having been stamped and initialled to prevent its being used again) is entered in the purchases daybook or journal, from which it will be credited to the supplier's account. Debit entries will be made, either individually or through periodic summaries, to the relevant nominal accounts.
- Unless the financial and costing records are integrated, a supplementary purchases analysis will be required as the medium for postings to job, departmental or stock accounts. The appropriate cost code numbers will be entered on the invoice at the time of approval, and where a purchase requisition exists they will be taken from that document.

3.2 Defective goods

When materials are defective the purchasing company will raise a debit note, the total of which will be debited to the supplier's account. It is common for the supplier, once he has agreed the company's charge, to issue his own credit note. The company will file this with a retained copy of its debit note, no additional accounting entries being necessary.

3.3 Payment

Unless there is a special agreement for payment to a particular supplier, payment will be made to all suppliers at regular intervals, usually monthly, the remittance covering the balance on each supplier's account at the end of the previous month.

No cheque should be drawn in favour of a supplier without an authority (eg a cheque requisition) first being obtained. Furthermore, all cheques should be signed by two responsible officials (eg two directors, or one director and the company secretary), although this will often in practice only happen for cheques above a certain value.

4 Stock recording

4.1 Introduction

There are three main methods of recording quantities of materials held in store – the bin card, the stock control card and the stores record card. The use of the word 'card' does not preclude the possibility of any/all of these being held on a computer.

4.2 The bin card

This is usually located near the point where the relevant stock item is stored. This records receipts and issues and shows the quantity of stock remaining after each transaction.

A simple form of bin card might be as shown below:

BIN CARD

Bin No: 342
Stock code: 21X123
Description: ½ inch bolts
Unit of issue: unit

Date	Ref	In	Out	Balance
01.1.X5				65
23.1.X5	R234		6	59
12.2.X5	R317		12	47
19.2.X5	R343		12	35
21.2.X5	GIN721	200		235

4.3 The stock control card

This will be kept in the stores office and incorporates additional data which will assist stock control and reordering. Possible basic information is shown in the following example:

Description	½ inch bolts	Max stock level	240
Material code	21X123	Min stock level	24
Location code	17	Ordering level	48
Bin No	342	Ordering quantity	200

Receipts			Issues			
Date	Qty	GR No	Date	Qty	Regn No	Balance in stock
01.1.X5						65
			23.1.X5	6	R234	59
			12.2.X5	12	R317	47
			19.2.X5	12	R343	35
21.2.X5	200	721				235

4.4 The stores record card

This incorporates the following additional information:

(i) quantities on order;

(ii) quantities demanded on material requisitions but which have not yet been issued because the items are not physically available (referred to as 'outstanding requisitions' or 'appropriations');

(iii) the 'free stock' balance which will be available when all outstanding purchase orders have been received and all outstanding appropriations have been satisfied.

An example of such a record is illustrated and explained in the following paragraphs.

This is sometimes known as a 'perpetual inventory system', although the expression is used in different ways by different writers.

STORES RECORD CARD

Description: 10cm Galvanised brackets
Code No: X3764

Reorder level: 230
Reorder quantity: 2,000

Date	On order – Qty ordered	On order – Qty received	On order – Balance on order	Receipts – Qty received	Receipts – Cumulative total	Issues – Qty issued	Issues – Cumulative total	Appropriations – Qty	Appropriations – Total outstanding	Free stock
1 Jan	2,000		2,000							2,000
4 Jan								300	300	1,700
15 Jan		1,600	400	1,600	1,600					
16 Jan						300	300	(300)	-	
22 Jan		400	-	400	2,000					
23 Jan								900	900	800
25 Jan								600	1,500	200
25 Jan	2,000		2,000							2,200
31 Jan						900	1,200	(900)	600	

This example records the following:

1 January   This is the first order for materials code number X3764. It is shown 'on order' and as the 'free stock' balance.

4 January   As 300 items were required, the 'appropriations' section shows this fact, while 'free stock' is reduced to 1,700.

15 January Part of the order (ie. 1,600 items) is received. This reduces the 'on order' balance to 400 while 1,600 items now appear in the 'receipts' section. (Note that this event does not affect the 'free stock' balance.)

16 January The 300 items needed are now requisitioned. The 'appropriations' balance falls to zero, while the 'issues' figure becomes 300. (Once again, the 'free stock' balance is not affected.)

You should now examine the entries for the remaining events in January. Note that when 600 items were appropriated on 25 January the 'free stock' balance fell to 200. As this figure was below the reorder level of 250, a fresh order for 2,000 was made on the same day.

The stores record card for this item of materials shows, as at 31 January:

(i)   800 units in stock (2,000 received less 1,200 issued) and 2,000 units on order – a total becoming available of 2,800 units;

(ii) 600 units appropriated but not yet issued, and 2,200 units unappropriated ('free stock'), accounting for the 2,800 units.

5 Periodic and continuous stock taking

5.1 Control of stocks

If stocks are to be controlled effectively it is unwise to rely entirely on stock records, however comprehensive. From time to time it is necessary to check the physical existence of the stocks and to make sure that the quantity seen is the same as the quantity recorded as in stock. There are three main methods for doing this:

(a)   storekeeper's own checks;

(b)   stocktaking ('physical inventory check') of all items at or near the year-end or at other regular intervals;

(c)   continuous independent stocktaking throughout the year (best done when stocks are at their lowest points).

5.2 Storekeeper's own checks

The storekeeper may be required to check from time to time that his physical stock holdings do agree with his bin cards or other records. A regular complete check would probably be too onerous, and he will often make a check only when the record shows that stocks have fallen to the reorder level.

Under some systems a predetermined minimum holding of each item will be kept in a separate bin, so that when he begins making issues from that bin he knows it is time to reorder and will make sure that the bin card shows the correct position. The disadvantages of any such system are:

- that there is no independent check on the storekeeper's work;
- the storekeeper may merely amend his records without reporting discrepancies;
- in consequence the stores ledger in the cost department may be incorrect.

5.3 Annual physical inventory (periodic)

Although annual stocktaking is quite common and may be necessary for financial accounting purposes, it has a number of disadvantages, particularly when many different items of stock are held. In particular:

- it may be necessary to close down operations whilst the stocktaking is in process;
- because many stock checkers will be needed, they may include people who have little knowledge of the items they are checking or who have little interest in the accuracy of their work. This stock count may therefore be inaccurate;
- discrepancies may be revealed some time after they have occurred, and investigation into their causes may therefore be difficult;
- the value of losses revealed may have a major effect on profits previously reported.

5.4 Continuous stocktaking

The procedure for continuous stocktaking is as follows:

(a)   a small team of people is appointed for the permanent task of stock checking. Alternatively employees in the cost office may be detailed to carry out stock checks from time to time when they can be released from other duties;

(b)   although the particular items to be checked each day may be chosen somewhat randomly, an attempt is made to ensure that over a year:

    (i)   all items of stock are checked;

    (ii)   fast-moving stock items are checked more frequently than those less in demand;

(c) a person selected to carry out a stock check is authorised to enter the stores for that purpose, but is not told the balance of stock recorded on the ledger card;

(d) after counting the stock, the person concerned reports back to the office with the number of items counted by him;

(e) if there is a discrepancy between the physical stock count and the recorded figure, the matter is investigated at once.

Very often, the discrepancy mentioned in (e) is due to materials requisition notes not having been processed at once. The fact that storemen do not know when particular items of stock are to be checked usually encourages them to deal with the requisition notes at once, without allowing a pile of them to accumulate on their counter.

The advantages of continuous stocktaking are:

- the physical check for annual stocktaking becomes unnecessary;
- disruption caused by annual stocktaking is avoided;
- regular skilled stocktakers can be employed, thus reducing likely errors;
- more time is available, thereby reducing errors and allowing investigation;
- discrepancies and losses are revealed sooner;
- production hold-ups are eliminated.

5.5 Stock losses

Stock may become 'lost' for a variety of reasons:

- Stock is stolen from stores
- Stock receipts or issues have been incorrectly recorded and hence the wrong number of items accounted for
- Deterioration (especially in the case of perishable items)
- Damage during stock counts or stock movements.

Stock losses should be accounted for as a stock issue on the record cards seen earlier. They should be accounted for as soon as they become apparent. However, it will often be the case that losses will only be detected at stocktake and will thus be accounted for at the stocktake date.

6 Stock control

6.1 Main objectives of stock control

(a) To maintain adequate stocks and thus minimise the risk of shortages which could disrupt production or cause customer dissatisfaction;

(b) to avoid excessive stock levels, and consequent tying-up of capital;

(c) to relieve management of taking frequent procurement decisions for every item carried in stock.

The achievement of these objectives is assisted by setting rules for the frequency of placing purchase orders and for the quantities to be ordered.

The two main methods are:

(a)   the periodic review system;

(b)   the reorder level system.

6.2   Periodic review

Under the periodic review system **purchase orders are placed** at **fixed intervals of time** (say monthly), and the quantity to be ordered on any occasion will be decided by reviewing the trend of demand for or usage of the item concerned.

This should help to avoid over-ordering, but if there should be an unexpected increase in demand the stock of an item may be exhausted before the next regular ordering date (or during the inevitable delay between placing an order and actually receiving the goods). It may be necessary, therefore, to hold a **buffer stock** or 'safety margin' to cover possible fluctuations in demand.

6.3   Reorder level system

The reorder level system involves deciding a level of stockholding at which new purchase orders shall be placed. Whenever stock falls to this '**reorder level**' an order will be placed for a **fixed quantity of the stock**. The 'reorder quantity' will have been decided having regard to the normal delivery delay and the expected usage of the stock during that delivery period.

Provided the delivery delay and the rate of usage are normal, the new delivery should be received before the existing stock is exhausted. To provide a safety margin against contingencies, however, a '**minimum level**' of stock holding will be fixed. If at any time stocks fall below that level the storekeeper will consider the need for a special emergency order.

The reorder quantity will ensure that when the goods are received the stock holding will be restored to an amount sufficient to last for a reasonable period ahead. This upper figure is known as the '**maximum level**'. If at any time the holding exceeds the maximum level, this provides a warning that demand must have declined, and the reorder quantity will have to be reviewed.

6.4   Stock levels

Therefore, there are four things that a company will need to decide on for each line of stock:

- Reorder level (ROL). When the level of stock falls to this amount, a fresh order should be made.
- The maximum stock level. Above this, capital is being tied up unnecessarily.
- The minimum stock level. Below this level, the company is in urgent need of replacing stock.
- The reorder quantity (ROQ). How many units should the company order at one time?

The above will be affected by two factors:

- Lead time – the time lag between the stock being ordered and being delivered.
- Usage – how quickly stock is being used up.

For example, if the company uses a large amount of a particular raw material (a high level of usage) the company might decide to have high levels in stock If the supplier takes a long time to deliver the stock (a high lead time) the company may have a high reorder level. Once the materials have been ordered it will still take a long time to receive them. During this time stock is still being used up. A high reorder level should prevent the company running out of raw materials.

18

6.5 Formulae used for stock control

These are not given in the examination and so must be learned. Notice that they should be calculated separately for each stock item, or group of related items.

- Reorder level (ROL)

  Maximum usage × maximum lead time.

  When stock falls to this level a fresh order is placed with the suppliers. The amount that is ordered is called the reorder quantity (ROQ).

- Maximum stock level

  ROL + ROQ − (minimum usage × minimum lead time).

  This is the maximum amount of stock that the company should hold. If the company is holding more than this amount of stock they will be wasting money by tying up capital unnecessarily.

- Minimum stock level

  ROL − (average usage × average lead time).

  Note that if the average is not given then use (maximum + minimum)/2.

  If stock levels fall below this amount then the company is in danger of running out of stock. An emergency stock order should be made to tide the company over until the next regular order is due.

In the examination if you are asked to calculate any stock holding quantities, you will probably be asked to comment on the stock holding policy of the company. If in doubt assume that the company is doing things incorrectly! For example they may be placing a fresh order when they are over the maximum required level or not placing any orders when they are below the reorder level.

6.6 Reorder quantity

The choice of reorder quantity may be derived using the EOQ model, which weighs up the conflicting patterns of costs associated with varying order quantities. This is covered in the next section.

6.7 Example

DL Holdings Ltd

Maximum usage per day	100 units
Minimum usage per day	50 units
Minimum lead time	20 days
Maximum lead time	30 days
Present reorder quantity (ROQ)	4,000 units

Required

Calculate the re-order level, maximum and minimum stock levels.

6.8 Solution

- Reorder level (ROL)

    Maximum usage × maximum lead time. In DL Holdings this is 100 × 30 = 3,000 units, ie reorder when stock level falls to 3,000 units. At this level a fresh order for 4,000 units will be placed.

- Maximum stock level (ROL + ROQ) − (minimum usage × minimum lead time). In DL Holdings this is 3,000 + 4,000 − (50 × 20) = 6,000 units.

    Note that by the time the delivery is made, DL will have at most 3,000 − (50 × 20) = 2,000 units in stock (the company places its order when stock falls to 3,000 units and uses 50 units a day for the 20 days it takes to receive fresh supplies). The order of 4,000 units will take them up to the maximum stock level. If demand is greater than 50 units a day or the delivery takes longer than 20 days the stock level will be less than 2,000 units when the delivery arrives, putting DL below the maximum level.

- Minimum stock level

    ROL − (average usage × average lead time). In DL this is 3,000 − (75 × 25) = 1,125 units. If stock levels fall below 1,125 units for whatever reason the company would have to place a rush order to restore stock levels.

7 The economic order quantity (EOQ)

7.1 Costs of holding and ordering stock

There are two types of cost associated with stock: ordering costs and holding costs.

Ordering costs

Each time the company places an order it has associated costs (representing administrative time, carriage etc).

The more orders that are placed the higher the total of these ordering costs becomes. It therefore makes sense to place just a few (large) orders to minimise these.

To minimise total ordering costs, large stock levels should be held.

Holding costs (also known as carrying costs)

Having a large amount of stock incurs costs since capital is tied up in the stock (ie money could have been sitting in the bank earning interest). Holding costs are therefore usually given as a percentage of the purchase price. To minimise these it makes sense to make lots of small purchases.

To minimise total holding costs, low stock levels should be held.

It should be clear that there is a conflict here: as ordering costs increase (by placing more smaller orders) holding costs will decrease and *vice versa*. There is a point at which the combined ordering and holding costs are at a minimum.

7.2 Example

Imagine that a company requires 4,000 units of a raw material in a year. The purchase price of the raw material is £10 per unit. Ordering costs are £12 each time an order is placed and holding costs are 6% of the purchase price.

The company is investigating possible reorder quantities and wish to minimise cost.

Required

Investigate the total cost of different ordering policies.

7.3 Solution

First look at the costs involved for the year if 4,000 units are purchased each time. There will be three different kinds of cost.

- The cost of purchasing the material.

    4,000 units at £10 per unit = £40,000.

- Total ordering costs

    If 4,000 units are ordered in one go then this will satisfy demand for the entire year. In this case only one order will need to be placed at a cost of £12. (Note that to find the number of orders required you should divide demand by the reorder quantity.) Total ordering costs will therefore be 1 × £12 = £12.

- Total holding costs

    If 4,000 units are ordered for the year then there will be an average of 2,000 units in store over the year (4,000 at the start of the year falling to nil by the end). The holding cost of *each* of these units is 6% of its purchase price, ie 6% × £10 = £0.60.

The total holding cost will therefore be 2,000 × £0.60 = £1,200. (Note that in general the average number of units in stock is half the reorder quantity.)

The total cost, if 4,000 units are ordered in one go is therefore £40,000 + £12 + £1,200 = £41,212.

Now do the same assuming that just one unit is ordered at a time:

- Total purchase price = 4,000 × £10 = £40,000.
- Total ordering costs = 4,000/1 × £12 = £48,000 (note that 4,000 orders will be required)
- Total holding cost = 0.5 × £0.60 = £0.30 (note that the average stock holding is half a unit)
- Total cost = £40,000 + £48,000 + £0.30 = £88,000.30.

We can repeat this for other re-order quantities and build up a table for the relevant ordering and holding costs.

Note: the purchase price has been ignored because it is the same for all order quantities, and therefore is not relevant in finding the minimum cost.

Q	N	TOC	A	THC	
	4000 ÷ Q	£12 × N	$\frac{Q}{2}$	0.6 × A	TOC + THC
Order quantity	Number of orders	Total ordering cost	Average units in stock	Total holding cost	Total cost
		£		£	£
200	20	240	100	60	300
400	10	120	200	120	240
600	6.67	80	300	180	260
800	5	60	400	240	300
1000	4	48	500	300	348

Based on the above it can be seen that ordering 400 units at a time gives the lowest total cost. This re-order quantity is known as the *economic order quantity* (EOQ).

7.4 Graphical illustration

The graph below illustrates the total ordering costs, total holding costs and total costs for the above order quantities.

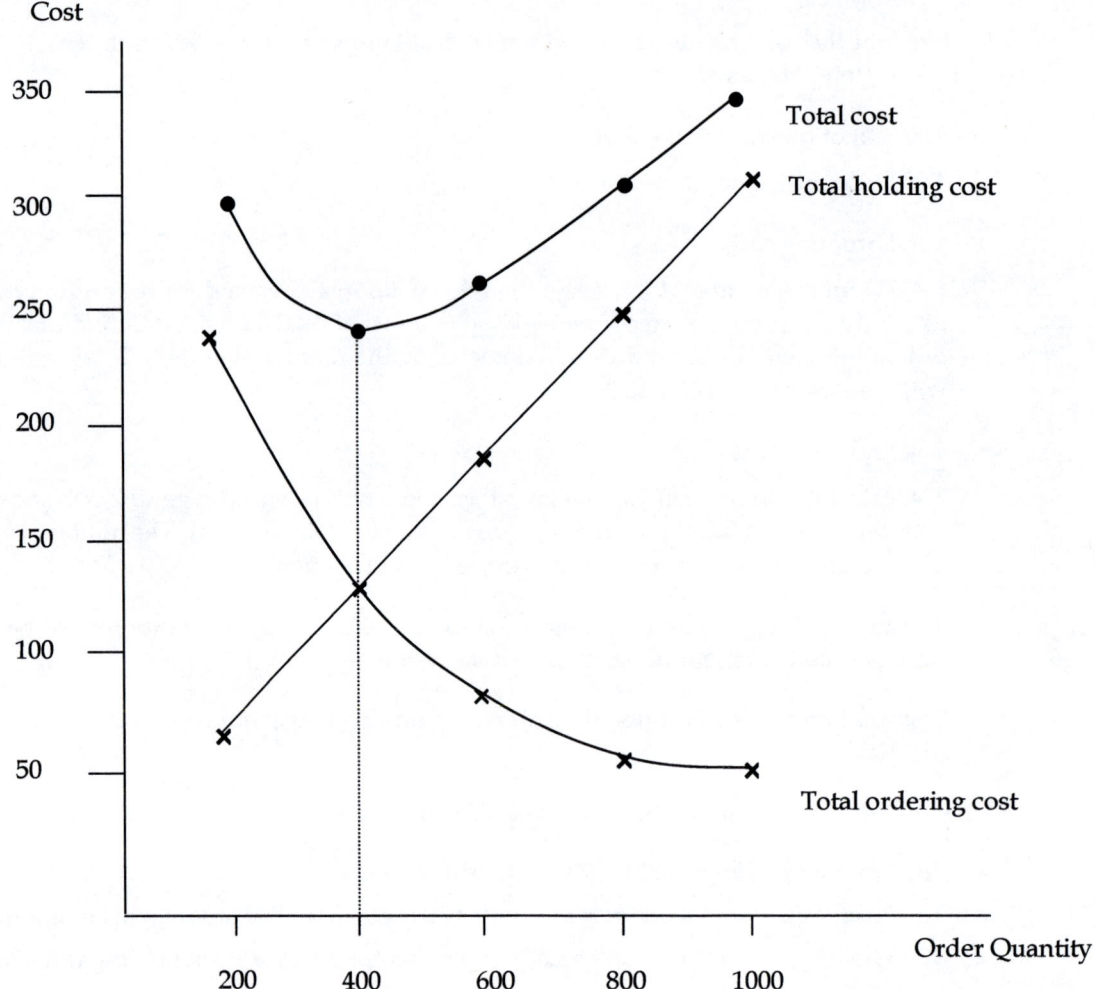

7.5 EOQ formula

Rather than going through all of the above there is a formula for calculating the EOQ quickly (this is given to you in the examination).

Economic order quantity $= \sqrt{\dfrac{2 \times C_O \times D}{C_H}}$

Where:

C_O = cost per order
D = annual demand
C_H = cost of holding one unit for a year

In our example above

C_O = £12
D = 4,000 units
C_H = £10 × 6% = £0.60

Substituting these into the formula gives:

Economic order quantity $= \sqrt{\dfrac{2 \times 12 \times 4,000}{0.6}}$ = 400 units as before.

✓ It should be noted that the economic quantity is just one possible reorder quantity and the company can decide to ignore it. If you are only given the economic order quantity in the exam then use this in place of the reorder quantity in stock control formulae.

7.6 Discounts

If a supplier is offering a discount on the purchase price of a product remember the following points.

- The discount affects the holding cost – since the purchase price is reduced the holding cost per unit goes down.
- The total cost of purchasing the goods will be reduced because of the discount. (This may make it worthwhile to order a different amount from the EOQ).

7.7 Example

In the above example assume that the supplier would grant a discount of 5% if orders were placed for 2,000 units at a time. Does this affect the choice of optimum re-order quantity?

7.8 Solution

Total cost = purchase price + ordering cost + holding cost

Taking account of the discount we can revise our calculations for the reorder quantity of 2,000 as follows.

- Purchase price per unit = £10 × (100 – 5)% = £9.50
  Total purchase cost = 4,000 × £9.50 = £38,000.
- Number of orders = 4,000/2,000 = 2
  Total ordering cost = 2 × £12 = £24
- Average number of units in stock = 2,000/2 = 1,000 units
  Holding cost per unit = £9.50 × 6% = £0.57
  Total holding cost = 1,000 × £0.57 = £570

Total cost = £38,000 + £24 + £570 = £38,594

Since this is less than the lowest total previously (£40,200) the company should accept the discount and adopt a reorder quantity of 2,000 units.

8 Issue of material from stock

8.1 Introduction

Withdrawals of materials from store for use on particular cost units or in particular cost centres will be requested on a **materials requisition note**.

8.2 Accounting for material transfers

If, for a particular job, the materials requisitioned turn out to be excessive, the surplus items should be returned to stores, the appropriate document for this purpose being a **materials returned note**. The particulars in this document will be similar to those for a materials requisition note but the document will probably be printed in red to avoid confusion.

Sometimes an item of material that is surplus to the requirements for one job can more conveniently be used immediately on another job. In this case, a **materials transfer note** should be prepared, giving details similar to those in a materials returned note, but showing the details of both transferor and transferee jobs.

Whereas a returned note requires reversing entries in the relevant job and stock accounts and in the two control accounts, the transfer note will call for entries in the two job accounts (ie. credit the transferor job and debit the transferee job), but the stock account and the control accounts will not be affected.

8.3 The stores ledger account

In addition to, or in substitution for, records of physical movements of stock, it is common for the cost accounting department to have a **stores ledger.** This will contain an account for each stock item on which both quantities and values will be shown.

A simple example of a stores ledger account would be as follows:

							Stores ledger account number:		
ITEM (description and reference code)									
UNIT OF ISSUE (unit, weight, length, etc)									
Receipts					Issues				
Date	Document reference	Qty	Price per unit	Amount £	Date	Document reference	Qty	Price per unit	Amount £

The purposes of such a record are:

(a) to ensure that the cost of units purchased is correctly reflected in the costs charged to the jobs or departments specified on stores requisitions;

(b) to provide a valuation of stocks in hand at any time.

8.4 Pricing issues

The cost of units purchased will normally be derived from suppliers' invoices and will normally be the quoted price, excluding VAT, less trade discounts plus any delivery charges incurred. VAT and cash discounts will be dealt with in the financial accounts.

Where there are many purchases of a particular item at differing prices a decision has to be taken as to which price shall be used in 'costing' individual issues. There are a number of possible methods, of which the following are discussed below:

(a) FIFO;
(b) LIFO;
(c) weighted average;

8.5 FIFO method

The FIFO (first in, first out) method assumes the **materials are used logically in the order in which they are received.**

In other words, the price paid for the first receipt of a particular item of stock is used for charging quantities of that item to different jobs until the total amount of the receipt has been accounted for. The price paid for the next consignment inwards is then used until the total of that consignment has been used.

The effect of using this method is that the closing stock at the end of the accounting period will be valued according to the prices paid for the most recent purchases; furthermore, in time the total figure for materials issues (in monetary terms) will equal the total purchase cost.

For example the stores ledger card below relates to material A on which there is no opening stock. Three purchases are recorded at different prices, and the two issues and the closing balance would be valued as shown below.

	Purchases				Issues		
Date	Quantity (units)	Price each (pence)	Amount £	Date	Quantity (units)	Price each (pence)	Amount £
2 Jan	1,000	20	200				
1 Feb	400	24	96	15 Feb	600	20	120
28 Feb	800	28	224	15 March	400	20	80
					200	24	48
					600		128
				31 March Balance c/f	200	24	48
					800	28	224
					1,000		272
	2,200		520		2,200		520

> You should appreciate that, although the FIFO method treats materials as being issued on a chronological basis, this does not necessarily mean that physical issues follow the same order as physical receipts. While it may be sensible (indeed, essential) that perishable items be used literally on a first in, first out basis, many items of stock of a longer lasting nature are mingled together, with the result that it would be more difficult (and unnecessary) to analyse the deliveries from which particular issues were obtained.

Although the FIFO method is simple to understand, it has the following disadvantages:

(a) in times of rapidly increasing prices, materials may be charged out at an early, and unrealistic price, resulting in the particular job showing a 'windfall' profit (especially if the selling price was fixed having regard to current costs);

(b) it may be necessary to 'split' an issue showing two prices in respect of the same supply to a job;

(c) two jobs started on the same day may show a different cost for the same quantity of the same material.

8.6 LIFO method

The LIFO (last in, first out) method is, in effect, the reverse of the FIFO method. Under the LIFO method, the **materials price used first is that paid for the most recent acquisition**. When the relevant quantity has been accounted for, the price of the next most recent consignment inwards is used (unless in the meantime there has been another purchase, in which case the price of that purchase will be taken). Under this method the example from paragraph used for the FIFO would appear as follows:

	Purchases				Issues		
Date	Quantity (units)	Price each (pence)	Amount £	Date	Quantity (units)	Price each (pence)	Amount £
2 Jan	1,000	20	200				
1 Feb	400	24	96	15 Feb	400	24	96
28 Feb	800	28	224		200	20	40
					600		136
				15 Mar	600	28	168
				31 Mar			
				Balance c/f	200	28	56
					800	20	160
					1,000		216
	2,200		520		2,200		520

The justification claimed for the LIFO method is that, by using the latest price for costing materials to jobs, the figure obtained is more likely to be in line with other costs (eg wages and overheads) and with selling prices. As with FIFO, LIFO is a method whereby, in time, the total cost to jobs equals the total of purchases. The storekeeper still issues the oldest stock first, of course. These are pricing methods and relate to cost office accounting only.

In addition to having disadvantages (b) and (c) mentioned above, the LIFO method results in closing stocks being shown at the earliest prices which means that, in times of rapidly increasing or decreasing prices, the stock figure bears no resemblance to the current cost of replacement. The method also involves keeping a record of unused stock at the earliest relevant price.

8.7 Weighted average method

Under this method, the **average is recomputed only when a new purchase is made**, by adding the deemed value of stock presently held (at the previously calculated average price) to the total cost of the new purchase. The new average price is then obtained by dividing this sum by the sum of the existing quantity and the quantity now being bought in. Therefore, there is no question of 'dropping' a price (as is done with the FIFO and LIFO methods) when the relevant quantity at that price is assumed to have been issued.

	Purchases				Issues		
Date	Quantity (units)	Price each (pence)	Amount £	Date	Quantity (units)	Price each (pence)	Amount £
2 Jan	1,000	20	200				
1 Feb	400	24	96	15 Feb	600	(W1) 21.1	126.60
28 Feb	800	28	224				
				15 Mar	600	(W2) 24.6	147.60
				31 Mar			
				Balance c/f	1,000	24.6	246.00
	2,200		520		2,200		520.20

Workings

1   Issue 1 is priced at $\dfrac{£200 + £96}{1,000 + 400} = £0.211$

2   Issue 2 is priced at $\frac{£520-£126.60}{2,200-600} = £0.246$

The rounding difference is only 20 pence under this method and will be dealt with automatically in recalculating a new average when the next purchase is made.

Note: The computations for this method are perhaps most easily carried out by carrying a running balance column on the right hand side of the ledger – see the answer to Practice Question 2.

8.8 Effect of FIFO, LIFO and weighted average on gross profit

Remember that the whole reason for valuing issues is to include their cost when calculating the cost of producing an item.

Under the FIFO method the issues were valued at the earliest price held in stock. This may result in the material cost of the product being too low and customers being undercharged which could potentially lead to cash flow problems in the future. The stock under this method is valued at the most up to date prices which has the advantage of being acceptable for use in the financial accounts. The gross profit under this method will be higher than the LIFO and weighted average methods due to the fact that the cost of sales is based on the earliest prices held in stock (assuming prices are rising).

Under the LIFO method the issues were valued at the most up to date costs and so these realistic costs are passed to the customers. The stock under this method is valued at the oldest prices which is not acceptable for use in financial accounting. The gross profit under this method will be lower than the FIFO and weighted average methods due to the fact that the cost of sales is based on the most up to date prices held in stock (again, assuming rising prices).

The weighted average method combines FIFO and LIFO and it is reasonably accurate as the prices are always being updated. The gross profit under this method will fall in between FIFO and LIFO and is acceptable for financial accounting purposes. However, this method is time consuming due to the need to recalculate the issue value after each purchase.

Practice questions 1 - 7 *(The answers are in the final chapter of this book)*

1   Stores records

What is meant by the terms *perpetual inventory* and *continuous stocktaking*?   **(6 marks)**

2   FIFO and LIFO

(a)   Define the FIFO and LIFO methods of pricing issues of materials to production.

(b)   Comment upon the advantages and disadvantages of the LIFO method.

(c)   From the data given below, write up the account for Material No. 1234, using the weighted average method of pricing issues.

20X1

1 Sept	Stock on hand	100	litres, valuation £100
18 Sept	Issue	60	litres
30 Sept	Receipt	40	litres, cost £1.20 per litre
12 Oct	Issue	60	litres
31 Oct	Receipt	80	litres, cost £1.30 per litre
4 Nov	Receipt	20	litres, cost £1.50 per litre
19 Nov	Issue	70	litres **(12 marks)**

3 Component ABC

From the information shown below which relates to component ABC, prepare statements using the weighted average cost of stock accounting to show the following:

(i) the amount to be charged to cost of production;

(ii) the value of the closing stock.

Date	Receipts into stores units	Unit cost	Issues to production units
1 May	100	41	
10 May	75	42	
15 May			50
20 May			65
23 May	40	45	
30 May			50

You may assume that the company had no opening stock of component ABC.

(8 marks)

4 Stock accounting methods

It is sometimes suggested that the use of the FIFO and average cost methods of stock accounting give rise to misleading results in the profit and loss account; and that the LIFO method would be preferable.

You are asked to explain and comment on this statement. **(10 marks)**

5 Stock ordering

(a) You are required to explain in outline the differences between the periodic review system and the reorder level system of determining the timing and quantities of purchase orders for stock.

(b) What do you understand by the *economic order quantity*, and what elements would enter into its calculation? **(12 marks)**

6 Component BCD

(a) From the following information relating to component BCD you are required to calculate:

(i) the reorder level;

(ii) the reorder quantity;

(iii) the minimum level;

(iv) the average stock held.

Maximum stock has been set at:		5,500	units
Usage per month	Maximum	1,100	"
	Minimum	900	"
Estimated delivery period	Maximum	4	months
	Minimum	2	months

(b) What do you consider to be the essential practices of efficient storekeeping? Explain by giving at least four examples. **(17 marks)**

7 Mr G

On 1 January Mr G started a small business buying and selling a special yarn. He invested his savings of £40,000 in the business and, during the next six months, the following transactions occurred:

Yarn purchases			Yarn sales		
Date of receipt	Quantity of boxes	Total cost £	Date of despatch	Quantity of boxes	Total value £
13 January	200	7,200	10 February	500	25,000
8 February	400	15,200			
11 March	600	24,000	20 April	600	27,000
12 April	400	14,000			
15 June	500	14,000	25 June	400	15,200

The yarn is stored in premises Mr G has rented and the closing stock of yarn, counted on 30 June, was 500 boxes.

Required

Calculate the value of the material issues during the six-month period, and the value of the closing stock at the end of June, using the following methods of pricing:

(i) first in, first out;

(ii) last in, first out; and

(iii) weighted average (calculations to two decimal places only). **(18 marks)**

9 Summary

You should now be able to:

- Distinguish between direct and indirect materials
- Explain raw material accounting and control procedures
- Explain and calculate re-order quantity, re-order level, maximum stock, minimum stock and economic order quantity
- Explain FIFO, LIFO and weighted average stock valuation methods
- Calculate stock, cost of sales and gross profit under LIFO, FIFO and weighted average

Multiple choice questions *(The answers are in the final chapter of this book)*

1. There are 27,500 units of Part Number X53 on order with the suppliers and 16,250 units outstanding on existing customers' orders.

   If the free stock is 13,000 units, what is the physical stock?

   ✓ A   1,750

   B   3,250

   C   14,000

   D   29,250

The following information is to be used for questions 2 and 3

A national chain of tyre fitters stocks a popular tyre for which the following information is available:

Average usage	140 tyres per day
Minimum usage	90 tyres per day
Maximum usage	175 tyres per day
Lead time	10 to 16 days
Re-order quantity	3,000 tyres

2. Based on the data above, at what level of stocks should a replenishment order be issued?

   A   2,240

   ✓ B   2,800

   C   3,000

   D   5,740

3. Based on the data above, what is the maximum level of stocks possible?

   A   2,800

   B   3,000

   ✓ C   4,900

   D   5,800

4. A firm has a high level of stock turnover and uses the FIFO (first in first out) issue pricing system. In a period of rising purchase prices, the closing stock valuation is:

   ✓ A   close to current purchase prices

   ✗ B   based on the prices of the first items received

   ✗ C   much lower than current purchase prices

   ✗ D   the average of all goods purchased in the period

CHAPTER 3

Accounting for labour

EXAM FOCUS

This chapter explains the accounting and control procedures for labour costs, along with an explanation of the different types of labour incentive schemes. Regardless of the type of organisation which you may be given in the examination all of them will incorporate some kind of labour input. For this reason labour will be an integral part of all examination questions. If a written question was set in this area of the syllabus it would tend to focus on the advantages and disadvantages of various payment methods and the treatment of indirect labour costs eg overtime premium.

LEARNING OUTCOMES

This chapter covers the following Learning Outcomes of the CIMA Syllabus.

> Explain labour accounting and control procedures
>
> Discuss and calculate factory incentive schemes for individuals and groups

In order to cover these Learning Outcomes the following topics are included.

> Identify the different remuneration methods used
>
> Explain the different sources which are used to accurately record labour cost information
>
> Distinguish between direct and indirect labour costs
>
> Examine the different incentive schemes used to reward staff on an individual or group basis
>
> Explain the difference between labour cost accounting and payroll accounting
>
> Perform the accounting entries for labour costs

1 Remuneration methods

1.1 Introduction

There are three main ways of paying staff, as follows:

- Fixed-rate salary (eg £20,000 per year or £350 per week).
- Time rate (employees paid in relation to the number of hours worked).
- Piecework rate (employees paid in relation to production).

1.2 Piecework rates

Piecework rates have the advantage that employees should work harder in order to produce more and therefore earn more.

The major problems with piecework rates are as follows.

- Output per employee must be measured accurately.
- Quality of output can suffer (because employees rush to complete work without sufficient regard to quality).

There are some industries where piecework would be extremely difficult to implement. For example, how would teachers be paid under a piecework scheme?

1.3 Time rates

In the examination, this is the most common method of paying the workers.

The standard method of payment is at a rate per hour. This is known as the basic rate. Time rates can be supplemented by various additional rates.

1.4 Basic rate

Mr Jones works 40 hours at a rate of £5.80 per hour = £232 per week.

Say that Mr Jones assembles computer monitors and each monitor requires two hours of assembly. The cost card for each monitor would include 2 × £5.80 = £11.60 for labour (in addition to materials etc).

1.5 Overtime rate

Mr Jones receives time and a third for any hours worked over 40. How much does he receive for a 45 hour week?

		£
Basic rate for all hours worked	45 × £5.80	261.00
Overtime premium for overtime hours only	5 × £5.80 × 1/3	9.67
Total		270.67

Note that the calculation of wages should be set out as above since basic pay is a direct labour cost whilst the overtime premium is treated separately.

Also note the terminology: Mr Jones 'receives time and a third' for his overtime hours, which means that for those hours his pay is his normal basic rate plus one third thereof in addition.

If Mr Jones assembles a monitor during the overtime period worked the labour cost to be included in the cost card would still be £11.60. The overtime premium he receives for this work will be treated as an overhead.

2 Recording labour cost information

2.1 Introduction

In most production and service businesses, records are needed of the time spent by each employee at work (attendance time) and time spent on operations, processes or products (job/chargeable time). Such timekeeping provides basic data for statutory records, payroll preparation, ascertainment and control of labour costs of an operation, service unit or product, overhead distribution (where based on wages or labour hours) and statistical analysis of labour records for determining productivity.

2.2 Attendance records

Attendance may be recorded by using a register, in which employees note their times of arrival and departure, or by means of a time recording clock which stamps the times on a card inserted by each employee. Alternatively, employees may be required to submit periodic time sheets showing the amounts of normal and overtime work; and these may also include job times as described below.

2.3 Job/chargeable time records

Job time bookings can either be done manually or by the use of a time-recording clock; the method adopted will depend on the size of the organisation and the nature of the work, a clock being more suitable when there are numerous jobs performed each day.

Chargeable time in a service industry (eg accountants, solicitors etc) is likely to be recorded on a timesheet.

3 The distinction between direct and indirect labour cost

3.1 Direct labour costs

Hours spent directly on making a product are charged directly to that product (ie included directly in the cost of the product). This amount would be included on any cost card for that job.

For example, Employee A earns £5 per hour. If he spends six hours assembling a product, the cost card of that product includes £5 × 6 = £30 for direct labour.

3.2 Indirect labour costs

There are other jobs that take place within an organisation, such as administration, supervision etc. These are called indirect labour costs and are treated as overheads.

Indirect production labour (such as supervision of direct employees) will be treated as a production overhead.

It is very important for the cost accountant to treat costs in a consistent manner. There are a number of conventions which you are expected to follow for the examination. These revolve around the treatment of indirect labour costs (remember that direct labour costs are included in a cost card). The two possible treatments are as follows.

- Regard as a period cost.
- Regard as a production overhead.

Period costs do not appear in any cost cards and are simply written off to the profit and loss account (ie reducing profit).

Production overheads can appear in cost cards. They may also be included in the stock value of an item and so appear in closing stock valuation.

3.3 Treatment of different types of indirect labour cost

Overtime is usually paid at some rate over the normal (time and a half or double time). The excess over the normal rate is overtime premium, which is shown in a separate column in the payroll.

Charging of the overtime premium will vary according to the circumstances.

Some examples are given below:

(a) allocate directly to the job if the overtime is worked on the customer's specific instructions;

(b) allocate to a separate general production overhead account if arising from general pressure of work;

(c) allocate to the department responsible for the delay which necessitated working overtime;

(d) charge to the department where the work is done, if resulting from a controllable fault arising in that department;

(e) charge directly to costing profit and loss account, if due to circumstances beyond the control of any department (eg. power failure, fire, national strike, etc).

Idle time should obviously be prevented as far as possible. It is important to analyse the causes of idle time so that necessary corrective action can be taken. There are three groups of causes of idle time:

(a) productive causes (eg. machine breakdown, power failure or time spent waiting for work, tools, materials or instructions);

(b) administrative causes (eg. surplus capacity, policy changes, unforeseen drop in demand);

(c) economic causes (eg. seasonal fluctuations in demand, cyclical fluctuations in demand, changes in demand because of tax changes).

Some of these causes are controllable (and therefore 'normal'), while others are uncontrollable (and are regarded as being 'abnormal').

Controllable idle time is shown under a separate account and charged as an overhead, although it may be charged to a department if it arose through the fault of that department.

Uncontrollable idle time is charged direct to the costing profit and loss account.

Bonus payments to both direct and indirect production workers are treated as production overheads.

Bonus payments to non-production workers are treated as period costs.

Other payments - items such as National Insurance contributions, pensions etc are treated as follows.

- Direct labour: add to hourly wage rate
- Indirect production labour: include in production overheads
- Indirect non-production labour: period cost

Gross wages are the total wages earned by employees.

Net wages are the wages actually paid to employees after allowing for deductions such as tax, National Insurance etc.

4 Incentive schemes

4.1 Bonus schemes

Individuals can receive bonuses if they work more quickly than expected. This might result in expected output being produced more quickly than planned or more units being produced in the time available.

It is more usual to pay bonuses to groups of workers rather than to individuals. This is usually based on the amount by which actual production exceeds standard production. For example, a bonus might be calculated by a formula such as the following.

$$\text{Bonus} = 50\% \times \frac{\text{Excess units}}{\text{Expected units}}$$

This bonus percentage is applied to the basic rate earned during the period.

4.2 Example

Three employees work in a group. Each earns £6 per hour. Their expected output is 10 units per hour. Mr Smith worked 42 hours, Mrs Jones 41 hours and Miss Green 47 hours. Their actual output was 1,400 units.

Required

Calculate the total amount earned by Miss Green

4.3 Solution

The total number of hours worked is 130 hours. The expected number of units to be made is 1,300. The number of actual units made is 1,400. Therefore there is an excess of 100 units.

$$\text{Bonus} = 50\% \times \frac{100}{1,300} = 3.85\%$$

Miss Green earns the following:

		£
Basic rate	47 × £6	282.00
Bonus rate	£282 × 3.85%	10.86
		292.86

4.4 Piece rate schemes

Basic piece rate schemes

Employees are paid for each unit of output produced. A similar idea is the commission that a salesperson receives on each item sold.

For example Mr Wolsey earns £1 for each model car he assembles. He assembles 175 cars in a particular week. Pay = £1 × 175 = £175. The cost card for each model car would include £1 for labour.

Piecework is often linked to standard labour times.

4.5 Example

Mr M works in a factory producing carved wooden animals. In week 25 his production is as follows.

Items produced	Standard time per unit (hours)
6 stags	2.0
5 otters	1.5
12 owls	1.0
6 golden eagles	2.0

He is paid £5 per standard hour of production.

Required

How much is he paid in week 25?

4.6 Solution

Output	Standard hours
6 stags (6 × 2)	12.0
5 otters (5 × 1.5)	7.5
12 owls (12 × 1)	12.0
6 golden eagles (6 × 2)	12.0
Total standard hours	43.5

43.5 standard hours @ £5 per hour = £217.50.

Notice that the labour cost of an otter would be 1.5 hours @ £5 per hour = £7.50 per unit.

4.7 Guaranteed minimum pay

Workers who are paid piecework are often guaranteed a minimum amount of pay. This is in case of problems in production or demand which prevent employees from working. In the example above, suppose that Mr M is guaranteed a minimum of £200 per week. In week 25 he has earned more than this and so receives £217.50.

If the minimum wage for the week was £250 then he would receive £250 in week 25 since his earnings would have been below this.

4.8 Halsey and Rowan bonus schemes

These are schemes to reward groups of workers.

Under the Halsey scheme, the bonus would be calculated as follows:

$$\text{Bonus} = \frac{\text{Time allowed} - \text{Time taken}}{2} \times \text{time rate}$$

Under the Rowan scheme, the bonus would be calculated as follows:

$$\text{Bonus} = \frac{\text{Time taken} \times \text{Time saved} \times \text{Time rate}}{\text{Time allowed}}$$

4.9 Example

Basic rate = £5.00 per hour

Time allowed for job A = 1 hour

Time taken to complete the job = 36 minutes = 0.6 hours

Required

Calculate the amount of bonus earned under both the Halsey scheme and the Rowan scheme.

4.10 Solution

Halsey scheme

			£
Bonus	=	$\frac{(1-0.6) \times £5.00}{2}$	1.00
Basic rate	=	0.6 × £5.00	3.00
Total payment			4.00

Rowan scheme

Time saved = (1 - 0.6) = 0.4 hours

			£
Bonus	=	$\dfrac{0.6 \times 0.40 \times £5.00}{1}$	1.20
Basic rate	=	$0.6 \times £5.00$	3.00
Total payment			4.20

5 Labour cost accounting and payroll accounting

5.1 Introduction

The calculation of pay due to employees each period is summarised on a **payroll** which forms the basis for accounting entries in the financial books. Although it is likely that only a total salaries or wages account will be debited, a separate payroll will usually be prepared for each main department in the business, so that some information will be available for an analysis of the total amount by cost centres.

Where payments are related to attendance time, the source document will be some form of attendance record, typically a time sheet or time card. Where payments are related to work done, the time record will need to be supplemented by detailed work records. For the cost accountant who needs to analyse payrolls over cost units such work records will be required regardless of the method of payment.

This sub-analysis is most frequently applied to the costs of manual labour and although the term 'labour cost' has traditional implications not always acceptable under contemporary conditions it has become established by long usage.

5.2 Accounting entries for labour cost

After analysing payrolls, attributing costs to particular cost units and any non-productive hours valued at rates of pay, the cost accountant will then analyse the gross pay which has been debited to the payroll control account into either direct wages (debit the job accounts) or indirect wages (debit overheads). The accounting entry will be as follows:

Debit	Accounts for the various jobs or work-in-progress
Debit	Expense accounts for non-production time (overheads)
Credit	Payroll control account

5.3 Example

In period 5, gross pay was £12,600. Of this, £9,500 is direct wages and the remainder is production overheads. You are required to prepare the wages control account for period 5.

5.4 Solution

Wages Control Account

	£		£
Bank	12,600	Work-in-progress	9,500
		Production overheads	3,100
	12,600		12,600

Practice question 1 *(The answer is in the final chapter of this book)*

1 Bonus payment

The term "tradesman's labourer" is generally understood to refer to those workers whose job it is to work with, and provide unskilled assistance to, a skilled tradesman.

Discuss the problems involved in paying a bonus (as an incentive for increased productivity) to a tradesman's labourer whose work is related to that of a skilled tradesman. Also consider the effectiveness of such a bonus. **(12 marks)**

6 Summary

You should now be able to:

- Identify the different remuneration methods used
- Explain the different sources used to accurately record labour cost information
- Distinguish between direct and indirect labour cost
- Explain the different incentive schemes used to reward staff on an individual or group basis
- Explain the difference between labour cost accounting and payroll accounting
- Prepare the accounting entries for labour costs

Multiple choice questions *(The answers are in the final chapter of this book)*

1. A job requires 2,400 actual labour hours for completion and it is anticipated that there will be 20% idle time. If the wage rate is £10 per hour, what is the budgeted labour cost for the job?

    A   £19,200

    B   £24,000

    C   £28,800

    D   £30,000

2. During a period £35,750 was incurred for indirect labour. In a typical cost ledger, the double entry for this is:

A	Dr Wages control	Cr Overhead control
B	Dr WIP control	Cr Wages control
C	Dr Overhead control	Cr Wages control
D	Dr Wages control	Cr WIP control

CHAPTER 4

Accounting for overheads using absorption costing

EXAM FOCUS

Overheads are a key cost in a company and therefore one of the most fundamental topics in this syllabus. Because of this they will feature in every examination either as a computational or as a written question. You must ensure that you understand the difference between allocation, apportionment and absorption. You must also be able to calculate any under or over absorption.

LEARNING OUTCOMES

This chapter covers the following Learning Outcomes of the CIMA Syllabus.

- Explain absorption costing
- Prepare cost statements for allocation and apportionment of overheads including reciprocal service departments
- Calculate and discuss overhead absorption rates
- Calculate under/over recovery of overheads

In order to cover these Learning Outcomes the following topics are included.

- Identify and explain the different types of overheads
- Explain why absorption costing is used to allocate overhead costs to products/services
- Explain why a single blanket overhead rate is not appropriate
- Identify and work through the stages of allocation, apportionment and absorption costing
- Calculate an appropriate overhead absorption rate (OAR) for each department
- Consider the effect of under/over absorption of overheads
- Perform the accounting entries for overheads

CIMA Paper 2 Text – Management Accounting Fundamentals

1 Overheads in product costs

1.1 Introduction

Why do we need to bother about overhead costs? Consider the example of RS Ltd.

RS Ltd is a manufacturing company that makes a single product called Product P. In manufacturing a unit of P the following costs are incurred.

		£
Direct labour	2 hrs @ £5 per hour	10
Direct materials	1 kg @ £5 per kg	5
Direct expenses		1
Prime cost		16

Note in the above that **prime cost** means the sum of all direct costs involved in manufacturing a product.

RS Ltd produces and sells 1,000 units in a month. What price should be charged?

RS could sell the product for £17. This would make a 'profit' of £1 per unit (£17 – £16 = £1) and so 1,000 units would make a 'profit' of £1,000.

But what about other costs RS Ltd will incur, such as heating, power for machinery, etc? These must also be included in the cost of a product.

In general these other costs are referred to as overheads. In Chapter 1 we talked about direct costs and indirect costs. Direct costs are things such as direct materials, etc and as you can see from the above these are charged directly to a product. Overheads represent *indirect* costs (all the other kinds of costs that a company spends money on).

Also in Chapter 1 we referred to fixed costs such as rent, etc. It should be obvious that fixed costs will be treated as overheads: the annual cost of renting a factory is not a direct cost of any particular product. We have also come across other kinds of overheads in the previous chapters. For example, indirect materials are overheads. Another major source of overheads is indirect labour costs, including:

- supervisor salaries
- overtime premiums.

1.2 Absorption of overheads

Once we have identified which costs are overheads the next step is to decide what to do with them. Ideally we would like to include them in the cost of a product, and hence in the product price. That way our customers will pay for them.

Note: This is in fact rather a glib statement. The fixed overheads will only be fully paid for by the customers if enough units are sold to recover the full amount of cost from sales proceeds.

1.3 Example

Assume that based on past experience RS Ltd (from previous example) estimates its overheads as follows.

	£
Heating	3,000
Power	2,000
Maintenance	500
Total	5,500

How might this affect the cost per unit?

1.4 Solution

Spread over the 1,000 units produced, this would equate to $\frac{£5,500}{1,000}$ = £5.50 per unit.

The cost of a unit of P would then be as follows.

		£
Direct labour	2 hrs @ £5 per hour	10.00
Direct materials	1 kg @ £5 per kg	5.00
Direct expenses		1.00
Prime cost		16.00
Overheads		5.50
Factory cost		21.50

If the company charges customers £22 per unit, £16 will cover the direct costs and £6.00 will be collected from each customer to pay for the overheads and to earn a profit. At the end of the period RS Ltd will have collected 1,000 × £22 = £22,000 sales revenue. Of this 1,000 × £16 = £16,000 would go to pay the direct costs. Of the remainder of the receipts, 1,000 × £5.50 = £5,500 would be used to pay the overheads. RS Ltd would be left with £22,000 − £16,000 − £5,500 = £500 which would represent the profit for the period.

1.5 More than one product

In the above example we attributed overheads to cost units on a simple unit basis. Will this still be appropriate where more than one type of product is made?

1.6 Example

Imagine that RS Ltd now starts producing another product, Product Q. Its direct costs are as follows.

		£
Direct labour	½ hr at £5 per hour	2.50
Direct material	0.1 kg at £5 per kg	0.50
Direct expenses		Nil
Prime cost		3.00

The company plans to make and sell 1,000 units of Product Q in a month.

The overheads stay as before (a total of £5,500). Calculate the costs per unit for each product.

1.7 Solution

The total number of units now being produced is 2,000 so the overhead cost per unit is now £5,500/2,000 = £2.75 per unit. The manufacturing costs of P and Q could now be calculated as follows.

Product P	£	Product Q	£
Prime cost	16.00	Prime cost	3.00
Overhead	2.75	Overhead	2.75
Total	18.75	Total	5.75

Overhead = 14.6% of cost (= 2.75/18.75)   Overhead = 47.8% of cost (= 2.75/5.75)

As you can see the overheads included in the cost for Product Q are almost as much as the direct costs of making it. If this is used to set the sale price of Product Q there is a strong chance that the product will be overpriced.

1.8 Absorption costs

You should be able to see that using the number of items produced to share out overheads is not a satisfactory method to use if the company is making more than one product. In fact the only time this method does work satisfactorily is when the products are similar and have a similar direct cost.

To overcome this problem there are other methods of calculating how much overhead should be attributed to a product. All of these try to relate the overhead to the direct costs of manufacture.

For example, if a product requires a large amount of labour it tends to cost more (since labour is often an expensive part of the manufacturing process). In this case, the more labour hours spent making a product, the larger the labour cost will be and so the more overhead should be attributed to the product. In this case an absorption rate based on direct labour hours may be used. This method is used particularly in labour intensive areas of the company.

Similarly, a major cost for many companies is the expense of running machinery. This has led to another common method of attributing overheads, that of using machine hours. The idea is that the more machine hours it takes to produce a product the more overhead should be attributed to it. A machine hour rate could be used here.

In the examination the most common methods of attributing overheads to products are to use direct labour hours or machine hours.

1.9 Validity of the use of absorption rates

Remember that the purpose of this exercise is to pass on overhead costs to customers by including them in product costs (and hence in product prices). However, the product still has to be priced realistically in order to be attractive to customers. Using labour or machine hours we try to relate the overheads to the cost of manufacture.

Notice in all of this that we never know the 'true' overhead cost of any particular product, because the whole point about overheads is that they do not relate directly to any particular product. We know our true expenditure on overhead costs, in total, but spreading this total across the individual units of product is a matter of applying various 'rules of thumb'. We say that overheads are *absorbed* into the cost of products and our objective is to find a 'fair' method of achieving this.

2 Absorption of overheads

2.1 Calculating an absorption rate

As we have already explained, one possible method of absorbing overhead costs into products is to use direct labour hours as a basis. The steps in this procedure are as follows.

- Establish the total overhead costs for a period.
- Establish the total number of direct labour hours to be worked in that period.
- Work out a rate per direct labour hour (Overhead Absorption Rate).
- Use this to say how much overhead should be absorbed by each unit of product.

This final step is achieved by noting how many direct labour hours will be worked on each unit.

2.2 Example

Calculate the direct labour hour rate for RS Ltd and the cost per unit for P and Q.

2.3 Solution

Each unit of Product P requires two hours of labour, so 1,000 units will require 2,000 hours in total. Similarly Product Q requires 1,000 × 0.5 = 500 hours. Total direct labour hours = 2,500.

The overhead absorption rate (OAR) is therefore $\frac{£5,500}{2,500}$ = £2.20 per labour hour.

In other words, for each direct labour hour included in the cost of a product, we will absorb £2.20. This £2.20 is added to the cost of the item. Note that this is in addition to the labour cost for each product.

Product P	£	Product Q	£
Prime cost	16.00	Prime cost	3.00
Overhead 2 hrs @ 2.20	4.40	Overhead (0.5 hrs @ 2.20)	1.10
Total	20.40	Total	4.10

Overhead = 21.6% of cost   Overhead = 26.9% of cost

As you can see, this has resulted in a more equitable split of overheads, so that Product Q is not overpriced.

Remember that the idea of this process is to collect enough money from customers to pay these overheads. In the above example the total amount collected from customers will be as follows.

		£
Product P	1,000 units × £4.40 per unit	4,400
Product Q	1,000 units × £1.10 per unit	1,100
Total		5,500

This is the same amount as the overheads we are expecting to pay out.

2.4 Alternative overhead absorption rates

There are various methods of calculating overhead absorption rates. Each will give a different overhead cost per unit. The six main methods are:

1. Cost per labour hour
2. Cost per machine hour
3. Percentage of direct labour cost
4. Percentage of material cost
5. Percentage of prime cost
6. Cost per unit

They use the same basic method – calculating an Overhead Absorption Rate (OAR), although for the percentage method, the OAR will be a percentage or proportion.

2.5 Example

Using the percentage of prime cost for RS Ltd, we can calculate the overhead cost per unit as follows:

$$\text{OAR} = \frac{\text{Total Overheads}}{\text{Total Prime Cost}}$$

$$\text{OAR} = \frac{£5,500}{£16,000 + £3,000} = 0.2895 = 28.95\% \text{ of prime cost}$$

This means that to calculate the overhead cost per unit, we simply multiply the prime cost per unit by 0.2895.

	Product P £	Product Q £
Prime Cost	16.00	3.00
Overhead	4.63	0.87
Total Cost	20.63	3.87

As you can see, the cost per unit is still a fairly equitable split of overheads.

2.6 Which method is correct?

There is not one right answer to this question. It depends on the circumstances. In an exam, if you had to choose your own method, use either labour hours or machine hours, whichever seems most appropriate for the question.

3 Under/over absorption (recovery) of overheads

3.1 Predetermined overhead absorption rates

It is important to note *when* the calculation of overhead absorption rates is done. It must be done at the start of a period, so that the company can charge the same price throughout the period. Because of this, overheads are calculated using *budgeted* figures for costs and for production levels. Since these rates are set at the start of a period they are referred to as *predetermined*.

Now *actual* activity levels or *actual* overhead costs incurred by the business differ from our budget estimates then our calculation will have been incorrect. This leads to the concept of under absorption and over absorption of overheads.

3.2 Example

Budgeted overheads	£10,000
Budgeted units of production	5,000

This gives a budgeted overhead absorption rate of £2 per unit. This £2 is added to the cost (and therefore to the price) of each unit.

At the end of the period the actual overheads and production are calculated. Assume the actual figures were as follows (Situation 1).

Actual overheads	£12,000
Actual units produced	5,500

Compute the under or over absorption of overheads.

3.3 Solution

Since we were absorbing £2 for each unit made and sold, we have absorbed 5,500 × £2 = £11,000. But the actual overhead is £12,000 so we have absorbed £1,000 less than we need to pay the bills. This is referred to as **under absorption**.

Our profit and loss account includes the cost of units produced, including overheads absorbed into product costs. But in this case overheads absorbed are less than the overheads actually incurred, and so our profit and loss account is inaccurate: costs are understated. To remedy this we must show an extra £1,000 cost in the profit and loss account for overhead under absorbed.

3.4 Example

Now assume instead that 5,600 units were produced and overheads actually cost £10,000 (Situation 2).

Compute the under/over absorption of overheads.

3.5 Solution

In this case the amount absorbed = £2 × 5,600 = £11,200. It can be seen that we have absorbed £11,200 – £10,000 = £1,200 more than needed. This is referred to as **over absorption**. If we have over absorbed overhead we would credit the additional £1,200 to the profit and loss account to increase the profit for the period.

3.6 Proforma for over/under absorption

A proforma for calculating over/under absorption is shown below:

Actual overhead expenditure	X
Less: Overheads absorbed (actual production × OAR)	(X)
Overheads under/(over) absorbed	X

where OAR = overhead absorption rate = $\dfrac{\text{Budgeted overheads}}{\text{Budgeted production}}$

If this is positive we have over absorbed and must adjust the profit and loss account to *increase* profits. If it is negative we have under absorbed overheads and must *reduce* the profit shown in the profit and loss account.

3.7 Accounting entries

The production overhead control account will be as follows:

Production overhead control account

Creditors or Bank	X	Work-In-Progress	X
(Overhead incurred)		(Overhead absorbed)	

The account is balanced off at the end of every period. The balance is the over or under absorption of overheads.

3.8 Example

In the examples above, the accounts will be as follows:

Situation 1

Production overhead control account

	£		£
Creditors (actual expenditure)	12,000	Work-In-Progress (absorbed) (5,500 × £2)	11,000
		Profit and Loss (Under absorption)	1,000
	12,000		12,000

Situation 2

Production overhead control account

	£		£
Creditors (actual expenditure)	10,000	Work-In-Progress (absorbed)	11,200
		(5,600 × £2)	
Profit and Loss (Over absorption)	1,200		
	11,200		11,200

4 Departmental absorption

4.1 Introduction

So far we have been dealing with overheads for the entire company. Most companies though spend different amounts in different parts of the organisation (cost centres). We will usually have to calculate a separate absorption rate for each different cost centre.

It is not necessary to use the same absorption base for each department. For example, a machining department will probably use a machine hours OAR, whereas a labour intensive department will use a labour hour rate.

4.2 Example

ABC Ltd makes three products A, B and C. Each passes through two departments - Machining and Assembly.

	Machining	Assembly
Time taken in each department		
Product A	1 hour	1 hour
Product B	2 hours	½ hour
Product C	None	4 hours

Production is expected to be as follows.

	Units
Product A	1,000
Product B	2,000
Product C	500

Overheads are expected to be as follows.

	£
Machining	100,000
Assembly	150,000
Total	250,000

Required

(a) Calculate the overhead absorbed by each product.

(b) Calculate the total absorbed altogether by the three products.

4.3 Solution

Notice that the two departments are separate and therefore a separate rate is calculated in each one.

		Machining			Assembly		
Stage 1							
Overhead (given)		£100,000			£150,000		
Stage 2							
Total hours	A	1,000 × 1	=	1,000	1,000 × 1	=	1,000
	B	2,000 × 2	=	4,000	2,000 × ½	=	1,000
	C	500 × 0	=	0	500 × 4	=	2,000
Total				5,000			4,000

Stage 3

Absorption rate =   £100,000/5,000   £150,000/4,000
                    £20 per hour   £37.50 per hour

The rate of £20 per hour in Machining applies to any product that spends any time in that department. Similarly, for every hour that any product spends in Assembly, overheads of £37.50 are added to the product cost.

Stage 4

Each unit of Product A will absorb the following overheads.

		£
Machining	1 hour @ £20	20.00
Assembly	1 hour @ £37.50	37.50
Total absorbed		57.50

Therefore £57.50 is added to the cost of Product A to allow for overheads.

Each unit of Product B will absorb the following overheads.

		£
Machining	2 hours @ £20	40.00
Assembly	½ hour @ £37.50	18.75
Total absorbed		58.75

Therefore £58.75 is added to the cost of Product B to allow for overheads.

Each unit of Product C will absorb the following overheads.

		£
Machining	0 hours @ £20	-
Assembly	4 hours @ £37.50	150.00
Total absorbed		150.00

Therefore £150.00 is added to the cost of Product C to allow for overheads.

The total that is absorbed by all three products is as follows.

		£
Product A	1,000 × £57.50	57,500
Product B	2,000 × £58.75	117,500
Product C	500 × £150.00	75,000
		250,000

This is the total of the overheads in the two departments.

4.4 Blanket overhead absorption

An alternative to the above is what is termed a *blanket rate for absorption*. This means that a single absorption rate is calculated for the entire factory regardless of departments.

For ABC Ltd this would be as follows.

Stage 1	Total overhead	£250,000
Stage 2	Total labour hours	9,000
Stage 3	Rate per hour = £250,000/9,000 = £27.78 per hour	
Stage 4	Product A absorbs (1 + 1) = 2 hours @ £27.78	£55.56
	Product B absorbs (2 + ½) = 2½ hours @ £27.78	£69.45
	Product C absorbs (0 + 4) = 4 hours @ £27.78	£111.12

Again the total absorbed between the three products will come to £250,000. (As an exercise you should check this.)

5 Allocation and apportionment of overheads

5.1 Introduction

When we were looking at production overheads above, we were given the total amount of overhead in each cost centre. But how do we attribute particular overhead costs to particular cost centres?

- Overheads may arise solely in a particular cost centre. An example might be the salary of a supervisor working exclusively in the assembly cost centre, or the indirect materials used by a cost centre. Such overheads are **allocated** to that cost centre.
- Other overheads may relate to several cost centres. Examples might include rent, rates, heating costs, etc. Such overheads are **apportioned** (shared) between cost centres.

Overheads should be apportioned on a fair basis. In other words they should be shared out in a way that reflects the use of the overhead by each department.

5.2 Apportionment bases

The following are often used as bases for apportioning overheads.

- Floor area
- Value of machinery
- Hours spent working for a particular cost centre
- Number of requisitions
- Machine time

Each particular overhead should be apportioned on the most appropriate basis. For example, canteen costs might be shared among different departments according to the number of employees in each department. Other examples are given below.

Type of cost	Basis of apportionment
Maintenance	Number of hours spent working for a department/machine time
Insurance	Value of machinery
Rent	Floorspace
Personnel	Number of employees/requests
Stores	Number of requests/amount of materials used

In the above we are trying to relate the overhead to a sensible way of sharing it out. For example, rent relates to a factory as a whole. The bigger the area occupied by a particular department the more of the rent charge it should be apportioned. Similarly if one department has a large number of employees it should be apportioned more of the canteen costs (since there are more people in that department to feed).

Again note that a company may ignore this and simply divide total overheads for the factory by total labour hours (or other number of units). Remember that this is known as a factory-wide or blanket rate.

5.3 Non-production overheads

Non-production overheads (administration, etc) are usually quoted as a percentage of production cost. For example non-production overheads might be absorbed as 10% of production cost for an item.

5.4 Service departments

Once we have done this we will have to look at the treatment of those departments that do not produce anything to be sold externally (eg departments such as maintenance and stores). These departments are known as **service departments** and their costs are re-apportioned to production centres using a fair basis. This treatment of costs is shown later.

5.5 Allocation apportionment and reapportionment

The process of allocation, apportionment and re-apportionment is shown below.

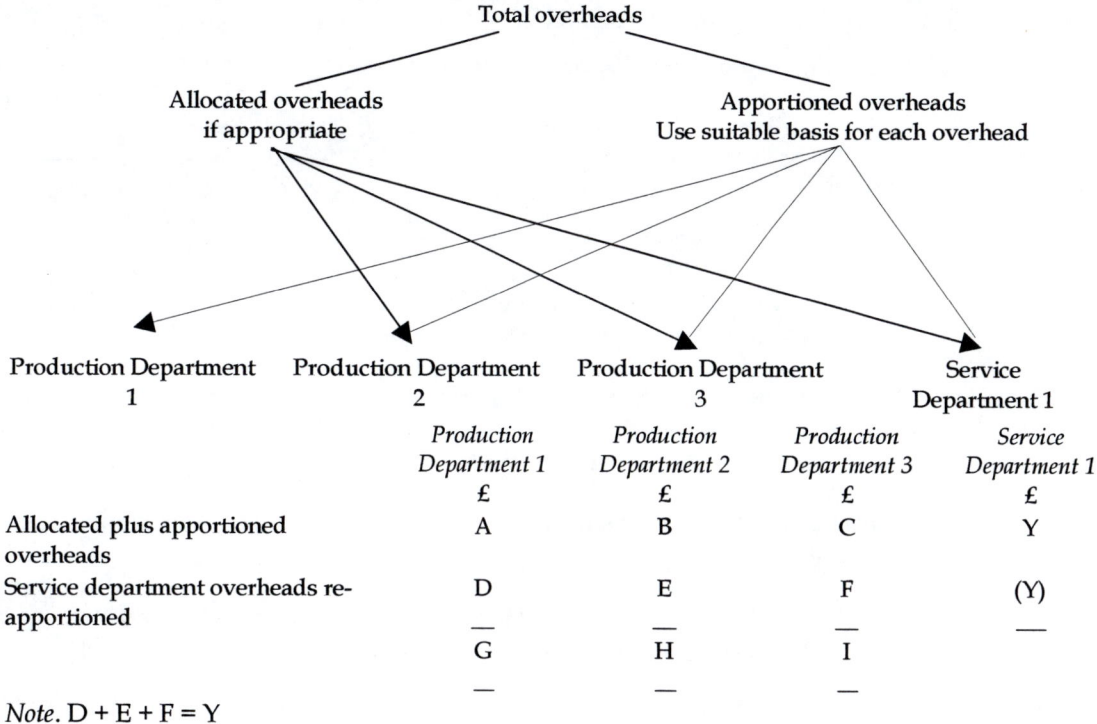

	Production Department 1 £	Production Department 2 £	Production Department 3 £	Service Department 1 £
Allocated plus apportioned overheads	A	B	C	Y
Service department overheads re-apportioned	D	E	F	(Y)
	G	H	I	

Note. D + E + F = Y

5.6 Example

SB Ltd has two production departments (Assembly and Finishing) and two service departments (Maintenance and Canteen). The following costs are expected to be incurred.

	£
Indirect materials	20,000
Rent	15,000
Electricity	10,000
Machine depreciation	5,000
Building depreciation	10,000
Direct labour	55,000

The following information is available.

	Assembly	Finishing	Maintenance	Canteen
Area (square metres)	1,000	2,000	500	500
Kw hours consumed	1,000	4,000	Nil	5,000
Machine value	£45,000	£35,000	£11,000	£9,000
Number of staff	20	30	10	-
Indirect materials consumed	7,000	8,000	3,000	2,000

Required

Calculate total overheads for each cost centre.

5.7 Solution

Overhead Analysis Sheet

Overhead	Total £	Basis of apportionment	Assembly £	Finishing £	Maintenance £	Canteen £
Indirect materials	20,000	Allocate (a)	7,000	8,000	3,000	2,000
Rent	15,000	Area (b)	3,750	7,500	1,875	1,875
Electricity	10,000	Kw hours (c)	1,000	4,000	-	5,000
Machine dep'n	5,000	Machine value (d)	2,250	1,750	550	450
Building dep'n	10,000	Area (e)	2,500	5,000	1,250	1,250
Direct labour	55,000	(f)	-	-	-	-
Total			16,500	26,250	6,675	10,575

Total overhead = £60,000

Notes

(a) We are given the amount of indirect materials used by each cost centre. This allows us to allocate the cost straight to each cost centre.

(b) Rent is something that is shared by the whole factory and therefore the cost must be apportioned between the cost centres. The first thing to decide is what basis to use. Since rent is related to area, floorspace would be a sensible basis to use.

There are two techniques for apportioning overheads, and you should use whichever you are happier with.

The first technique is to use proportions. For the rent we need to divide up the rent of £15,000 in the proportions 1,000 : 2,000 : 500 : 500.

This works as follows:

- Calculate the total floor area for the factory.
- For each cost centre calculate what fraction of the total floor area this represents.
- Multiply this fraction by £15,000.

In the present case this would be as follows.

Total floor area is 1,000 + 2,000 + 500 + 500 = 4,000 square metres.

Assembly uses 1,000 square metres, ie 1,000/4,000 of the total area. Assembly is apportioned £15,000 × 1,000/4,000 = £3,750.

Similarly, finishing is apportioned £15,000 × 2,000/4,000 = £7,500 and Maintenance and Canteen are apportioned £15,000 × 500/4,000 = £1,875 each.

The second method is as follows:

Calculate the rent per square metre, as shown:

$$\text{Rent per sq m} = \frac{\text{Total rent}}{\text{Total square metre}} = \frac{£15,000}{1000 + 2000 + 500 + 500}$$

$$= \frac{£15,000}{4,000} = £3.75$$

As assembly department is 1,000 square metres, its proportion of the rent will be 1,000 × £3.75 = £2,750.

Continue this for each department.

(c) The most appropriate basis for apportioning the electricity between the cost centres will be the Kw hours consumed since these are a measure of the amount of electricity used.

The total Kw hours consumed = 1,000 + 4,000 + 0 + 5,000 = 10,000 hours. Assembly will be apportioned £10,000 × 1,000/10,000 = £1,000, etc.

(d) Machine depreciation will be based on the value of the machinery and again needs to be apportioned between the cost centres.

The total machine value is £2,250 + £1,750 + £550 + £450 = £5,000. This results in Assembly being apportioned £5,000 × 2,250/5,000 = £2,250, etc.

(e) Since the whole building is being depreciated, building depreciation should be related to the area of each cost centre. It does not matter that we have already used area once. There is no restriction against using it again if it is the most appropriate basis for apportioning this cost.

(f) You may have thought that using number of employees was a good way to share out the direct wages bill, but remember that we are only interested here in *overheads*. Direct wages will already be included in the costs of the products that are made by the company. (Similarly direct materials are ignored for overheads.) If the question had included *indirect* labour then that would be included as an overhead and could be apportioned using the number of people working in each cost centre.

Practice question 1 *(The answer is in the final chapter of this book)*

Peter Radford

Peter Radford makes running shoes and is halfway through his budgeting process for the coming year. He has estimated his fixed production overheads as follows.

	£000
Factory rent	18
Factory light and heat	38
Depreciation	
Premises	15
Machines	41
Maintenance	
Premises	30
Machines	30
Cleaning	25
Supervisory salaries	80
Production control	84
Warehousing	40
Insurance	24
Works canteen	32
	457

There are three production departments (all housed in the same building) for which levels of activity and other relevant information are shown below.

	Cutting	Assembly	Packing
Number of staff	23	38	14
Production hours	40,000	75,000	25,000
Area (sq ft)	4,000	5,000	6,000
Number of supervisory staff	2	2	1
Net book value of machinery (£000)	150	50	5

The vast majority of the materials in the warehouse are used by the Cutting Department but 5% are used by Packing and 10% by Assembly.

The Maintenance Department spends its time equally repairing machinery in the Cutting and Assembly Departments with very little time spent in Packing. Half the insurance costs relate to premises and half to machinery. The Cutting and Packing Departments make twice as much mess per square foot as the Assembly Department (relevant to cleaning costs).

Radford makes four types of shoe: the Christie and the Martin for men, and the Gunnell and the Murray for women.

Required

Prepare a schedule showing the apportionment of budgeted fixed production overheads between the three production departments (work to the nearest £000).

6 Service cost centres

6.1 Reapportioning service centre costs

So far we have calculated costs in both production and service cost centres. However, only production cost centres produce cost units. Therefore we must re-apportion all service cost centre costs into production cost centres.

6.2 Example

In the previous example (SB Ltd), suppose that the following additional information is available.

Time spent servicing equipment: Assembly 60%, Finishing 40%

The canteen equipment is serviced by outside specialist contractors.

Required

Re-apportion both service centre costs to production cost centres.

6.3 Solution

A suitable basis for sharing out canteen costs is the number of employees. A suitable basis for sharing out the maintenance costs is the time spent servicing equipment.

First re-apportion canteen costs since the canteen provides services for maintenance but maintenance do not work for the canteen.

Overhead	Basis		Assembly £	Finishing £	Maintenance £	Canteen £
Total from above			16,500	26,250	6,675	10,575
Canteen	Personnel	20:30:10	3,525	5,288	1,762	(10,575)
Sub-total			20,025	31,538	8,437	
Maintenance	Time	60:40	5,062	3,375	(8,437)	
Total			25,087	34,913		

Total overhead = £60,000

All costs are now in production cost centres and we can proceed with the final three stages in the process of absorbing overheads into products.

6.4 Overhead absorption

Continuing with the example above, SB Ltd expects production in the next year to be 1,000 units of Product A and 2,000 of Product B.

Product A requires 15 minutes of assembly and one hour of finishing.

Product B requires two hours of assembly and half an hour of finishing.

Using the overhead apportioned to each department above, how much overhead is charged to each product?

This is calculated as in Section 4 of this chapter.

	Assembly		Finishing	
Step 1				
Total overhead (from above)	£25,087		£34,913	
Step 2				
Calculate total hours				
1,000 Product A	$1,000 \times 15/60 =$	250	$1,000 \times 1 =$	1,000
2,000 Product B	$2,000 \times 2 =$	4,000	$2,000 \times ½ =$	1,000
Total		4,250		2,000
Step 3				
Calculate rate per hour	£25,087/4,250		£34,913/2,000	
	= £5.90 per hour		= £17.46 per hour	

⚠ Whilst exam candidates can generally cope well with the allocation and apportionment parts of this procedure, it is often at the calculation of absorption rates that they come unstuck. Ensure you are quite happy with the above computation.

Step 4	Product A	£	Product B	£
Overhead absorbed by each product				
Assembly = £5.90 per hour	15/60 × £5.90 =	1.48	2 × £5.90 =	11.80
Finishing = £17.46 per hour	1 × £17.46 =	17.46	½ × £17.46 =	8.73
Total per unit		18.94		20.53

Note that the total absorbed by Products A and B is (1,000 × £18.94) + (2,000 × £20.53) = £60,000.

Practice question 2 *(The answer is in the final chapter of this book)*

Ensign

Ensign Ltd has partly completed its budgeting process and has also allocated and apportioned estimated fixed production overheads between its five departments as follows.

Department	Overheads
	£000
Machine shop	311
Assembly department	422
Stores	46
Maintenance	61
Canteen	40
	880

The service department costs now have to be split to leave all overheads charged to production departments only. The time spent by each service department looking after other departments is as follows.

	Machine %	Assembly %	Stores %	Maintenance %	Canteen %
Stores	72	24	–	4	–
Maintenance	60	40	–	–	–
Canteen	35	50	10	5	–

Budgeted production hours are as follows.

Machine shop	40,000
Assembly department	60,000

The firm wishes to find hourly fixed overhead absorption rates for the two production departments.

Required

Apportion service department costs over production departments, and find overhead hourly rates for those two departments.

6.5 Reciprocal servicing

The situation is more complicated if two service centres provide services to each other. This is called *reciprocal servicing*. (We avoided this complication above by stating that maintenance services for the canteen are provided by an *external* supplier.)

6.6 Example

In SB Ltd above suppose that a review of timesheets shows that maintenance spends its time as follows.

Assembly 50%, Finishing 40%, Canteen 10%.

Required

Recalculate the amount of overhead apportioned to each department.

6.7 Solution

Now maintenance works for canteen and canteen works for maintenance. This will be tackled by using the 'repeated distribution' method – service department costs get apportioned and reapportioned until the amounts get so small that they can be ignored/rounded off to zero.

Overhead	Basis		Assembly £	Finishing £	Maintenance £	Canteen £
Total from above			16,500	26,250	6,675	10,575
Canteen	Personnel	20:30:10	3,525	5,288	1,762	(10,575)
Subtotal			20,025	31,538	8,437	–
Maintenance	Time	50:40:10	4,218	3,375	(8,437)	844
Canteen	Personnel	20:30:10	281	422	141	(844)
Maintenance	Time	50:40:10	71	56	(141)	14
Canteen	Personnel	20:30:0 (numbers are so small, ignore maintenance)	6	8	–	(14)
Total			24,601	35,399	–	–

Note that no costs can be left in service departments, they must all be apportioned to production departments.

We would now carry on the calculation as before to find total hours, etc.

Practice question 3 *(The answer is in the final chapter of this book)*

Pirie

Pirie uses an absorption costing system. As a consequence he needs to find a standard fixed overhead cost per unit figure for his various products. His fixed overhead budget for the year shows the following.

	£000
Light and heat	30
Canteen expenses	52
Insurance	72
Consumable stores	118
Supervisors' salaries	152
Other indirect labour	248
Rent and rates	306
Depreciation	452
Total	1,430

Other budget information shows the following.

Department	A	B	C	Stores	Maintenance
Floor space (000 sq ft)	8	4	8	8	2
Number of direct employees	56	46	48	8	8
Number of supervisors	4	2	2	1	1
Number of indirect employees	8	4	8	2	2
Materials consumed (£000)	1,140	1,035	1,275	–	300
Book value of plant and equipment (£000)	1,400	1,600	600	200	200
Maintenance hours (000)	5	7.4	3.6	–	–
Production labour hours (000)	100	80	100	–	–

A, B and C are the three production departments. Consumable stores are to be apportioned on the basis of materials consumed. Fixed overheads will be recovered on labour hours. Insurance costs comprise £24,000 for machinery and £48,000 for buildings, whilst depreciation costs represent £368,000 for machinery and £84,000 for buildings.

Required

(a) Split fixed costs between the five departments (production and service), then find the budgeted fixed overhead cost for each of the three production departments for the coming year. (Carry out your apportionment calculations to the nearest £100.)

(b) Calculate the fixed overhead hourly rate for each of the three production departments, then the fixed overhead cost per unit for one of Pirie's three products, the Gordon, for which details are given below.

Product	Douglas	Alastair	Gordon
Annual production (000)	5	5	10
Labour time per unit			
Department A	5	5	5
Department B	2	2	6
Department C	4	4	6

(c) Find the fixed overhead costs per unit if Pirie decides that the fixed overhead recovery of each department should be based on units produced rather than labour hours.

(d) State why the first set of calculations is more suitable and explain the nature of the problem that might arise in the initial calculations as far as treatment of service department costs is concerned.

7 Preparing a cost card

7.1 Introduction

We are now in a position to prepare cost cards and quotes for customers. Often this will involve calculating the final sales price in addition to costs. The most straightforward way to approach this in the exam is to use a logical approach to ensure you have covered everything. Look at material, labour and overheads separately.

7.2 Example

Griffey Ltd operates a job costing system.

The following records of costs are all for March 20X8.

	£	
Indirect materials	50,000	(5,000 kg purchase)
Direct labour	75,000	(6,000 hours worked)
Indirect labour	40,000	(5,000 hours worked)
General production overheads	200,000	

There are three departments in Griffey Ltd: Assembly, Finishing and Maintenance. Relevant details are given below.

	Assembly	Finishing	Maintenance
Indirect material used (kg)	3,000	1,500	500
Direct labour hours	4,000	2,000	Nil
Maintenance hours	3,000	1,000	

General *production overheads* and indirect labour costs are split evenly between all three departments.

Production overheads are recovered on the basis of direct labour hours.

Non-production overheads are recovered on the basis of 125% of production cost.

One particular direct material is Material XR34. Griffey Ltd uses the LIFO method of stock valuation. Stock records for Material XR34 in March are as follows.

1 March	Opening balance	500 kg	Total value of £1,500
5 March	Receipt	400 kg	Total cost of £1,220
10 March	Issues to production	300 kg	
12 March	Receipt	300 kg	Total cost £918
21 March	Issues to production	500 kg	

Sales price is calculated to give profit of 20% of sales price for each job undertaken by Griffey Ltd.

Required

(a) Calculate an appropriate overhead absorption rate in each production department.

(5 marks)

(b) Prepare a stores record card for Material XR34 and calculate the total value of materials issued. **(5 marks)**

(c) Job 1763 was started and completed during March 20X8. The following details are available.

Material XR34

200 kg issued on 10 March

500 kg issued on 21 March

Labour

The following number of hours were spent working on Job 1763.

	Direct labour hours
Assembly	11
Finishing	4

Calculate the sale price of Job 1763. **(5 marks)**

(Total : 15 marks)

7.3 Solution

Part (a)

	Assembly £	Finishing £	Maintenance £
Indirect materials (W1)	30,000	15,000	5,000
General production overheads and indirect labour (W2)	80,000	80,000	80,000
Total	110,000	95,000	85,000
Re-apportion maintenance 3:1	63,750	21,250	(85,000)
Total	173,750	116,250	
Direct labour hours	4,000	2,000	
Rate per direct labour hour	£43.44	£58.13	

(W1) Cost per kg of indirect materials = total cost/total kg = £50,000/5,000 = £10 per kg.

(W2) Since these are both to be split equally, total = £200,000 + £40,000 = £240,000
£240,000/3 = £80,000 each.

Part (b)

Date	Ref			In stock	
1 March	(i)	Opening balance	(i)	500 kg @ £3 per kg (W1)
5 March	(ii)	Receipt	(i)	500 kg @ £3 per kg
		400 kg @ £3.05 (W2)	(ii)	400 kg @ £3.05 per kg
10 March		Issue	(i)	500 kg @ £3 per kg
		300 kg @ £3.05 (ii)	(ii)	100 kg @ £3.05 per kg
12 March	(iii)	Receipt	(i)	500 kg @ £3 per kg
		300 kg @ £3.06 (W3)	(ii)	100 kg @ £3.05 per kg
			(iii)	300 kg @ £3.06 per kg
21 March		Issue	(i)	400 kg @ £3 per kg
		300 kg @ £3.06 (iii)		
		100 kg @ £3.05 (ii)		
		100 kg @ £3 (i)		

(W1) Cost per kg = Total value/kg = £1,500/500 = £3 per kg

(W2) Cost per kg = £1,220/440 = £3.05 per kg

(W3) Cost per kg = £918/300 = £3.06 per kg

Total value of materials issued:

300 kg	@	£3.06	=	918
400 kg	@	£3.05	=	1,220
100 kg	@	£3	=	300
800 kg				£2,438

Part (c)

Cost card for Job 1763

Direct material XR34

		£
200 kg issued on 10 March	200 kg @ £3.05	610.00
500 kg issued on 21 March	300 kg @ £3.06	
	100 kg @ £3.05	
	100 kg @ £3.00	1,523.00
		2,133.00

Direct labour

Labour (11 + 4) hours @ £12.50 per hour (W1)			187.50
Overheads			
Assembly	11 hours @ £43.44	477.84	
Finishing	4 hours @ £58.13	232.52	
			710.36
Production cost			3,030.86
Selling and administration		125% × £3,030.86	3,788.58
Total cost			6,819.44
Margin (W2)		£6,819.44 × 20/80	1,704.85
Sales price			8,524.29

(W1) Labour rate per hour = total cost/hours worked = £75,000/6,000 = £12.50 per hour.

(W2) Margin = 20% of price

Cost = 80% of price

∴ Margin = $\dfrac{20}{80} \times \text{Cost}$

Practice question 4 *(The answer is in the final chapter of this book)*

PQR

Knowing that you are studying cost accounting, a friend who manages a small business has sought your advice about how to produce quotations in response to the enquiries which her business receives. She believes that she has lost orders recently through her use of a job cost estimating system which was introduced, on the advice of her auditors, seven years ago.

This system adds a plant-wide percentage of 125% to prime costs in order to arrive at a selling price. This percentage is intended to cover all overheads for the three production departments (P, Q, and R), all the selling, distribution and administration costs and the profit.

You recommend that an analysis of overhead cost items be undertaken with the objective of determining a direct labour hour rate of overhead absorption for each of the three departments that work passes through. You have already discovered that selling, distribution and administration costs equate to roughly 20% of total production costs, and that a margin of 20% of sales value is required.

There are 50 direct workers in the business plus indirect production people. From the books, you find the following information.

Cost/expense	Annual amount £	Basis for apportionment where allocation is not given
Repairs and maintenance	62,000	P £42,000 Q £10,000 R £10,000
Depreciation	40,000	Cost of plant and equipment
Consumable supplies	9,000	Direct labour hours
Wage related costs	87,000	12.5% of direct wages costs
Indirect labour	90,000	Direct labour hours
Canteen	30,000	Number of direct workers
Business rates and insurance	26,000	Floor area

Other information/estimates

	Department P	Department Q	Department R
Estimated direct labour hours	50,000	30,000	20,000
Direct wages costs	£386,000	£210,000	£100,000
Number of direct workers	25	15	10
Floor area in square metres	5,000	4,000	1,000
Plant and equipment at cost	£170,000	£140,000	£90,000

Required

(a) Calculate the overhead absorption rates for each department based on direct labour hours.

(b) Prepare a sample quotation for Job 976, utilising your answer to (a) and the following information.

Estimated direct material costs	£800
Estimated direct labour hours	30 in Department P 10 in Department Q 5 in Department R

Calculate what would have been quoted for Job 976 under the 'auditors' system' and comment on your friend's suspicions about lost business.

8 Summary

You should now be able to:

- Explain the meaning of overheads
- Identify and explain the different types of overheads
- Explain why absorption costing is used
- Identify and work through the stages of absorption costing
- Consider the effect of under/over absorption
- Perform the accounting entries for overheads

Chapter 4 Accounting for overheads using absorption costing

Multiple choice questions *(The answers are in the final chapter of this book)*

1. A firm absorbs overheads on labour hours. In one period 11,500 hours were worked, actual overheads were £138,000 and there was £23,000 over-absorption. The overhead absorption rate per hour was:

    A £10

    B £12

    C £13

    D £14

2. A company absorbs overheads on machine hours which were budgeted at 11,250 with overheads of £258,750. Actual results were 10,980 hours with overheads of £254,692.

    Overheads were:

    A under-absorbed by £2,152

    B over-absorbed by £4,058

    C under-absorbed by £4,058

    D over-absorbed by £2,152

3. A method of dealing with overheads involves spreading common costs over cost centres on the basis of benefit received. This is known as:

    A overhead absorption

    B overhead apportionment

    C overhead allocation

    D overhead analysis

CHAPTER 5

Absorption and marginal costing

EXAM FOCUS

Marginal costing is a different method of costing to absorption costing. Questions in the examination will often combine calculation of overheads with methods of treating them in the accounts. Marginal costing is particularly relevant for decision-making purposes and this can be seen in later chapters. Decision-making is a feature of every examination and therefore marginal costing provides the foundation needed to tackle questions in this area.

LEARNING OUTCOMES

This chapter covers the following Learning Outcomes of the CIMA Syllabus.

- Calculate product costs under absorption and marginal costing
- Explain the contribution concept
- Compare and contrast absorption and marginal costing
- Prepare profit and loss accounts from the same data under absorption and marginal costing and reconcile and explain the differences in reported profits

In order to cover these Learning Outcomes the following topics are included.

- Describe marginal costing
- Identify the differences between absorption and marginal costing
- Prepare the profit and loss statement using marginal costing and absorption costing
- Reconcile and explain any difference in the profit/loss reported under each system
- Advantages of absorption and marginal costing

1 Contribution and profit

1.1 Contribution

The concept of contribution is one of the most fundamental in cost accounting. Contribution measures the difference between the sales price of a unit and the variable costs of making and selling that unit.

Illustration

Sales price	£10
Direct costs	(£6) (materials, labour etc)
Contribution	£4

The concept of contribution is an extremely important one in cost and management accounting. It is important to remember that since contribution measures the difference between sales price and the variable cost of making a unit, **if a product has a positive contribution it is worth making** (since it will contribute some amount, however small, towards paying the fixed overheads).

1.2 Profit

The above does not include fixed overheads, so how do we account for them?

Assume that we sell 10,000 units of the above product, and that fixed overheads amount to £30,000.

Total contribution is 10,000 × £4 = £40,000

The fixed costs must be paid out of this £40,000 contribution. If there is any money left over this will represent profit.

Profit = total contribution − fixed costs = £40,000 − £30,000 = £10,000

1.3 Changes in activity level

It should be clear from the above that **there is a direct link between the total contribution and the number of items sold.** If sales doubled to 20,000 units the total contribution would also double to £80,000.

What would happen if we looked at the profit for one unit? If fixed overheads are absorbed on a unit basis we would add £30,000/10,000 = £3 per unit for fixed overheads.

The profit for one unit would be as follows:

	£
Sales price	10
Direct costs (materials, labour etc)	6
Contribution	4
Fixed overheads	3
Profit per unit	1

What happens to profit if one extra unit is made and sold (ie we make and sell 10,001 units)? Does the profit go up by £1?

At first glance it looks obvious that the answer is yes, but remember that £3 of the revenue from each unit has been set aside to pay for fixed overheads. Once sales of 10,000 units have been achieved this is no longer needed, because the fixed overheads have been paid.

So what does happen if the company makes and sells an extra unit? Total contribution would go up by £4, but the fixed overheads would not change. **Profit would therefore also go up by £4 (ie the same as contribution).**

There is therefore **no direct link between profit and output.** If output doubles, profits do not necessarily double. We will see this in later chapters of this book.

2 The differences between absorption and marginal costing

Absorption and marginal costing are two different ways of valuing finished goods in stock. This difference in treatment leads to two different ways of preparing profit statements.

- Marginal costing values stock at the amount it costs to produce each unit (the marginal cost). This means including direct materials, direct labour, direct expenses and any *variable* production overheads. No fixed overheads are absorbed into product costs.

- Absorption costing adds an amount to the cost of each unit to represent the fixed production overheads incurred by that product. Remember that the amount added to each unit is based on estimates made at the start of the period. If these estimates are incorrect we may have under or over absorption. Absorption costing is a requirement of SSAP9.

3 Profit/loss statement - marginal and absorption costing

3.1 Layout of profit statement – marginal costing

The proforma layout for calculating profit and loss under marginal costing is as follows (with illustrative figures).

	£	£
Sales		100,000
Opening stock (at marginal cost)	10,000	
Add production (at marginal cost)	80,000	
	90,000	
Less closing stock (at marginal cost)	(15,000)	
Variable cost of sales		(75,000)
Contribution		25,000
Less: Actual fixed production costs	6,000	
Actual fixed non-production costs	8,000	
		(14,000)
Profit for the period		11,000

3.2 Layout of profit statement – absorption costing

Using absorption costing, the layout is somewhat different.

	£	£
Sales		100,000
Opening stock (at absorption cost)	14,000	
Add production (at absorption cost)	90,000	
	104,000	
Less closing stock (at absorption cost)	(21,000)	
Cost of sales		(83,000)
		17,000
Add over absorbed overheads (or less under absorbed overheads)		3,000
Gross profit		20,000
Less actual fixed non-production costs		(8,000)
Profit for the period		12,000

Note in the above the different treatment of fixed production and fixed non-production overheads. Also note that you will have either over or under absorption for a product (one product cannot have both).

3.3 Reconciliation of profit/loss under absorption and marginal costing systems

These two methods of calculating profit will usually give different amounts. This is because marginal costing includes the actual fixed overheads spent in a period whereas absorption costing carries them forward in closing stock (they are treated as costs in the next period). There may also be fixed overheads brought forward in opening stock.

We will need to be able to reconcile these profits for the examination.

The proforma for this reconciliation is as follows.

	£
Marginal costing profit	X
Add: change in stock × fixed overheads per unit	X
Gives absorption costing profit	X

Notice that the change in stock is calculated as closing stock units less opening stock units. If the change in stock is negative then this will be a negative figure (in which case marginal costing gives a higher profit figure).

3.4 Worked example of profit and loss statements

		Per unit
Sales price		£15
Materials		£4
Variable production costs		£2
Budgeted fixed production overheads		£40,000 per month
Budgeted production and sales		10,000 units per month
Actual production	9,000 units in Month 1	11,000 units in Month 2
Actual sales	8,000 units in Month 1	12,000 units in Month 2
Actual fixed production overheads		£40,000 each month
No opening stock		

Required

(a) Produce a marginal costing standard cost card.

(b) Produce an absorption costing standard cost card.

(c) Produce a marginal costing and an absorption costing profit and loss account for Month 1, and reconcile the two.

(d) Produce a marginal costing and an absorption costing profit and loss account for Month 2, and reconcile the two.

3.5 Solution

Part (a): marginal costing standard cost card

	£	£
Sales price		15
Materials	4	
Variable production costs	2	
Variable production cost of sales		(6)
Contribution per unit		9

Part (b): absorption costing standard cost card

	£	£
Sales price		15
Materials	4	
Variable production costs	2	
Fixed production overheads (W)	4	
Cost of sales		(10)
Profit per unit		5

Working

The fixed overhead absorbed by each unit is as follows.

$$\frac{\text{Budgeted fixed overheads}}{\text{Budgeted production}} = \frac{£40,000}{10,000} = £4 \text{ per unit}$$

Again, remember that these are estimates. If you look at the actual units produced each month it is never equal to 10,000. This is irrelevant, because absorption costing uses the *expected* amounts.

When calculating the profit we will need the number of units in closing stock. This is given by: opening stock + production − sales.

In Month 1 this will be 0 + 9,000 − 8,000 = 1,000 units.

Remember that closing stock in Month 1 becomes opening stock in Month 2. So closing stock in Month 2 will be: 1,000 + 11,000 − 12,000 = 0 units.

✓ If you are not given opening stock in a question assume it equals 0 units. You should also assume, unless told otherwise, that unit revenues and costs are as budgeted.

Part (c): marginal costing profit and loss account for Month 1

	£	£
Sales (8,000 × £15)		120,000
Opening stock	–	
Variable production costs (9,000 × £6)	54,000	
Closing stock (1,000 × £6)	(6,000)	
Variable cost of sales		(48,000)
Contribution		72,000
Fixed costs		(40,000)
Profit		32,000

Absorption costing profit and loss account for Month 1

	£	£
Sales (8,000 × £15)		120,000
Opening stock	–	
Production costs (9,000 × £10)	90,000	
Closing stock (1,000 × £10)	(10,000)	
Cost of sales		(80,000)
		40,000
Under absorption:		
Amount absorbed (9,000 × £4)	36,000	
Actual expenditure	40,000	
		(4,000)
Profit		36,000

Reconciliation of profits

	£
Marginal costing profit	32,000
Add: fixed overheads in change in stock levels (1,000 × £4)	4,000
Absorption costing profit	36,000

Part (d): marginal costing profit and loss account for Month 2

	£	£
Sales (12,000 × £15)		180,000
Opening stock (1,000 × £6)	6,000	
Variable production costs (11,000 × £6)	66,000	
Closing stock	–	
Variable cost of sales		(72,000)
Contribution		108,000
Fixed costs		(40,000)
Profit		68,000

Absorption costing profit and loss account for Month 2

	£	£
Sales (12,000 × £15)		180,000
Opening stock (1,000 × £10)	10,000	
Production costs (11,000 × £10)	110,000	
Closing stock	–	
Cost of sales		(120,000)
		60,000
Over absorption		
Amount absorbed (11,000 × £4)	44,000	
Actual expenditure	40,000	
		4,000
Profit		64,000

Reconciliation of profits

	£
Marginal costing	68,000
Deduct: fixed overheads in change in stock levels	
(1,000 × £4)	(4,000)
Absorption costing profit	64,000

(Closing stock = 0 units – opening stock of 1,000 units gives a decrease of 1,000 units.)

4 Advantages of absorption and marginal costing

4.1 Advantages of absorption costing

1. SSAP 9 requires its use for financial reporting.

2. The importance of fixed costs is revealed.

3. Where sales are seasonal and production steady the profit figure, being more consistent with production, will be more reasonable.

4.2 Advantages of marginal costing

1. Simplicity – avoiding apportionments and absorption problems.

2. Fixed costs logically relate to time and are so charged.

3. Profit figures more consistent with fluctuating sales.

4. Better for decision making.

The choice between the two will depend on the requirements of and production/sales profile of the particular organisation.

Practice questions 1 - 3 *(The answers are in the final chapter of this book)*

1 Absorption costing

The following information has been provided.

	Cost per unit £
Direct material	8.50
Direct labour	27.20
Variable production overhead	11.30
Variable selling costs	2.20
Fixed production overhead	14.00
Fixed selling costs	4.95

Selling prices are set such that net contribution is 20% of revenue.

Required

Calculate each of the following in £/unit.

(a) Prime cost   35.70
(b) Full production cost   61.00

(c) Full cost of making and selling 68.15
(d) Marginal cost of making and selling 49.20
(e) Absorption cost stock value 61.00
(f) Selling price 61.50
(g) Unit profit −6.65
(h) Unit contribution 12.30

2 Marginal costing

At the start of the year there were 500 units in stock. Budget and actual production was 10,200 units and sales were 9,600 units during the year. The standard cost of a unit is £15 (absorption costing) or £12 (marginal costing). All units were sold for £20. Fixed production costs were as budgeted.

Required

Calculate gross profit for the two costing methods and explain any difference.

3 McTack

McTack manufactures typewriters and has produced a budget for the quarter ended 31 March 20X4 (Quarter 1) as follows.

	£	£
Sales (100 units @ £500 per unit)		50,000
Production cost of 120 units		
Materials	12,000	
Labour	24,000	
Variable overhead	6,000	
Fixed overhead	6,000	
	48,000	
Less closing stock (20 × £400)	(8,000)	
		(40,000)
Profit		10,000

There was no opening stock on 1 January 20X4 and it is expected that the long-term average quarterly production and sales level will be 120 units.

He produces budgets for production, sales and stock for the next three quarters of the year as follows (the sales price, variable costs per unit and fixed costs being the same as for Quarter 1).

Quarter	2 (units)	3 (units)	4 (units)
Opening stock	20	30	30
Production	120	120	120
Sales	110	120	130
Closing stock	30	30	20

Required

(a) Produce a schedule showing the cost of production per unit and the contribution/profit per unit using marginal costing and absorption costing.

(b) Produce budgeted profit and loss accounts for the four quarters of the year using marginal costing and absorption costing.

(c) Explain the difference in the budgeted profit figures for Quarter 1 as calculated on the two different bases. **(18 marks)**

5 Summary

You should now be able to:

- Explain marginal costing
- Identify the difference between absorption and marginal costing
- Prepare the profit and loss statement using marginal costing and absorption costing
- Reconcile and any difference in the profit/loss reported under each system

Multiple choice questions *(The answers are in the final chapter of this book)*

1   A company made 17,500 units at a total cost of £16 each. Three quarters of the costs were variable and one quarter fixed. 15,000 units were sold at £25 each. There were no opening stocks.

By how much will the profit calculated using absorption costing principles differ from the profit if marginal costing principles had been used?

A   The absorption costing profit would be £22,500 less

B   The absorption costing profit would be £10,000 greater

C   The absorption costing profit would be £135,000 greater

D   The absorption costing profit would be £10,000 less

2   When comparing the profits reported under marginal and absorption costing during a period when the level of stocks increased,

A   absorption costing profits will be higher and closing stock valuations lower than those under marginal costing

B   absorption costing profits will be higher and closing stock valuations higher than those under marginal costing

C   marginal costing profits will be higher and closing stock valuations lower than those under absorption costing

D   marginal costing profits will be lower and closing stock valuations higher than those under absorption costing

3   Z Ltd manufactures a single product, the budgeted selling price and variable cost details of which are as follows:

	£
Selling price	15.00
Variable costs per unit:	
Direct materials	3.50
Direct labour	4.00
Variable overhead	2.00

Budgeted fixed overhead costs are £60,000 per annum charged at a constant rate each month. Budgeted production is 30,000 units per annum.

In a month when actual production was 2,400 units and exceeded sales by 180 units, the profit reported under absorption costing was:

A   £6,660

B   £7,570

C   £7,770

D   £8,200

CHAPTER 6

Job, batch and contract costing

EXAM FOCUS

In the first five chapters of this book we have looked at how costs are calculated for items such as materials, labour and overheads. The next stage will be to consider the ways in which these principles can be adapted to cope with different production techniques ie job, batch or contract costing. Whilst numerical questions on job and batch costing tend not to be as frequent as ones on contract costing, it is vital to ensure that you understand the nature of job and batch costing and the principles involved.

LEARNING OUTCOMES

This chapter covers the following Learning Outcomes of the CIMA Syllabus.

> Compare and contrast job, batch and contract costing systems
>
> Prepare ledger accounts for job, batch, contract (in accordance with SSAP9) costing systems

In order to cover these Learning Outcomes the following topics are included.

> Define the term "specific order costing"
>
> Define job costing and explain the treatment and accounting entries for costs
>
> Define batch costing and explain the treatment and accounting entries for costs
>
> Define contract costing and explain the treatment and accounting entries for costs
>
> Discuss particular problems encountered in contract costing, including profit recognition

1 Specific order costing

Specific order costing can be defined as:

> "The basic cost accounting method applicable where work consists of separately identifiable contracts, jobs or batches."
>
> CIMA Official Terminology

The sub-divisions of specific order costing are:

(i) job costing
(ii) contract costing
(iii) batch costing

2 Job costing

2.1 Definition

Job costing can be defined as:

> "A form of specific order costing in which costs are attributed to individual jobs."
> CIMA Official Terminology

2.2 Illustration

Jobbing operations are characteristic of certain types of engineering, for example fabricating a jig, tool or die to meet a customer's special requirements; manufacturing a special-purpose machine or building a special-purpose vehicle body. There are also general-purpose machine shops holding themselves available to carry out any type of machining operation as and when required. Certain trades also do 'one-off' jobs like house decoration, plumbing or domestic electrical work. Repair shops (for example, those which repair damaged vehicles or carry out periodic service operations) also perform a series of separately identifiable jobs.

In addition to these manufacturing based jobs, job costing can also be applied to services. An accountant or solicitor will keep a separate record of costs incurred on each job carried out for each client.

2.3 Cost collection

It is necessary to establish the cost of each job separately, either for the purpose of fixing a selling price or to ensure that the costs incurred on the job are kept within the price fixed in advance. It is also important to identify how much labour time (and in some cases machine time) is booked as **direct labour** to jobs, because **idle time** will enter into the amount of overheads to be recovered over the year as a whole.

The costing of separate jobs is the most fully developed application of cost accountancy since it involves:

(a) a separate cost record for each individual job;

(b) detailed time analysis and material usage records to identify the labour and material costs which relate specifically to each job.

2.4 Job cost card

Every job will have its own job card which will record all of the cost information – see illustration below. The costing information on the job card is then used at the month end to place a value on uncompleted jobs ie work in progress.

		Materials Estimate £1,250		Labour Estimate £100		Overhead Estimate £176		Other charges Estimate £25	

JOB CARD

Customer: Green & Co Ltd Job No: 342
Description: Transfer machine Promised delivery date: 3.11.X1
Date commenced: 25.9.X1 Actual delivery date: 13.11.X1
Price quoted: £2,400 Despatch note no: 7147

Date	Ref	Cost £	Cum £	Hrs	Cost £	Cum £	Cost £	Cum £	Cost £	Cum £
20X1						Hourly rate £11				
	b/f		1,200	17		110		187		13
6 Nov	MR 1714	182	1,382							
7 Nov	Consultant's test fee								10	23
8 Nov	MR 1937	19	1,401							
9 Nov	MRN 213	(26)	1,375							
10 Nov	Labour analysis			5	28	138	55	242		

Summary £ **Comments**
Materials 1,375
Labour 138
Overhead 242
Other charges 23
  ─────
  1,778
Invoice price
(invoice number 7147 dated 12.12.X1) 2,400
  ─────
Profit 622

Note the build-up of cost in the job card:

Direct materials	1,375
Direct labour	138
Direct expenses	23
Overheads	242
	1,778

Job costing uses the principles of costings explained in previous chapters, with overheads absorbed, in this case, at £11 per hour. The job is the cost unit.

3 Batch costing

3.1 Definition

Batch costing can be defined as:

> "A form of specific order costing in which costs are attributed to batches of products."
> CIMA Official Terminology

3.2 Illustration

The most common forms of batch are:

(a) where customers order a quantity of identical items, or

(b) where an internal manufacturing order is raised for a batch of identical parts, sub-assemblies or products to replenish stocks.

3.3 Cost collection

The procedure for costing batches is similar to job costing. The batch is treated as the job and the costs for the batch are collected on the job card which is then subsequently used to value work in progress.

4 Contract costing

4.1 Definition

Contract costing can be defined as:

"A form of specific order costing in which costs are attributed to individual contracts."
CIMA Official Terminology

Contract costing is similar to job costing except that the timescale, size and value of the contracts involved exceeds those of job costing. Typical applications are construction companies and civil engineering projects.

Because of the long timescale and size of the contracts there is a necessity for the valuation of work done at certain points in the contract so that invoices can be raised and progress payments received. Without this the contract may experience liquidity problems.

4.2 Cost collection

Every contract has its own account which is used to record all of the relevant cost information. The following types of costs are common to most contract costing systems:

- preparation of work specification and possibly of outline drawings;
- preparation of tender documents;
- negotiation of contract terms.

Some of the special features of contract cost accounting are as follows:

- *Materials delivered direct to site.* These will be charged direct to the contract account from the supplier's invoice.

- *Direct expenses.* In the case of site work there may be items of expenditure which are incurred on the site and are direct costs of the contract. These could include the purchase or hire of a site office or of special equipment and the supply of services such as electricity and water to the site. Under this heading also could be payments to a subcontractor for carrying out work not done by the company's own work force. The wages of a site manager and of any work force specially recruited for or seconded to the contract would of course be direct labour costs of the contract.

- *Stores transactions.* Materials may be requisitioned from a central store for use on the contract. Some of these materials (or of the materials purchased directly for the contract) may eventually prove surplus to the contract requirements. They should be identified and returned to store.

- *Use of plant on site.* Dealt with in detail below.

4.3 Use of plant on contract

There are two possible accounting methods for dealing with plant and machinery used on a contract.

(a) Where an item of plant is purchased for the purpose of a particular contract and has little further value to the business at the end of the contract, the cost of that item will be charged as a direct expense of the contract. At the end of the contract any proceeds of its sale will be credited to the contract account. Similarly any plant owned by the business and transferred to the contract for use over its remaining useful life will be charged to the contract at book value, and again any proceeds of its disposal will be credited to the contract account. Maintenance and running costs will be charged to the contract account.

(b) Where an item of plant is bought for or used on a contract, but on completion of the contract it has further useful life to the business, then on completion of the contract it will be valued and transferred either to another contract or into the fixed assets of the business. Alternatively the plant may be capitalised by the business and depreciation charges made to the contract on which it is used. In either case maintenance and running costs will be charged to the contract concerned.

4.4 Calculations and accounting entries

Having examined the particular features associated with contracts, it is now time to study the calculations that you may be required to perform in the examination. There are two particular problems that you need to master in the context of accounting for contracts:

(a) the calculation of the profit to be taken as the contract progresses;

(b) the accounting entries.

We examine the calculation of profit and the accounting entries below.

Terminology

Before moving on to the calculations you must understand some of the terminology:

(a) *Contract price* – This is the price agreed for the contract. It is the 'selling price' of the contract.

(b) *Work certified* – As the contract progresses, the architect or consultant will estimate, at regular intervals, the amount of work that has been completed by the contractor. It is expressed at selling price. For example, if the total contract price is £2,000,000 for a three year contract, the architect may certify that £300,000 worth of work has been completed at the end of the first year. The work certified will be invoiced to the customer as the contract progresses.

(c) *Payments on account* – The contractor will naturally want to be paid in stages as the work progresses. These payments are called payments on account, or progress payments.

(d) *Retentions* – In order to safeguard the persons paying for the contract, an agreed amount (typically 5%) will be deducted from each invoice, and will only be paid when the contract is finished and is seen to be satisfactory.

4.5 Attributable profit on contracts

SSAP 9 defines this as:

> "that part of the total profit currently estimated to arise over the duration of a contract (after allowing for likely increases in cost so far as not recoverable under the terms of

the contract) which fairly reflects the profit attributable to that part of the work performed at the accounting date."

The accounting problem presented by long-term contracts which may extend over a number of years is that if profit is only recognised at the end of the contract then profits reported in any one year will bear little or no relationship to the activity which has taken place during that year. Thus, in theory, it is clearly desirable to recognise the profit on a contract as it accrues over the life of the contract.

4.6 Reasonable certainty

The requirement to recognise attributable profit prior to the completion of a contract is considered by many accountants to be imprudent. Therefore, it must be stressed that attributable profit should not be recognised until the outcome of the contract can be assessed with **reasonable certainty**. Furthermore, where the outcome can be assessed with reasonable certainty before the conclusion of the contract, and attributable profit is taken up, the judgement involved should be exercised with **prudence**.

4.7 Calculation of attributable profit

(a) Calculate total profit currently estimated to arise over the duration of the contract. This is done by taking into account not only the total costs to date and the total estimated further costs to completion, but also the estimated future costs of rectification and guarantee work, and any other future work to be undertaken under the terms of the contract. These are then compared with the total sales value of the contract.

(b) Calculate that part of total profit in (a) which is attributable to the work performed at the accounting date.

SSAP 9 states that the profit taken up needs:

(i) to reflect the **proportion** of the work carried out at the accounting date; and

(ii) to take into account any **known inequalities** of profitability in the various stages of a contract.

Point (b)(i) above may present problems in the examination because the examiner may present information in different ways. There are two common ways of apportioning the total profit to the period under consideration:

(a) by reference to costs; and

(b) by reference to the contract price.

4.8 Example

Consider the following information:

Contract A is to run from 1.1.X1 to 31.12.X5

Contract price	£10m
Work certified at 31.12.X1	£2m
Costs incurred at 31.12.X1	£1m
Further costs expected to be incurred by 31.12.X5	£6m

You are required to calculate the attributable profit at 31.12.X1.

4.9 Solution

(a) Step 1: Calculate the total profit on the contract

	£'000
Contract price	10,000
Total costs £1,000 + £6,000	7,000
Total profit	3,000

(b) Step 2: Apportion the total profit for the year ended 31.12.X1

(i) by reference to costs:

$$£3m \times \frac{\text{Costs to 31.12.X1}}{\text{Total contract costs}}$$

$$£3m \times \frac{£1m}{£7m} = £428,571$$

(ii) by reference to contract price:

$$£3m \times \frac{\text{Work certified to date}}{\text{Total contract price}}$$

$$£3m \times \frac{£2m}{£10m} = £600,000$$

✓ The examiner should make it clear which method he wants to be used. If he does not, then either is acceptable.

4.10 An alternative calculation of attributable profit

✓ The examiner may not give you sufficient information to calculate the total profit and apportion it to the period. Consider the following information:

	£'000
Contract price, 4 year contract	200,000
Work certified, end of year 1	40,000
Costs incurred at end of year 1	30,000
Costs of work completed but not certified at end of year 1	4,000

You cannot calculate the total profits on the contract because you are not told the further costs to be incurred.

The calculation of attributable profit is as follows:

	£'000	£'000
Work certified at end of year 1		40,000
Cost of work certified to end of year 1		
Total costs for year 1	30,000	
Less costs incurred but not certified	4,000	
		26,000
Attributable profit for year 1		14,000

4.11 Foreseeable losses

In accordance with the prudence concept, if it is expected that there will be a loss on a contract as a whole, provision should be made for the whole of the loss as soon as it is recognised irrespective of:

(a) whether or not the work has yet commenced on such contracts;

(b) the proportion of work carried out at the accounting date;

(c) the amount of profits expected to arise on other contracts.

5 Contract costing worked examples

5.1 Example 1

The Amazon contract year ending 31 December 20X1

	£'000
Total contract price	1,000
Costs incurred to 31.12.X1	320
Estimated costs to completion	480
Progress payments received to 31.12.X1	300
Work certified at 31.12.X1	360

You are required to prepare a profit statement for the year to 31.12.X1

5.2 Solution 1

	£'000	£'000
Total contract price		1,000
Less: Costs to 31.12.X1	320	
Estimated costs to completion	480	
		800
Total estimated profit on contract		200

As measured by costs,

$\dfrac{320}{800}$ of the contract has been completed

Thus, attributable profit = $\dfrac{320}{800} \times £200,000 = £80,000$

So, £80,000 profit will be taken to the profit and loss account for year ending 31 December 20X1. The profit and loss account will also include in turnover the sales value of work done so far, ie. the value of work certified (£360,000). Cost of sales will therefore be a balancing figure of £280,000 (£360,000 – £80,000).

Profit statement for year ended 31.12.X1

	£'000
Turnover	360
Cost of sales	(280)
Attributable profit	80

5.3 Example 2

The Amazon contract year ending 31 December 20X2

	£'000
Costs incurred to 31.12.X2	665
Estimated costs to completion	95
Progress payments received to 31.12.X2	750
Work certified at 31.12.X2	810

You are required to prepare a profit statement for the year ended 31.12.X2.

5.4 Solution 2

	£'000	£'000
Total contract price		1,000
Less: Costs to 31.12.X2	665	
Estimated costs to completion	95	
		(760)
Total estimated profit on contract		240

Attributable profit to date = $\dfrac{665}{760} \times £240{,}000 = £210{,}000$

The profit dealt with in the profit and loss account for the year ending 31 December 20X2 will be:

	Total to 31.12.X2 £'000	Recognised at 31.12.X1 £'000	Year ended 31.12.X2 £'000
Turnover	810	360	450
Cost of sales (bal figure)	600	280	320
Attributable profit	210	80	130

Notice that the estimates of the outcome of the contract have changed from 20X1 to 20X2. This does not necessarily mean that the outcome could not have been foreseen with reasonable certainty in 20X1. What happened was that in 20X1 prudence was exercised in estimating the further costs to complete the contract. As things turned out the cost pattern proved to be slightly more favourable than expected and so extra profit was taken in 20X2 instead of in 20X1. Nevertheless prudence should always be exercised when estimating the likely outcome of a contract.

5.5 Example 3

The Bourne contract year ending 31 December 20X1

	£'000
Total contract price	500
Costs incurred to 31.12.X1	100
Estimated costs to completion	450
Progress payments received and receivable at 31.12.X1	70

You are required to calculate the attributable profit or loss for the year ending 31.12.X1

81

5.6 Solution 3

	£'000	£'000
Total contract price		500
Less: Costs to 31.12.X1	100	
Estimated costs to completion	450	
		550
Total estimated loss on contract		(50)

This loss must be recognised immediately and in full and so the loss of £50,000 would be included in the profit and loss account for year ending 31 December 20X1.

6 Accounting entries

6.1 The contract account

The contract account is simply debited with all expenses incurred on the contract. At the end of each period, the costs included in the attributable profit (if any) for the period is transferred to the profit and loss account and the stock of materials on site and contract work in progress are carried down into the next period.

Contract No 32 account

	£		£
Materials	x	Stock of materials c/f	x
Labour	x	Cost of sales (profit and loss a/c)	x
Expenses	x	WIP c/f (balancing figure)	x
	x		x

6.2 The turnover account

As the work progresses, an architect will usually certify that each stage of the contract has been completed. These certificates will give a sales value of the work done to date. This amount represents the constructor's turnover and the accounting entry is:

		£	£
Dr	Amounts recoverable	x	
Cr	Turnover		x

6.3 The amounts recoverable account

As the work is certified, the customer is invoiced. Any retention, usually 5% or 10% of the work certified, is held back (or retained) by the customer until the whole contract has been successfully completed. The retention represents a kind of insurance for the customer in case the contractor is unable to complete the contract or in case any rectification work may be needed at the end of the contract.

The manner in which these events are reflected in the books is very straightforward and may be shown as follows:

		Dr	Cr
		£	£
(i)	Dr Debtors	x	
	Cr Amounts recoverable		x
	– with the amount invoiced to the customer		
(ii)	Dr Cash	x	
	Cr Debtors		x
	– with the payment received from the customer		

(iii) At the end of each year the amount of turnover is taken to the profit and loss account.

(iv) After calculating attributable profit and hence, cost of sales, a transfer for this amount is made from the contract account to the profit and loss account:

Dr Profit and loss account	x	
Cr Contract account		x

– with cost of sales charge

Practice questions 1 and 2 *(The answers are in the final chapter of this book)*

1   Jeremy Bilt

Jeremy Bilt is a building contractor who operates under the name Froughnup Ltd, and specialises in flat conversions.

On 1 July he started work on the conversion of 91 Queens Gate into self-contained flats. At the end of his financial year (31 December) the contract is not complete, and you are given the following information at that date:

	£
Contract price	50,000
Materials purchased	12,150
Materials from other sites	1,040
Labour	8,460
Plant hire	1,070
Direct expenses	3,900
Administration expenses applicable	140
Stock of materials on site at the year-end	1,560

By the year-end, architects had certified work carried out up to 31 December to the extent of £30,000 which had been received in cash by Froughnup Ltd, subject to a 5% retention.

Jeremy estimates that the additional costs which will be incurred in order to complete the contract are as follows:

	£
Materials	5,940
Labour	5,670
Plant hire	750
Other expenses	2,920
	15,280

Required

You are required to prepare the relevant accounts for No 91 Queens Gate at 31 December and show how the profit taken to the credit of profit and loss account is calculated.

2 Contractors Ltd

Contractors Ltd have been engaged upon a construction project which has been designated in their books 'Contract 59'. The contract was commenced on 1 February 20X0, and expenditure on it was as follows:

	To 31.12.X0 £	Estimated to complete £
Materials purchased	18,692	25,250
Materials issued from store	1,496	–
Wages	8,457	14,420
Direct expenses	4,835	8,030
Charges for administration expenses	1,780	2,750
Plant purchased for the contract on February 1 20X0	10,800	–
Work certified	38,000	

On 31 December 20X0, there were wages accrued of £640 (included in the estimated costs to complete) and the stock of materials on the site amounted to £1,580.

The plant was purchased specially for this contract. The contract is expected to last a further 17 months at the end of which time the plant will have an estimated realisable value of £5,760.

The total contract price is £98,250 and attributable profit is to be calculated by reference to costs incurred.

Required

Prepare a contract account for the period ended 31 December 20X0 and to show your calculations of the amount of profit taken to the credit of the profit and loss account.

(20 marks)

7 Summary

You should now be able to:

- Define the term "specific order costing"
- Explain and identify costs under a job costing system
- Explain and identify costs under a batch costing system
- Explain contract costing and prepare the contract account, calculate the amount of profit to be recognised and calculate the value of work in progress.

Chapter 6 Job, batch and contract costing

Multiple choice questions *(The answers are in the final chapter of this book)*

1 The following items may be used in costing jobs:

   (i)   Actual material cost

   ✗(ii) Actual manufacturing overheads

   (iii) Absorbed manufacturing overheads

   (iv) Actual labour cost

   Which of the above are contained in a typical job cost?

   A (i), (ii) and (iv) only

   B (i) and (iv) only

   C (i), (iii) and (iv) only

   D All four of them

The following data is to be used for sub-questions 2 and 3 below.

A firm uses job costing and recovers overheads on direct labour.

Three jobs were worked on during a period, the details of which were:

	Job 1	Job 2	Job 3
	£	£	£
Opening work-in-progress	8,500	0	46,000
Material in period	17,150	29,050	0
Labour for period	12,500	23,000	4,500

The overheads for the period were exactly as budgeted, £140,000.

2 Jobs 1 and 2 were the only incomplete jobs.

   What was the value of closing work-in-progress?

   A £81,900

   B £90,175

   C £140,675

   D £214,450

3 Job 3 was completed during the period and consisted of 2,400 identical circuit boards. The firm adds 50% to total production costs to arrive at a selling price.

   What is the selling price of a circuit board?

   A It cannot be calculated without more information.

   B £31.56

   ✓C £41.41

   D £58.33

4 A construction company has the following data concerning one of its contracts:

Contract price   £2,000,000
Value certified   £1,300,000
Cash received   £1,200,000
Costs incurred   £1,050,000
Cost of work certified £1,000,000

The profit (to the nearest £1,000) to be attributed to the contract is:

A   £250,000

B   £277,000

C   £300,000

D   £950,000

CHAPTER 7

Service costing

EXAM FOCUS

There has been a shift in recent examination papers to accommodate the increase in service industries. Therefore it is highly likely that service costing will feature in some way in the exam. The important aspect to focus on here is although the title of this chapter refers to "service costing", in fact no new costing methods are involved, it is merely additional application of the methods already described in previous chapters. The important difference will usually be in deciding a suitable cost unit measure for the service unlike manufacturing companies who have a tangible unit of output to cost.

LEARNING OUTCOMES

This chapter covers the following Learning Outcomes of the CIMA Syllabus.

> Prepare and contrast cost statements for service and manufacturing organisations

In order to cover these Learning Outcomes the following topics are included.

> Define service costing
>
> Identify appropriate cost units in service costing
>
> Classify costs in service organisations

1 The examination

As an examination candidate you are not expected to have specialist knowledge of a wide range of industries; but you may be given the technical details relevant to a special business situation and be asked to establish costs in an appropriate manner. The purpose of this chapter is to make clear that no new costing principles are involved when you move from one type of business to another, but merely a logical thought process in deciding what are the relevant cost units and how may the elements of cost in materials, wages and expenses be analysed and classified in order to establish the cost of these cost units.

2 Service costing

2.1 Introduction

This is defined as:

> "Cost accounting for services or functions, eg canteens, maintenance, personnel. These may be referred to as service centres, departments or functions."
>
> CIMA Official Terminology

Thus the service provided may be for sale, eg hotel accommodation, or it may be internally provided.

2.2 Service cost units

It can sometimes be difficult to identify a cost unit that represents a suitable measure of the service provided and for this reason a composite cost unit is often used. A **composite cost unit** for example in the hotel industry would be "occupied bed night". Other examples include passenger mile for a transport company, meals served for a restaurant, patients days for a hospital etc. The nature of the service provided will determine the cost unit used.

2.3 Cost collection

As with job or batch costing the costs are collected in relation to the service provided and in order to calculate the unit service costs we simply calculate the average cost per unit as follows:

$$\text{Unit service cost} = \frac{\text{Total costs per period}}{\text{No of service units supplied in the period}}$$

2.4 Illustration

The following diagram represents the cost centre structure of a transport operation.

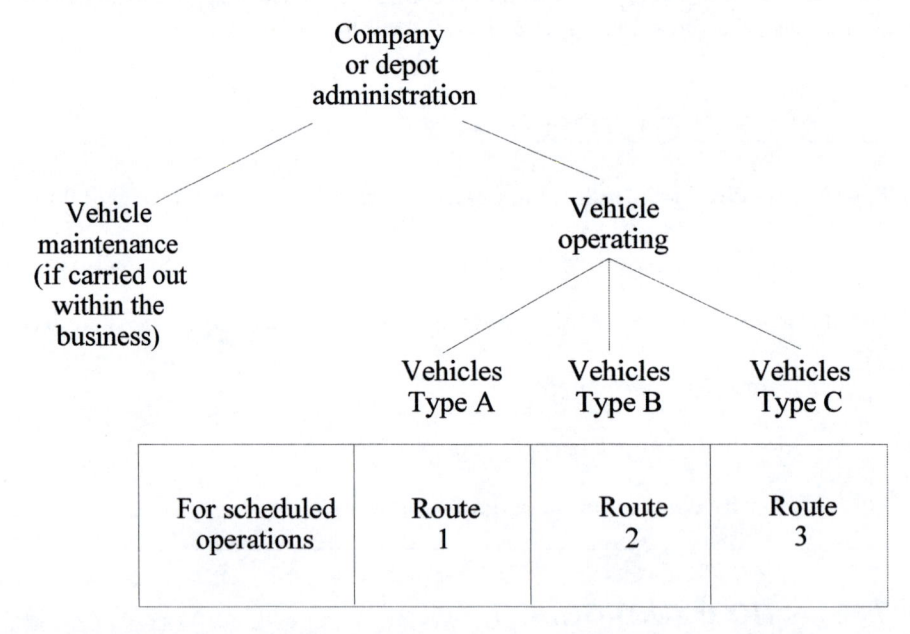

```
                    Company
                    or depot
                  administration
                   /         \
         Vehicle              Vehicle
       maintenance           operating
      (if carried out       /    |    \
        within the      Vehicles Vehicles Vehicles
         business)      Type A   Type B   Type C
```

| For scheduled operations | Route 1 | Route 2 | Route 3 |

Work done by the vehicle maintenance department, like that of any maintenance department, may be charged to the vehicle operating cost centres either by costing specific jobs or by apportionment on the basis of technical estimates.

The analysis of vehicle operating costs by type of vehicles or by route may be done formally by creating separate cost centres or may be a memorandum statistical calculation.

In some texts, it is suggested that each vehicle should be a separate cost centre. This is probably excessive, but certain statistical information will be required for individual vehicles such as kilometres run, fuel consumption per kilometre and down-time due to breakdowns or routine maintenance. This information can be obtained from the log book kept for each vehicle or may be held in the plant register.

3 Internal service activities

3.1 Types of service function

Although transport was dealt with earlier as a separate business, it should be noted that a transport department will often exist as a service function within a manufacturing or other type of business. This does not affect the cost accounting procedures that are needed. The only difference is that as an independent entity the transport business will sell its services at a commercial price, whilst as a service department it will probably transfer them to other departments in the business at cost.

Consider any other activities which might in some cases be carried on as independent businesses but which will frequently be performed internally for reasons of cost, security or flexibility of control. Under this heading we could include the costing of factory and plant maintenance, research and development or works canteen.

3.2 Advantages of internal service costing

Why should we want to establish a cost for 'internal' services – ie services that are provided by one department for another, rather than sold externally to customers? In other words, what is the purpose of service costing?

Service costing has two basic purposes:

(a) *To control costs in the service department* – The establishment of a distribution cost per tonne mile, a canteen cost per employee, a maintenance cost per machine hour, or a mainframe computer operating cost per hour, etc. enables us to:

  (i) compare actual costs against a target; and

  (ii) compare actual costs in the current period against actual costs in previous periods;

 in order to establish control measures.

(b) *To control costs of the user departments, and prevent the unnecessary use of services* – If the costs of services are charged to the user departments in such a way that the charges reflect the use actually made by each department of the services then:

  (i) if the service charges for a user department are high, the user might be encouraged to consider whether it is making an excessively costly and wasteful use of the service;

  (ii) the overhead costs of user departments will be established more accurately. Indeed some service department variable costs might be identified as directly attributable costs of the user department.

Practice questions 1 and 2 *(The answers are in the final chapter of this book)*

1 Retail store

A private company operates a departmental retail store in a large provincial town. What type of costing system would you suggest for the analysis of its results, and what statistical measures would you use in comparing the profitability of its various departments? **(12 marks)**

2 Delivery service

A transport company operates a regular delivery service from its warehouse at point A to a destination at point B, the total annual mileage covered (including 100 outward and return journeys) being 18,000 miles per 10-ton vehicle.

For the outward journey the vehicle is always fully loaded and in addition there is a regular demand for return loads of 400 tons per vehicle per annum. The standard charge to customers is 24p per ton/mile. The costs of operating this service are as follows:

Vehicle fixed charges	£5,400 per annum
Drivers' wages, including normal overtime	£10,260 per annum
Vehicle running costs	33p per mile

The company is willing to pay a bonus to drivers of up to 30% of any additional profit for obtaining additional return loads.

Required

(a) What annual profit would be earned per vehicle without any additional return loads?

(b) What annual bonus would be payable to a driver who consistently obtained an additional 5-ton return load?

(c) What annual bonus would be payable if the additional 5-ton return load involved a detour of 20 miles (on which no income would be earned) and £2 additional overtime pay on each occasion? **(18 marks)**

4 Summary

You should now be able to:

♦ Explain service costing, identify composite cost units and how costs are classified in service organisations

Multiple choice questions *(The answer is in the final chapter of this book)*

The following data is to be used for questions 1 and 2.

A small management consultancy has prepared the following information:

Overhead absorption rate per consulting hour	£12.50
Salary cost per consulting hour (senior)	£20.00
Salary cost per consulting hour (junior)	£15.00

1   The firm adds 40% to total cost to arrive at a selling price.

Assignment number 652 took 86 hours of a senior consultant's time and 220 hours of junior time.

What price should be charged for assignment number 652?

A   £5,355

B   £7,028

C   £8,845

✓D   £12,383

Chapter 7 Service costing

2   During a period 3,000 consulting hours were charged out in the ratio of 1 senior to 3 junior hours. Overheads were exactly as budgeted.

What was the total gross margin for the period?

A   £34,500

B   £48,300

C   £86,250

D   £120,750

3   The following data relates to two activity levels of an out-patients' department in an hospital:

Number of consultations by patients	4,500	5,750
Overheads	£269,750	£289,125

Fixed overheads are £200,000 per period.

The variable cost per consultation:

A   is approximately £15.50

B   is approximately £44.44

C   is approximately £59.94

D   cannot be calculated without more information

CHAPTER 8

Process costing

EXAM FOCUS

Process costing is one of the most complex areas of the syllabus and tends to be the area of cost accounting that most students find hardest to understand. However, it appears on a regular basis in exams, and therefore it is an area worth looking at repeatedly to make sure that you can have a reasonable attempt at any question asked. Apart from computational questions, you may face written questions as well. Developing good examination technique when approaching questions will help you to score maximum marks.

LEARNING OUTCOMES

This chapter covers the following Learning Outcomes of the CIMA Syllabus.

> Prepare ledger accounts for a process costing system NB the average cost method will only be used for process costing and students must be able to calculate normal losses and abnormal loss/gains and deal with opening and closing stocks.

In order to cover these Learning Outcomes the following topics are included.

> Explain continuous operation/process costing

> Demonstrate using a simple example how costs are collected in the ledger account (process account).

> Consider the type of losses experienced in process costing and their effects

> Consider the treatment of abnormal gains

> Identify the effect of scrap values/disposal costs for losses

> Discuss the use of the equivalent unit concept in dealing with opening and closing work in progress

> Prepare the accounting entries for the various accounts associated with process costing using the average cost method

> Explain and account for joint products and by-products

1 Process costing

1.1 Definition

Process costing is defined as:

> "The costing method applicable where goods or services result from a sequence of continuous or repetitive operations or processes. Costs are averaged over the units produced during the period, being initially charged to the operation or process."
>
> CIMA Official Terminology

Process costing is sometimes referred to as continuous operation costing as the goods produced result from a sequence of continuous or repetitive operations or processes.

Examples include the chemical, cement, oil, paint and textile industries.

1.2 Illustration

Process costing is used when a company is mass producing the same item and the item goes through a number of different stages. Here is an example.

First stage   Input some material valued at £1 per kg

Process (do some work to) the material (which costs money)

Output the material now valued at £2 per kg

Second stage   Input material from the first stage valued at £2 per kg

Process the material in a different way, increasing the cost again

Output the material now valued at £4 per kg

Final stage   Input material from the second stage valued at £4 per kg

Process the material again, increasing the cost

Output the material now valued at £9 per kg. This now goes into finished goods ready to be sold. Cost of sales is £9 per kg.

There are two main complications.

- What happens if some of the material to the process is lost?
- What happens if the process is not complete at the end of a period?

1.3 Ledger accounts in process costing

To keep track of the costs we are going to prepare a process account for each process. This resembles a T account with extra columns. The reason for the extra columns is that we have to keep track of how many units we are working on as well as their value.

The usual costs appearing in such an account are those for materials, labour and overheads. (Labour and overheads are often combined under the heading 'conversion costs'.) In the case of materials we record both units and monetary amount; in the case of conversion costs we record the monetary amount only, because they do not add any units.

1.4 Example

Typically a process account might appear as follows.

Process 2 account

	Kg	£		Kg	£
Input materials from Process 1	2,000	2,950	Output materials to Process 3	2,500	4,544
New materials	500	550			
Labour		564			
Overheads		480			
	2,500	4,544		2,500	4,544

In this simple case, the output to process 3 would be costed at:

$$\frac{£4,544}{2,500} = £1.8176 \text{ per unit}$$

2 Normal and abnormal losses

2.1 Normal losses

In many industrial processes, some input is lost or damaged during the production process. The first thing we will look at in process costing is the concept of normal losses and abnormal losses or gains.

Normal loss represents items that you expect to lose during a process, and its cost is therefore treated as part of the cost of good production.

2.2 Example

At the start of a heating process 1,000kg of material costing £16 per kg is input. During the process, conversion costs of £2,000 are incurred. Normal loss (through evaporation) is expected to be 10% of input. During March 1,000kg were input and output was 900kg.

Prepare the process account for March.

2.3 Solution

To prepare the process account we need to balance the units and then balance the cost.

Firstly, to balance the units we put input units on the left and output units on the right. Normal loss also appears on the right.

The process account will look as follows.

Process account – March (units only)

	Kg	£		Kg	£
Input	1,000		Output	900	
Conversion costs	–		Normal loss	100	
	1,000			1,000	

As you can see the units put in on the left total those on the right; our units balance.

Now we can go on to put in costs and values.

The input was valued at £16 per kg, giving a cost of input of £16,000. Conversion costs are £2,000. Normal loss is valued at zero – its cost will be absorbed into good production. Output is valued at cost divided by expected output (ie cost/(input – normal loss)).

In this example output is valued at £18,000/900kg = £20 per kg

The total value of the output is therefore 900 × £20 = £18,000

The completed process account now looks as follows.

Process account – March

	Kg	£		Kg	£
Input	1,000	16,000	Output	900	18,000
Conversion costs		2,000	Normal loss	100	–
	1,000	18,000		1,000	18,000

Notice that the units and the monetary amounts balance.

2.4 Abnormal loss

Any actual loss in excess of the normal (expected) loss is known as abnormal loss. This is **not** treated as part of normal production cost and is separately identified and costed throughout the process. Its cost is then written off to profit and loss.

2.5 Abnormal loss - example

In April, 1,000kg were input (at £16 per kg) to the same process as above and actual output was 800kg.

Required

Prepare the process account for the month of April.

2.6 Solution

Again look at the units only to start with.

Process account – April (units only)

	Kg	£		Kg	£
Input	1,000		Output	800	
Conversion costs	-		Normal loss	100	
	1,000			900	

As you can see, 1,000kg were input to the process but only 900kg have been accounted for coming out of the process. The extra 100kg is an *abnormal loss*. It represents items that we did not expect to lose. In this example it may have been that the temperature was set too high on the process, causing more of the input to evaporate.

To make the units balance we therefore include 100 units on the right of the process account to represent this abnormal loss.

Process account – April (units only)

	Kg	£		Kg	£
Input	1,000		Output	800	
			Normal loss	100	
Conversion costs	-		Abnormal loss	100	
	1,000			1,000	

Now that the units balance we can examine the costs.

Input, normal loss and output are valued at the same amount as before. The value for abnormal loss is the same as that of output, ie £20 per kg.

Process account – April

	Kg	£		Kg	£
Input	1,000	16,000	Output	800	16,000
			Normal loss	100	-
Conversion costs	-	2,000	Abnormal loss	100	2,000
	1,000	18,000		1,000	18,000

The units and values are now balanced. The £2,000 value of the abnormal loss represents lost output. This output cannot be sold (it has evaporated) and therefore the profits of the company will be reduced. In the accounts, the value of abnormal loss is debited to the profit and loss account.

2.7 Abnormal gain

An abnormal gain occurs where losses are less than expected. Its treatment is the same as abnormal loss only the debits and credits are reversed.

2.8 Example

In May 2,000 kg at £16 per kg were input to the heating process and £4,000 conversion costs incurred. This month output was 1,950 kg.

Required

Prepare the process account for the month of May.

2.9 Solution

We begin by looking at the units columns.

Process account – May

	Kg	£		Kg	£
Input	2,000		Output	1,950	
Conversion costs	–		Normal loss	200	
	2,000			2,150	

Again it can be seen that the two sides do not balance. This time the reason is that we have more output than expected. We would have expected to lose 10% of input (ie 200kg) so we expected output to be 1,800kg. In fact it was 1,950kg, an increase of 150kg. This additional output is an *abnormal gain*.

The completed process account is shown below.

Process account – May

	Kg	£		Kg	£
Input	2,000	32,000	Output	1,950	39,000
Conversion costs	–	4,000			
Abnormal gain	150	3,000	Normal loss	200	–
	2,150	39,000		2,150	39,000

Output and abnormal gain are both valued at £36,000/(2,000 – 200)kg = £20 per kg. Since we now have additional units to sell, the abnormal gain is credited to the profit and loss account. We have an additional 150 units to sell at £20 per unit.

3 Scrap value

3.1 Introduction

So far we have assumed that all losses are scrapped (ie they have nil value) but what happens if this is not the case?

3.2 Example

Maine Ltd processes a liquid. When it is produced a residue forms on top of the liquid. This is skimmed off and sold off for 90p/litre. Normal waste is 10% of input. Costs for batch 975D were as follows.

	£
Materials (10,000 litres @ £2 per litre)	20,000
Labour	2,000
Overheads	500
Total	22,500
Actual output	8,500 litres

Required

Prepare the process account.

3.3 Solution

The process account will include normal loss as before but this time it is **valued at its scrap value**. The sales value of the normal loss is then **subtracted** from the costs of the process before calculating value per unit.

In the example we would receive 1,000 litres @ £0.90 = £900 for selling the normal loss. This is entered in the process account. The same amount is then subtracted from the process costs, leading to the following valuation.

$$\text{Value per unit} = \frac{£20,000 + £2,000 + £500 - £900}{10,000 - 1,000} = £2.40 \text{ per litre.}$$

Although we actually have 1,500 loss units to sell (1,000 litres of normal loss plus 500 units of abnormal loss), we only include the sales value of the **normal** loss in this calculation.

Process account

	Ltrs	£		Ltrs	£
Input Material	10,000	20,000	Output @ £2.40	8,500	20,400
Labour	–	2,000	Normal loss @ £0.90	1,000	900
Overheads		500			
			Abnormal loss @ £2.40	500	1,200
	10,000	22,500		10,000	22,500

3.4 Normal and abnormal loss accounts

We now require two additional T accounts to show the value of the normal and abnormal loss in this situation. These match the costs of the losses (from the process account) against the scrap proceeds. Here we show separate accounts for each type of loss, sometimes they will be combined into one 'process loss' account.

3.5 Example

Show the normal and abnormal loss accounts for Maine Ltd.

3.6 Solution

Normal loss (scrap)

	Ltrs	£		Ltrs	£
Normal loss from process account	1,000	900	Cash proceeds	1,500	1,350
Abnormal loss	500	450			
	1,500	1,350		1,500	1,350

Note: This account may also be called a "scrap" account.

This T account takes the total sales of 1,500 units and cash proceeds received of £1,350 and divides it between the normal and abnormal loss units.

Abnormal loss

	Ltrs	£		Ltrs	£
Abnormal loss from process = full value of lost units @ £2.40	500	1,200	Cash received for abnormal loss @ £0.90	500	450
			P&L (balancing figure)		750
	500	1,200		500	1,200

✓ If the scrap value of the losses was nil, then we would have written off £1,200 to the profit and loss account. However, in this case we were able to sell the abnormal loss for £0.90 per unit. Since we received £450 for selling the abnormal scrap, we are only £750 worse off than if we sold all the lost units at full value.

In effect we are worse off by (£2.40 – £0.90) = £1.50 per unit lost. Since the abnormal loss was 500 units then we are worse off by 500 × £1.50 = £750 which matches the P&L figure in the abnormal loss account.

✓ In the above, the normal and abnormal loss accounts are being used purely to calculate the debit or credit to the profit and loss account. Remember they are not needed if the losses have no scrap value since the value of abnormal loss may be debited straight to the profit and loss account.

Practice questions 1 and 2 *(The answers are in the final chapter of this book)*

1 X plc

X plc processes a chemical. Input to a batch was as follows.

	£
Materials (10,000 litres)	10,000
Labour and overheads	800
Total	10,800

Normal loss is 10% of input.

Actual output = 8,700 litres. The remaining liquid was skimmed off and sold for 36p per litre.

Required

Record this in a process account, a normal loss account and an abnormal loss account.

2 Chemical compound

A chemical compound is made by raw material being processed through two processes. The output of Process A is passed to Process B where further material is added to the mix. The details of the process costs for the financial period number 10 were as shown below.

Process A

Direct materials	2,000 kg @ £5 per kg
Direct labour	£7,200
Process plant time	140 hours @ £60 per hour

Process B

Input from process A	?
Direct material	1,400 kg @ £12 per kg
Direct labour	£4,200
Process plant time	80 hours @ £72.50 per hour

The departmental overhead for period 10 was £6,840 and is absorbed into the costs of each process on direct labour costs in each process.

	Process A	Process B
Expected output	80% of input	90% of input
Actual output	1,400 kg	2,620 kg

Assume no opening or closing work-in progress.

Normal loss is contaminated material which is sold as scrap for £0.50 per kg from Process A and £1.825 per kg from Process B.

Required

Prepare the following accounts.

(a) Process A

(b) Process B

(c) Normal loss (scrap)

(d) Abnormal loss/gain

(e) Finished goods (extract)

(f) Profit and loss (extract)

4 Equivalent units and work in process

4.1 Introduction

We begin with a word of warning. This next section on equivalent units is not easy to assimilate in one go: do not worry if you have to read it through a number of times.

Process costs are used for many products where the process may not be completed at the end of a period (eg manufacturing cars). We need some way of calculating the value of work in process at the beginning and at the end of a period.

To do this we use the concept of **equivalent units**.

Illustration

We have 1,000 units that are 50% complete at the end of a period. How many finished units is this equivalent to?

$1,000 \times 50\% = 500$ equivalent units (these are abbreviated to EUs).

In other words, we could have made 500 units and finished them instead of 1,000 half-finished units.

The calculation of equivalent units is quite straightforward.

Equivalent units = Number of physical units × percentage completion.

4.2 Example

DL Ltd is a manufacturer. In Period 1 the following production occurred.

Opening work in process (abbreviated as OWIP)	=	Nil
Started and finished units	=	1,000
Closing work in progress (abbreviated as CWIP)	=	2,000 units each 25% complete

Required

How many finished units is this equivalent to?

4.3 Solution

		EUs
Started and finished	1,000 × 100%	1,000
Starting closing WIP	2,000 × 25%	500
Total		1,500

Costs for Period 1 will be spread over 1,500 units. Later in this chapter we will see how this is done. For the moment it is important to consider what we are trying to do. We will spend money in Period 1 making products, of which some will be completed and some will be unfinished (ie in closing stock) at the end of the period.

How much do we charge customers buying the completed products and how much is the closing stock valued at?

4.4 Example

In Period 2 the following production occurred in DL Ltd.

Completed opening WIP

Started and finished 500 units

Closing WIP = 1,000 units 60% complete.

Required

How many EUs were produced?

4.5 Solution

		EUs
Finishing opening WIP	2,000 × 75%	1,500
Starting and finished units	500 × 100%	500
Starting closing WIP	1,000 × 60%	600
Total		2,600

> One of the most common mistakes in the examination is the incorrect treatment of opening WIP. If the WIP is 25% complete at the start of the period then to finish it (ie to complete it) will require an additional (100% − 25%) = 75% of input.

Notice then that for closing WIP we take how much work has been done and for opening WIP we take how much is *left to do*. Those units that are started and finished within the period are always 100% complete.

4.6 Valuing work in process and finished goods

If we can calculate the cost of an equivalent unit we can calculate the cost of finished goods and closing WIP.

The cost per equivalent unit is simply calculated as total cost divided by the number of EUs produced. Assume that in DL above the costs in Period 1 were £6,000.

Earlier we calculated that 1,500 EUs were produced in Period 1. This was made up as follows.

		EUs
Started and finished	1,000 × 100%	1,000
Starting closing WIP	2,000 × 25%	500
Total		1,500

Cost per EU = £6,000/1,500 = £4 per EU.

This can be used to calculate the value of the finished goods and closing WIP.

Value of goods started and finished = 1,000 × £4 = £4,000.

You can see that the value of finished goods is £4 per unit and the total value of finished goods is £4,000.

Value of closing WIP = 500 × £4 = £2,000.

This will go in the balance sheet for Period 1 and will become the value of opening WIP for Period 2.

> Note that closing WIP is valued using EUs and not physical units. Many students get this wrong in the exam.

Our process account for Period 1 would look as follows.

Process account – Period 1

	£		£
Costs	6,000	Finished goods	4,000
		Closing WIP c/f	2,000
	6,000		6,000

You can see that if there is no opening WIP the method is quite straightforward.

- Calculate total equivalent units.
- Calculate total costs.
- Calculate cost per equivalent unit.
- Value finished goods and closing WIP as number of EUs × cost per EU.

5 Opening WIP

5.1 Introduction

Above we calculated the closing WIP as 500 EUs worth £2,000. This will become the opening WIP for Period 2. When we continue production in Period 2, what will we do with the work we have already done and the costs already incurred?

We will use the average cost method to overcome this problem.

5.2 AVCO – average cost

Under this method we imagine that the opening WIP units were produced in Period 2, ie we include its costs and physical units in Period 2.

5.3 Example

Staying with DL Ltd, production in Period 2 was as follows.

		EUs	
Finishing opening WIP	2,000 × 75%	1,500	(£2,000 costs associated with these)
Starting and finishing units	500 × 100%	500	
Starting closing WIP	1,000 × 60%	600	
Total		2,600	

Assume that Period 2 production costs were £13,000.

Required

Prepare the process account.

5.4 Solution

Imagine that opening WIP was also produced in Period 2, ie include it as started and finished (100% completed in Period 2). In other words, include all 2,000 physical units and £2,000 costs.

As the problems can get more involved, it is useful to start with a 'physical flow of units' to get the categories of production sorted out:

Opening WIP	+	Units started	=	Units completed	+	Closing WIP
2,000	+	1,500 (500+100)	=	2,500	+	1,000

Units started and finished = 500 + 2,000 = 2,500 × 100% = 2,500 (assume all started and finished within Period 2).

Closing WIP equivalent units are still 1,000 × 60% = 600.

Total costs = £13,000 + £2,000 = £15,000 (including costs brought forward as though they had occurred in Period 2).

Cost per EU = £15,000/(2,500 + 600) = £4.839 per EU.

		£
Started and finished	2,500 × 100% × £4.839	12,097
Closing WIP	1,000 × 60% × £4.839	2,903
		15,000

Process account – Period 2

	£		£
Costs in Period 2	13,000	Finished goods	12,097
Costs from Period 1 b/f	2,000	Closing WIP	2,903
	15,000		15,000

Practice question 3 *(The answer is in the final chapter of this book)*

Process WIP

On 1 March 20X0 a process contained 50 units, each 20% complete. During March work started on another 300 units and at the end of the month there were still 75 units in the process, each 60% complete.

The total cost of materials input during March was £3,596 and the opening work in progress had a value of £100.

Required

Calculate the value of both finished goods and closing WIP.

6 Treatment of materials and other costs

6.1 Different degrees of completion

So far we have talked about 'production costs' in general. In most questions, however, these will be split between various types of cost.

Assume that a process involves some direct materials and some direct labour and overheads.

Labour and overhead costs added together are often called **conversion costs**.

Usually, all the material is put in at the beginning of the process, whereas the conversion is 'added' as the product advances through the process. This means there may be a **different amount of equivalent units for conversion and materials.**

A good example is making a cake. All the materials (cake mix, fruit etc) are put in at the beginning, whereas cooking the cake advances through the process over time. So if the cake takes two hours to cook, after one hour the cake is 50% complete as regards the heating but is 100% complete with regard to materials.

Because of this, we have to keep track of the equivalent units for materials and for conversion separately.

For example, imagine we have a process in which all the materials are input at the beginning and that at the end of November there are 200 units 75% complete.

For conversion there are 200 × 75% = 150 EUs.

For materials all 200 units are complete (since all material went in at the beginning), ie 200 EUs.

6.2 Example

Blue Ridge Ltd specialises in making disinfectants. Production requires several successive processes and the production details of the first process are as follows.

Opening work in process		200 units
Degree of completion:		
Materials (valued at £6,060)		75%
Conversion (valued at £2,940)		25%
Units started in period		1,200 units
Closing work in process		400 units
Degree of completion:		
Materials		100%
Conversion		50%
Costs incurred in April:		
Materials		£75,000
Conversion		£69,000

Required

Calculate the value of closing work in process and completed units.

6.3 Solution

First start, as always, with a physical flow of units:

Opening WIP + Units started = Units completed + Closing WIP

200 + 1,200 = 1,000 + 400

The 1,000 units completed is a balancing figure and includes the 200 units b/f in OWIP.

The effective units, costs and costs per unit are most clearly set out in a table as follows:

Input	Effective units			Costs			Costs per EU (£)
	Completed in period	c/f in CWIP	Total EU	b/f in OWIP	In period	Total costs (£)	
Materials	1,000	400 (100%)	1,400	6,060	75,000	81,060	57.90
Conversion	1,000	200 (50%)	1,200	2,940	69,000	71,940	59.95
						153,000	117.85

Work carefully through the table to ensure you are quite happy about where all the figures have come from.

Note that for the 'completed in period column' effective units = physical units, as the opening WIP units are being treated as being wholly processed in this period. These units are then added to the effective units for the CWIP, to arrive at the total EU units treated as having been processed in the period.

The costs associated with the OWIP are added in, line-by-line, to the costs incurred in the period, to give total costs. These are then divided by the total EU to get a cost per EU for each type of input cost, and a total cost for each completed unit.

The costs may now be attributed to the categories of output as follows:

			£	£
Completed units:	1,000 × £117.85			117,850
Closing WIP:	Materials	400 × £57.90	23,160	
	Conversion	200 × £59.95	11,990	
				35,150
				153,000

105

CIMA Paper 2 Text – Management Accounting Fundamentals

The process account would appear as follows. Note that if any units are entered in here, they would be *physical* units, not EU, as this would get too confusing!

Process account

	£		£
Materials b/f	6,060	Completed goods	117,850
Conversion b/f	2,940	Closing work in progress	35,150
Materials	75,000		
Conversion	69,000		
	153,000		153,000

7 Equivalent units and losses

7.1 Introduction

So far we have looked at examples with either equivalent units, OR with losses. The example below covers both in one question.

7.2 Example

MR Ltd produces its product using two processes. The following data relates to process 2 in April:

Opening Work-in-Progress:	2,400 Kg		
Materials	100% complete	value	£8,232 (incl process 1 costs)
Conversion	50% complete	value	£954
Transfers from process 1	224,000 Kg	value	£670,880
Transfers to finished goods	210,800 Kg		
Closing Work-in-Progress:	3,200 Kg		
Materials	100% complete		
Conversion	75% complete		

Costs incurred in the period:

| Additional Materials | £63,466 |
| Conversion | £170,598 |

Normal loss is 5% of total units completed and occurs on inspection, at the end of the process. Losses have no scrap value.

You are required to prepare the process 2 account for April.

7.3 Solution

First start, as always, with a physical flow of units, this time including the losses:

Opening WIP	+	Units started	=	Good units completed	+	Normal loss	+	Abnormal loss (bal)	+	Closing WIP
2,400	+	224,000	=	210,800	+	11,160 (W)	+	1,240	+	3,200

Working   *Normal loss = 5% of (OWIP + Units started − CWIP)*

The normal loss is 5% of total units completed – ie both good and loss units. This must be total input units – CWIP units, ie 2,400 + 224,000 – 3,200 = 223,200. Thus normal loss is 5% × 223,200 = 11,160 units.

⚠ Normal loss percentages can be computed on a number of different bases – read the question carefully!

The effective units, costs and costs per unit are set out in the following table. Note that you do not need a separate column for normal loss as its cost is absorbed into the cost of other units:

Input	Effective units					Costs				Costs per EU (£)
	Completed in period	AL	c/f in CWIP	Total EU		b/f in OWIP	In period	Total costs (£)		
Process 1/ materials	210,800	1,240	3,200 (100%)	215,240		8,232	670,880 + 63,466	742,578		3.45
Conversion	210,800	1,240	2,400 (75%)	214,440		954	170,598	171,552		0.80
								914,130		4.25

The costs may now be attributed to the categories of output as follows:

			£	£
Completed units:	210,800 × £4.25			895,900
Abnormal loss units:	1,240 × £4.25			5,270
Closing WIP:	Process 1/mats	3,200 × £3.45	11,040	
	Conversion	2,400 × £0.80	1,920	
				12,960
				914,130

The process account would thus appear as follows:

Process 2 Account

	Kg	£		Kg	£
Opening WIP	2,400	9,186	Finished Goods	210,800	895,900
Process 1	224,000	670,880	Closing WIP	3,200	12,960
Added materials		63,466	Normal Loss (W1)	11,160	0
Conversion		170,598	Abnormal Loss	1,240	5,270
	226,400	914,130		226,400	914,130

Note the treatment of abnormal loss. It is treated in the same way as before, in that the units are the balancing figure of the account, and they are valued the same as goods output.

Do not ignore the abnormal loss in the calculation of cost per equivalent unit because the unit (Kg) would have been worked on.

Practice questions 4 - 6 *(The answers are in the final chapter of this book)*

4   Cleansing

A cleansing agent is manufactured from the input of three ingredients. At 1 December there was no work in process. During December the ingredients were put into the process in the following quantities.

	Kg	£ per kg
Material A	2,000	0.80
Material B	3,000	0.50
Material C	6,000	0.40

Additionally, labour costs of 941 hours paid at £4 per hour were incurred. Overheads are recovered on the basis of 50% of labour cost. There was no loss in the process. Output was 8,600 kg.

The closing work in process is 100% complete for materials. In addition, one quarter of the closing work in process is 60% complete for labour and overheads. The remaining three quarters is 25% complete as to labour and overheads.

Required

Prepare the process account for December.

5 Process X

A company operates Process X. All material is introduced at the start of Process X.

Details for Process X are as follows.

Opening work in process is 6,000 units 60% complete.

Costs contained in opening WIP

Materials	£24,000
Conversion	£15,300
Units started during period	16,000
Material costs in period	£64,000
Conversion costs in period	£75,000

Closing WIP is 4,000 units 75% complete.

Required

Prepare the process account.

6 NH Ltd

NH Ltd has two processes.

Material for 12,000 items was put into **process 1**. There were no opening stocks and no process losses. Other relevant information is:

Transfers to process 2	9,000 items
Direct material cost	£36,000
Direct labour cost	£32,000
Overheads	£8,530

The unfinished items were complete as to materials and 50% complete as to labour and overheads.

Information for **process 2** is as follows:

Items complete	7,600 items
Normal loss (scrapped)	600 items
Labour cost	£27,510
Overheads	£15,000

The unfinished items were deemed to be 25% complete in labour and overheads.

Required

Prepare process accounts for each process.

8 Joint products and by-products

8.1 Introduction

It is typical of many manufacturing operations that a process may yield not only the main product desired but also one or more secondary products. This poses the question of how to apportion the process costs to the various products.

The process output will not be separately identifiable until a certain stage of processing is reached. This is sometimes referred to as the 'split-off point' and the undifferentiated costs incurred up to that point are known as **joint-product costs** or **pre-separation costs**.

It is not possible to determine positively what proportion of the pre-separation costs relates to each of the products emerging. It is therefore necessary to use arbitrary methods of apportioning pre-separation costs over the different products. This introduces, to a greater or lesser extent, an element of unreliability as to the accuracy of the costs of each product.

If the saleable value of both products is relatively significant, the outputs are usually called **joint products**. If the secondary product has a small market value relative to that of the principal product, that secondary item is referred to as a **by-product** of the principal item of output; in such cases a decision may be taken not to cost it separately.

8.2 Joint products

Joint products are those resulting from the same process and having substantially equal importance (in value) to the company. After the different products have been separated they may be sold in their (then) existing state or further processed in order to give them a higher sales value. Whereas post-separation costs are usually identifiable with the particular product to which they relate, pre-separation costs can only be apportioned in accordance with one of the recognised bases outlined as follows:

(a) According to sales value, which may be:

  (i) the market value at the point of separation;

  (ii) the market value after further processing has been carried out, ie. the final sales value;

  (iii) the 'net realisable value', or 'notional sales value' method ie. the final sales value less the post-separation costs;

(b) According to physical measurement, which may be:

  (i) actual, where there is a common unit of measurement for all products;

  (ii) weighted in accordance with some technical estimation which reduces all output to a common basis.

8.3 By-products

By-products are items of relatively low market value that are produced in conjunction with a main product having a significant value. As with joint products, by-products may be sold either in their then state or after further processing.

Pre-separation costs are not charged to the by-products, but any revenue obtained from the sale of those products is either:

(i) credited to the process account, thereby reducing the pre-separation charge to the main product; or

(ii) credited direct to profit and loss account.

Method (i) should be used if the by-product service is a normal occurrence. Method (ii) should be used if the revenue were unusual.

Practice question 7 *(The answer is in the final chapter of this book)*

Product X

(a) Distinguish between the cost accounting treatment of joint products and of by-products. **(3 marks)**

(b) A company operates a manufacturing process which produces joint products A and B, and by-product C.

Manufacturing costs for a period total £272,926, incurred in the manufacture of:

Product A	16,000 kgs	(selling price £6.10 per kg)
Product B	53,200 kgs	(selling price £7.50 per kg)
Product C	2,770 kgs	(selling price £0.80 per kg)

Required

Calculate the cost per kg (to 3 decimal places of a pound £) of products A and B in the period, using market values to apportion joint costs. **(5 marks)**

(c) In another of the company's processes, Product X is manufactured using raw materials P and T which are mixed in the proportions 1:2.

Material purchase prices are:

P   £5.00 per kilo

T   £1.60 per kilo

Normal weight loss of 5% is expected during the process.

In the period just ended 9,130 kilos of Product X were manufactured from 9,660 kilos of raw materials. Conversion costs in the period were £23,796. There was no work in process at the beginning or end of the period.

Required

Prepare the Product X process account for the period. **(6 marks)**

(Total : 14 marks)

9 Summary

You should now be able to:

- Explain continuous operation/process costing
- Demonstrate how costs are collected in the ledger account (process account)
- Consider the type of losses experienced in process costing and their effects
- Consider the treatment of abnormal gain ie where the normal loss is less than expected
- Identify the effect of scrap values/disposal costs for losses
- Prepare the accounting entries for the process account, normal loss account (aka the scrap account); and abnormal loss and gain account

Chapter 8 Process costing

- Discuss the implication of opening and closing work in progress
- Prepare the accounting entries for the process account, normal loss account; and abnormal loss and gain account using the weighted average method of valuing working progress
- Explain joint products and by-products

Multiple choice questions *(The answers are in the final chapter of this book)*

1. In process costing, the value attributed to any abnormal gain units is:

    A debited to the process account and credited to the abnormal gain account

    B debited to the abnormal gain account and credited to the normal loss account

    C debited to the normal loss account and credited to the abnormal gain account

    D debited to the abnormal gain account and credited to the process account

2. In process costing an equivalent unit is:

    A a notional whole unit representing incomplete work

    B a unit made at standard performance

    C a unit being currently made which is the same as previously manufactured

    D a unit made in more than one process cost centre

3. Process B had no opening stock. 13,500 units of raw material were transferred in at £4.50 per unit. Additional material at £1.25 per unit was added in process. Labour and overheads were £6.25 per completed unit and £2.50 per unit incomplete.

    If 11,750 completed units were transferred out, what was the closing stock in Process B?

    A £77,625.00

    B £14,437.50

    C £141,000.00

    D £21,000.00

4. The following details relate to the main process of X Ltd, a chemical manufacturer:

Opening work-in-progress	2,000 litres, fully complete as to materials and 40% complete as to conversion
Material input	24,000 litres
Normal loss is 10% of input	
Output to process 2	19,500 litres
Closing work-in-progress	3,000 litres, fully complete as to materials and 45% complete as to conversion

111

The numbers of equivalent units to be included in X Ltd's calculation of the cost per equivalent unit, using a *weighted average basis* of valuation, are:

	Materials	Conversion
A	21,400	20,850
B	22,500	21,950
C	22,500	20,850
✓ D	23,600	21,950

CHAPTER 9

Cost bookkeeping

EXAM FOCUS

In the first eight chapters we have looked at how costs are calculated for items such as materials, labour and overheads along with the differing costing methods used by manufacturing and service industries. In this chapter we will look at how these costs are recorded in ledger accounts. Apart from a numerical question on an integrated system of cost bookkeeping you may face a written question on the differences between integrated and interlocking systems of cost bookkeeping.

LEARNING OUTCOMES

This chapter covers the following Learning Outcomes of the CIMA Syllabus.

> Prepare accounting entries for an integrated accounting system
>
> Explain the difference between integrated and interlocking accounting systems

In order to cover these Learning Outcomes the following topics are included.

> Explain the difference between cost and financial accounts
>
> Explain the two types of cost bookkeeping systems:
>
> - Integrated
>
> - Interlocking (aka non-integrated)
>
> Identify the differences which occur between the financial and cost accounting in an interlocking system
>
> Prepare accounting entries using an integrated accounting system

1 Cost accounting systems

1.1 Introduction

There is no statutory requirement for companies to maintain cost records. Therefore it is quite usual for companies to maintain traditional financial accounts and only prepare cost accounts on an ad hoc basis. There are two systems used for recording cost information within organisations:

- Integrated accounts
- Interlocking accounts

1.2 Integrated accounts

This is a set of accounting records which provides both financial and cost accounts using a common input of data for all accounting purposes. For example if a purchase of raw material is made on credit, the following entries are made under an integrated system:

    Debit   Raw materials

    Credit Creditors

When the creditor is paid off the entries are as follows.

    Debit   Creditors

    Credit Bank

Note that these entries are identical to the entries you would make in a financial accounting system. An integrated system is designed to provide financial information to the financial accountant and cost information to the cost accountant at the same time.

1.3 Interlocking accounts

Interlocking accounts are a system in which the cost accounts are distinct from the financial accounts. The financial accountant has one set of accounts and the cost accountant another. Both sets are kept in agreement or should be reconciled regularly.

The main difference is that the cost accountant has one account which represents *all* the financial transactions. This is usually known as the **cost ledger control account** or the **financial ledger control account** (abbreviated to CLC or FLC). The same purchase of raw material on credit that we looked at above would be recorded under an interlocking set of accounts as follows.

    Debit   Raw materials

    Credit   Cost ledger control account

The credit side could be cash or credit. The cost accountant is not concerned with how the material is paid for, simply that there will be a matching credit somewhere in the financial accounts.

1.4 Differences between financial and cost accounts

Under an interlocking system there will often be differences between the two sets of accounts. Here are some of the reasons why.

- Stock valuation: only certain bases (FIFO, weighted average) are allowed in the financial accounts, whereas some other method (eg LIFO) may be preferred in the cost accounts.
- Depreciation is usually done as a year-end adjustment in financial accounts, whereas in the cost accounts depreciation may be included in the apportionment of overheads and charged to cost units throughout the year.
- Items appearing in financial accounts only. Typical examples are dividends, profit and losses on sales of assets, interest, fines, etc.
- Abnormal losses: these may be treated differently in the cost accounts and the financial accounts.
- Items appearing only in the cost accounts. These are infrequent and usually relate to imputed charges for such matters as rents and interest.

2 Recording transactions

2.1 Introduction

Firstly, it is important to remember that there are **no set formats or layouts** for preparing cost accounts, so you do not have to learn any particular forms of presentation. For example a wages control account may be included, or the wages may be taken straight to the relevant cost accounts (in this chapter there will be various ways of presenting the information).

It is also important to note that there is **not a standard terminology**. For example one question might refer to the raw materials control account whilst another question refers to the stores control ledger. As long as the marker is aware whether you are dealing with stocks of materials, labour etc, the name of the account is not vitally important.

2.2 Accounting entries – integrated accounts

Below is a list of accounts. For each one the relevant debits and credits have been shown. The number next to each debit or credit refers to the other side of the double entry. (It does *not* mean that you must make the entries in this order; it is purely for reference.) Note that, for simplicity, the debtors, creditors and bank accounts have **not** been shown.

Stores ledger control

	£		£
Opening balance	O/B	Issues of direct materials	3
Creditors: Purchase of materials	1	Issues of indirect materials	4
Returns to stores	2	Creditors: Returns to suppliers	5
		Closing balance	C/B

Wages control

	£		£
Bank: Wages paid to staff	6	Direct wages	8
Bank: Deductions paid to relevant authority	7	Indirect wages (indirect workers + overtime premium etc)	9

Note: no opening or closing balances on this account.

Work in progress control account

	£		£
Opening balance	O/B	Returns to stores (direct materials)	2
Direct materials	3	Transfer to finished goods	13
Direct labour	8	Closing balance	C/B
Bank: Direct expenses	11		
Production overheads absorbed	12		

Production overheads

	£		£
Issues of indirect materials	4	Production overheads absorbed	12
Indirect wages	9	Under absorption	14
Cash spent on overheads (rent etc)	10		
Over absorption	15		

Note that the over/under absorption of overheads will be a balancing figure. (Obviously you will only have one or the other, not both.) Note: no opening or closing balances on this account.

Finished goods

	£		£
Opening balance	O/B	Transfer to cost of sales	16
Transfer from work in progress	13	Closing balance	C/B

Cost of sales

	£		£
Transfer from finished goods	16	Transfer to profit and loss	23
Administrative overheads absorbed	17		

Note: no opening or closing balances on this account.

Administrative overheads

	£		£
Bank: Amount spent on sales/administrative overheads	18	Administrative overheads absorbed	17
Over absorption	19	Under absorption	20

Note: no opening or closing balances on this account.

Over/under absorption

	£		£
Under absorption of production overheads	14	Over absorption of production overheads	15
Under absorption of administrative overheads	20	Over absorption of administrative overheads	19
Over absorbed overheads to profit and loss (balancing figure)	21	Under absorbed overheads to profit and loss (balancing figure)	22

Again the amount transferred to the profit and loss account is a single balancing figure. Note: no opening or closing balances on this account.

Sales

	£		£
To profit and loss	25	Debtors: Sales	24

Note: no opening or closing balances on this account.

Profit and loss

	£		£
Under absorbed overheads to profit and loss (balancing figure)	22	Over absorbed overheads to profit and loss (balancing figure)	21
Transfer from cost of sales	23	Transfer from sales	25
Profit for period (balancing figure)	26	Loss for period (balancing figure)	27

Again only a single profit or loss figure will be required to balance the accounts. This is equivalent to the transfer of profit to the capital account in the financial accounts. Note: no opening or closing balances on this account.

The closing balances on the stores ledger, work in progress and finished goods will form part of the financial ledger list of balances.

2.3 Interlocking accounting

If an interlocking accounting system was being used, the entries relating to bank, debtors, creditors etc would instead be made in the cost ledger control account, which would then appear as follows:

Cost ledger control account

	£		£
Returns to suppliers	5	Opening balance	O/B
Sales made	24	Purchase of materials	1
Loss for period (balancing figure)	27	Wages paid to employees	6
Closing balance	C/B	Deductions paid to relevant authority (tax etc)	7
		Direct expenses	11
		Cash spent on overheads (rent etc)	10
		Cash spent on sales/administrative overheads	18
		Profit for period (balancing figure)	26

The opening balances on stores ledger, work in progress and finished goods total to the opening balance on cost ledger control. The same is true of the closing balances. This can be used to check for arithmetical errors.

2.4 Rationale for entries

Why do the above amounts go where they do? The following general principles should help you to remember.

- Direct costs go to work in progress.
- Indirect costs go to production overheads.
- Overheads are transferred from production overheads to work in progress using a suitable absorption rate.
- Work in progress is transferred to finished goods.
- Finished goods are transferred to cost of sales.

3 Examples

3.1 Example – integrated accounts

The following information relates to the cost accounting transactions of a company. The company uses an integrated set of accounts.

				£
1	Credit/cash transactions			
	Credit:	Materials purchased		146,000
		Production overheads		92,000
		Administrative overheads		73,000
		Sales revenue		390,000
	Cash:	Wage costs		80,000
2	Materials issued			
	Direct materials			137,000
	Indirect production materials			5,000
	Losses written off			3,000
3	Wages analysis			
	Direct wages			60,000
	Indirect production wages			20,000
4	Production overhead is absorbed at a rate of 180% of direct wages cost			
5	Transfers into finished goods stock			290,000
6	Finished goods sold during the period			280,000
7	Administrative costs are charged to cost of sales at 25% of production cost of sales			

117

8   All under/over absorption of overhead is transferred to a single over/under absorption account before being charged to the costing profit and loss account
9   The opening entries in the stock accounts were as follows.

	£
Stores ledger account	33,000
Work in progress ledger control account	18,000
Finished goods ledger control account	68,000

Required

Record the above transactions in the relevant accounts including the profit and loss account. You do not need to show debtors, creditors or bank (cash) accounts.

3.2 Approach to the solution

The following is a guide to how to prepare the answer which is shown in full later. You may find it useful to set up the relevant 'T' accounts and complete the double entry as you go through and then compare your answer with the given version.

Where to start?

A good idea is to start with the opening balances. Not only will you gain credit for entering the balances but also you will have an indication of which accounts must be prepared.

Open T accounts for the following.

- Stores ledger (raw materials)
- WIP (work in progress)
- Finished goods

These are assets and are shown as debits in the ledger accounts.

Credit/cash transactions

If materials are purchased they are increasing the raw materials asset so they must be a debit, with a credit to creditors account.

		£	£
Debit	Raw materials	146,000	
Credit	Creditors		146,000 (not shown)

Money has been spent on production overheads (rent etc) and again this signals that a new T account is required. These overheads are an expense and are therefore a debit in the production overheads account and a credit to creditors.

		£	£
Debit	Production overheads	92,000	
Credit	Creditors		92,000 (not shown)

Another new account is needed for administrative overheads. The cost of these is again debited to this account with the other side being an entry in the creditors.

		£	£
Debit	Administration overheads	73,000	
Credit	Creditors		73,000

Next, we have received some revenue from sales. We will need a sales account and the amount received will be credited to this account. The debit side will be in the debtors.

		£	£
Debit	Debtors	390,000	
Credit	Sales		390,000

Finally, we have paid cash for wages. This tells us that we need to set up a labour account. Wage costs are an expense and therefore a debit in the labour account with a corresponding credit in the CLC.

		£	£
Debit	Wages	80,000	
Credit	Cash		80,000

Dealing with materials issued

Materials issued from stores are credited to the stores account (they reduce the amount in stock). Direct and indirect materials are treated in different ways.

- Direct materials are used to make units of production, ie they are part of work in progress.

		£	£
Debit	WIP	137,000	
Credit	Stores		137,000

- Indirect production materials are production overheads.

		£	£
Debit	Production overhead	5,000	
Credit	Stores		5,000

We also have some losses that have been written off. If in any doubt in the exam, go back to basics. If stocks have been written off this means they can no longer be used and so they must be reducing the amount of stock; therefore we must credit the stock account. The debit entry must be in the profit and loss simply because we can no longer use those items of stock (this means we need a profit and loss account).

		£	£
Debit	Profit and loss	3,000	
Credit	Stores		3,000

Dealing with wages

Wages are treated in the same way as materials. Direct wages (basic wages of direct labour) go to WIP whereas indirect labour costs (wages of indirect workers, overtime premiums etc) go to production overheads.

Since the amounts are being transferred out of the wages account they are credited to the wages account and debited to the WIP/production overhead account.

		£	£
Debit	WIP	60,000	
Credit	Wages		60,000
Debit	Production overhead	20,000	
Credit	Wages		20,000

Dealing with production overheads

In previous chapters we have talked about production overheads and mentioned that overheads need to be absorbed into the costs of products (we have previously seen production overheads appearing in the cost cards of products). We 'store up' production overheads in the production overhead account before adding them to the cost of WIP.

These overheads can be counted as part of work in progress and so they are transferred from production overheads to WIP using some suitable method.

In this example we are told that overheads are absorbed at 180% of direct wages. Since we already know that direct wages are £60,000, we can calculate production overheads as 180% of £60,000 = £108,000.

		£	£
Debit	WIP	108,000	
Credit	Production overheads		108,000

Dealing with finished goods

Work in progress refers to products that are not complete. Once they are completed they become finished goods. This stage simply represents a transfer of WIP to finished goods.

Since the amount of finished goods is increasing it must be treated as a debit. Similarly the amount of WIP is decreasing and therefore represented by a credit entry.

		£	£
Debit	Finished goods	290,000	
Credit	WIP		290,000

Dealing with goods sold

In the same way as above, goods that are sold during the period must be leaving finished goods and so a credit entry is made in the finished goods account. Since these goods have now been sold they go into a newly set up cost of sales account as a debit (expense) entry.

		£	£
Debit	Cost of goods sold	280,000	
Credit	Finished goods		280,000

Dealing with non-production overheads

We stated in an earlier chapter that production overheads are the only ones which can be included in stock valuation, so administrative overheads (or any other non-production overheads) cannot go into the WIP account. These overheads are treated by simply adding their cost to that of goods sold during the period using a suitable method. In this case the administrative overheads are absorbed at 25% of the cost of sales (this is the normal manner of absorbing these types of overheads).

As with the treatment of production overheads the idea is simply to transfer overheads from where they have been collected (in this case the administrative overheads account) into the cost of sales account. Since the cost of sales account represents expenses the amount will be debited here and therefore credited in the overheads account. The relevant amount will be 25% of the cost of sales, ie 25% of £280,000 = £70,000.

		£	£
Debit	Cost of sales	70,000	
Credit	Administrative overheads		70,000

Dealing with over/under absorption

When we dealt with overheads we stated that they are based on estimates of what will happen. In this example the company has absorbed production overheads at 180% of direct wages and administrative overheads as 25% of cost of sales based on estimates of how much it expects to spend and how much it expects to produce.

Usually these estimates will prove to be incorrect and so the company will end up with not having charged enough or having charged too much. In this example the company has added £108,000 to the value of WIP (in effect adding £108,000 to the sales price of products and passing the costs on to customers). If this amount is less than the actual expenditure on the overheads then the company has under-absorbed.

To calculate under/over absorption, simply balance off the amounts in each overheads account.

The amount spent on production overheads is £20,000 + £5,000 + £92,000 = £117,000, whereas the amount absorbed is only £108,000. In other words the company has under absorbed. The balancing figure is a credit in the production overhead account. The debit in this case is taken to a separate under/over absorbed overheads account (sometimes it will be taken direct to the profit and loss account) and so we need an account for this.

		£	£
Debit	Under/over absorbed overheads	9,000	
Credit	Production overheads		9,000

Similarly, £73,000 has been spent on administrative overheads but only £70,000 has been absorbed, therefore £3,000 has been under-absorbed.

		£	£
Debit	Under/over absorbed overheads	3,000	
Credit	Administrative overheads		3,000

Closing balances

The following accounts will have balances carried forward.

- Raw materials
- Work in progress
- Finished goods
- (Creditors, debtors, bank – if they had been shown)

Balance off each of the first three accounts (you should have an entry on the credit side for each one).

		£
Credit	Raw materials	34,000
Credit	WIP	33,000
Credit	Finished goods	78,000

Finishing off

The following accounts still require to be balanced off.

- Cost of sales
- Under/over absorption
- Sales
- Profit and loss

Cost of sales goes into the profit and loss account. Balance the account and transfer the amount to the profit and loss account (it will appear as a debit, ie an expense.)

		£	£
Debit	Profit and loss account	350,000	
Credit	Cost of sales		350,000

The balance on the under/over absorption account must be transferred to the profit and loss. In this case we have a debit balance, which will become an expense in the profit and loss (this is correct since we under-absorbed overheads).

		£	£
Debit	Profit and loss	12,000	
Credit	Under/over absorption		12,000

Transfer sales into the profit and loss account. Since these are income they will appear as a credit in the profit and loss.

		£	£
Debit	Sales	390,000	
Credit	Profit and loss		390,000

The profit and loss account can now be balanced off. The balancing figure of £25,000 is on the debit side indicating a profit for the period. This will ultimately be transferred to the capital account.

3.3 Solution

Raw materials control

	£		£
Balance b/f	33,000	WIP (direct issues)	137,000
Creditors (materials purchased)	146,000	Production overhead	5,000
		Losses	3,000
		Balance c/d	34,000
	179,000		179,000

Work in progress

	£		£
Balance b/f	18,000	To finished goods	290,000
Materials	137,000	Balance c/d	33,000
Wages	60,000		
Production overhead (180% × direct wages)	108,000		
	323,000		323,000

Wages

	£		£
Bank (wages paid)	80,000	WIP (direct wages)	60,000
		Production overhead (indirect wages)	20,000
	80,000		80,000

Finished goods

	£		£
Balance b/f	68,000	To cost of sales	280,000
From WIP	290,000	Balance c/d	78,000
	358,000		358,000

Production overhead

	£		£
Wages	20,000	WIP	108,000
Materials	5,000	Over/under absorbed	9,000
Creditors (production overhead)	92,000		
	117,000		117,000

Cost of sales

	£		£
Finished goods	280,000	To profit and loss	350,000
Administrative overheads (25% of production costs)	70,000		
	350,000		350,000

Administration overheads

	£		£
Creditors	73,000	Cost of sales	70,000
		Under/over absorption	3,000
	73,000		73,000

Under/over absorption

	£		£
Production overheads	9,000	Profit and loss	12,000
Administration overheads	3,000		
	12,000		12,000

Profit and loss

	£		£
Material losses	3,000	Sales	390,000
Over/under absorption	12,000		
Cost of sales	350,000		
Profit	25,000		
	390,000		390,000

Sales

	£		£
Profit and loss	390,000	Debtors	390,000

3.4 Entries for interlocking accounts

If the above example had been an interlocking system, the creditors, debtors and cash entries would have been replaced by entries in a cost ledger control (CLC) account.

The opening (credit) balance on the CLC will be the sum of the opening (debit) balances on the cost ledger accounts, ie:

	£
Stores	33,000
WIP	18,000
Finished goods	68,000
CLC	119,000

The accounts have been shown below with those changes made.

Raw materials control

	£		£
Balance b/f	33,000	WIP (direct issues)	137,000
CLC (materials purchased)	146,000	Production overhead	5,000
		Losses	3,000
		Balance c/d	34,000
	179,000		179,000

Work in progress

	£		£
Balance b/f	18,000	To finished goods	290,000
Materials	137,000	Balance c/d	33,000
Wages	60,000		
Production overhead (180% × direct wages)	108,000		
	323,000		323,000

Wages

	£		£
CLC (wages paid)	80,000	WIP (direct wages)	60,000
		Production overhead (indirect wages)	20,000
	80,000		80,000

Finished goods

	£		£
Balance b/f	68,000	To cost of sales	280,000
From WIP	290,000	Balance c/d	78,000
	358,000		358,000

Production overhead

	£		£
Wages	20,000	WIP	108,000
Materials	5,000	Over/under absorbed	9,000
CLC (production overhead)	92,000		
	117,000		117,000

Cost of sales

	£		£
Finished goods	280,000	To profit and loss	350,000
Administrative overheads (25% of production costs)	70,000		
	350,000		350,000

Administration overheads

	£		£
Creditors	73,000	Cost of sales	70,000
		Under/over absorption	3,000
	73,000		73,000

Under/over absorption

	£		£
Production overheads	9,000	Profit and loss	12,000
Administration overheads	3,000		
	12,000		12,000

Profit and loss

	£		£
Material losses	3,000	Sales	390,000
Over/under absorption	12,000		
Cost of sales	350,000		
Profit	25,000		
	390,000		390,000

Sales

	£		£
Profit and loss	390,000	CLC (sales made)	390,000

Cost ledger control

	£		£
Sales	390,000	Balance b/f	119,000
Balance c/d	145,000	Materials purchased	146,000
		Wages paid	80,000
		Production overhead paid	92,000
		Administrative overhead paid	73,000
		Profit and loss account	25,000
	535,000		535,000

Note the transfer of the profit and loss account balance into the CLC.

3.5 Example - SIA Ltd

SIA Ltd
Trial balance as at 1 January 20X1

	£	£
Share capital		10,000
Reserves		5,000
Fixed assets	13,000	
Provision for depreciation		3,000
Cash	5,000	
	18,000	18,000

During the year to 31 December 20X1, the following results were obtained:

SIA Ltd
Actual profit and loss statement year ending 31 December 20X1

Sales: 8,000 units
Production: 8,000 units

	£	£
Sales 8,000 units at £4.875		39,000
Production cost		
Direct materials		8,500
Direct labour		7,500
Variable production overhead incurred - electricity		5,500
Fixed production overhead incurred		
Rent	2,000	
Supervisor's salary	12,000	
Depreciation	1,500	
		15,500
		37,000
Actual profit		2,000

The fixed assets comprise production machinery and are depreciated at £1,500 per annum.

Fixed production overheads are absorbed at the rate of 200% of direct labour cost.

All purchases and sales are on credit, and all cash is paid and received by the year-end. There are no stocks at the beginning or end of the year.

Required

Prepare all the accounting entries for the year to 31 December 20X1.

3.6 Solution

In the solution, to prevent unnecessary entries being put through the accounts which may obscure the basic double-entry, no attempt has been made to rule off the various accounts nor to carry down balance at the year-end. After working through a solution you will find it helpful to quickly check the balances on the various accounts and verify that a trial balance, if taken out, would in fact balance.

Share capital

	£		£
		b/f	10,000

Rent

	£		£
Cash	2,000	Total overhead	2,000

Reserves

	£		£
		b/f	5,000
		Profit	2,000

Supervisor's salary

	£		£
Cash	12,000	Total overhead	12,000

Fixed assets

	£		£
b/f	13,000		

Depreciation expense

	£		£
Provision	1,500	Total overhead	1,500

Provision for depreciation

	£		£
		b/f	3,000
		Depreciation expense	1,500

Material purchases

	£		£
Creditors	8,500	WIP	8,500

Creditors' control

	£		£
Cash	8,500	Materials	8,500

Production wages

	£		£
Cash	7,500	WIP	7,500

Debtors' control

	£		£
Sales	39,000	Cash	39,000

Electricity

	£		£
Cash	5,500	WIP	5,500

Cash book

	£		£
b/f	5,000	Wages	7,500
Debtors	39,000	Electricity	5,500
		Salary	12,000
		Rent	2,000
		Creditors	8,500

Total fixed overhead

	£		£
Rent	2,000	WIP (200% × 7,500)	15,000
Salary	12,000	Profit and loss account	
Depreciation	1,500	(under absorption)	500

Sales

	£		£
Profit and loss account	39,000	Debtors	39,000

Work in progress (WIP)

	£		£
Material	8,500	Finished goods	36,500
Wages	7,500		
Electricity	5,500		
Fixed overhead	15,000		

Finished goods

	£		£
WIP	36,500	Cost of sales	36,500

Cost of sales

	£		£
Finished goods	36,500	Profit and loss account	36,500

Profit and loss account

	£		£
Cost of sales	36,500	Sales	39,000
Under absorption	500		
Profit to reserves	2,000		

Practice questions 1 and 2 *(The answers are in the final chapter of this book)*

1   **A Ltd**

Using the information given below for the month of October, in respect of A Ltd,

(a)   write up the integrated accounts;   **(15 marks)**

(b) prepare a trading and profit and loss account for October; **(5 marks)**

(c) compile a trial balance as at 31 October. **(5 marks)**

(Total : 25 marks)

(1) *List of balances at 1 October 20X3*

	£000
Fixed assets - production	1,000
Provision for depreciation of fixed assets	400
Material stores control	100
Work-in-progress stock	50
Finished goods stock	20
Debtors	600
Creditors	290
Creditors for PAYE and National Insurance (see note for overseas students)	85
Wages control - credit balance (accrued direct wages)	20
Cash	5
Bank - overdrawn	300
Share capital	600
Profit and loss appropriation: credit balance	80

(2) *Transactions for the month of October*

	£000
Received from debtors	380
Paid to creditors	170
Expenses paid by cheque	
Production indirect costs	60
Administration	40
Selling	20
Bank interest on overdraft	10
Paid to creditor for PAYE and National Insurance	60
Depreciation of fixed assets (for production)	25
Materials received and invoiced	110
Materials issued to production	80
Materials issued to production maintenance	20
Transfers from work in progress to finished goods	230
Sales on credit	310
Sales for cash	10
Production cost of goods sold	200
Cash paid into bank	13

	Gross £000	PAYE National Insurance £000	£000
Direct wages paid	86	20	66
Direct wages accrued	22	-	22
Indirect wages paid (production)	24	4	20
Administrative staff salaries paid	12	4	8
Selling staff salaries	20	4	16
Employer's contribution, National Insurance			
Production			9
Administration			3
Selling			2

Production overhead is absorbed on the basis of 150% on direct wages; any under or over absorption is transferred to profit and loss account.

Administration and selling costs are not absorbed into product costs.

Note for overseas students

PAYE is the "Pay as You Earn" income tax system of collection at source adopted in the United Kingdom whereby tax is deducted from an employee's wages or salary by the employer and paid over to the Inland Revenue on behalf of the employee.

The National Insurance system is similar but the employer must also make a contribution in addition to the employee's contribution which is deducted at source.

2 Integrated accounts

"The adoption of integrated accounts in which one set of books is used for both financial and costing systems must have obvious advantages."

(a) What are the "obvious advantages" of integrated accounts?

(b) Detail three items of costing information which are unlikely to be incorporated into financial accounts.

(c) Detail three items of financial information which are unlikely to be incorporated into cost accounts.

(d) What is an alternative to integrated accounts and what are the special features of such a system? **(16 marks)**

4 Summary

You should now be able to:

- Explain the two types of cost bookkeeping systems
- Identify the differences which occur between the two systems
- Prepare accounting entries using an integrated accounting system

Multiple choice questions *(The answers are in the final chapter of this book)*

1 In an integrated cost and financial accounting system, the accounting entries for factory overhead absorbed would be:

A	Dr Work-in-progress control account	Cr Overhead control account
B	Dr Overhead control account	Cr Work-in-progress control account
C	Dr Overhead control account	Cr Cost of sales account
D	Dr Cost of sales account	Cr Overhead control account

2   A firm operates an integrated cost and financial accounting system.

The accounting entries for an issue of Direct Materials to Production would be:

✓ A	Dr Work-in-progress control account	Cr Stores control account
B	Dr Finished goods account	Cr Stores control account
C	Dr Stores control account	Cr Work-in-progress control account
D	Dr Cost of sales account	Cr Work-in-progress control account

3   In the cost ledger the factory cost of finished production for a period was £873,190. The double entry for this is:

A	Dr Cost of sales account	Cr Finished goods control account
✓ B	Dr Finished goods control account	Cr Work-in-progress control account
C	Dr Costing profit and loss account	Cr Finished goods control account
D	Dr Work-in-progress control account	Cr Finished goods control account

CHAPTER 10

Introduction to decision making and the limiting factor decision

EXAM FOCUS

In this chapter we look at an area which is expected to feature heavily on the examination paper. Your understanding of marginal costing will underpin the knowledge required in this area. You can expect both computational and written questions in this area. Computational questions will tend to focus on the limiting factor decision with written questions focusing on the explanation and understanding of the terminology used in decision making. The types of decision which you will be examined on are one-off short term decisions.

LEARNING OUTCOMES

This chapter covers the following Learning Outcomes of the CIMA Syllabus.

> Identify relevant costs and revenues
>
> Calculate the profit-maximising sales mix for a company with a single resource constraint which has total freedom of action

In order to cover these Learning Outcomes the following topics are included.

> Define a decision and explain the decision making process
>
> Explain and discuss the application of relevant cost terminology used in decision making
>
> Identify the decision rule applied in limiting factor problems and consider the steps used to solve them

1 Decision making

1.1 Introduction

A decision in the context of this paper may be defined as:

> "A choice between two or more alternatives with the objective being maximisation of profit or minimisation of cost."

All levels of management are involved in decision making. There are normally three tiers of management in any organisation:

1   **Strategic level**

   This level is involved in formulating, evaluating and selecting strategies for the purpose of preparing a long-term plan of action to attain objectives. This is also known as corporate planning.

2   **Tactical level**

   This level is involved in planning the utilisation of resources to achieve specific objectives in the most effective and efficient way.

3   **Operational level**

   This level is involved in planning the detailed specifications by which individuals are expected to carry out the predetermined cycles of operations to meet sectoral objectives.

1.2 The decision making process

The stages in the overall decision process are as follows:

1   **Defining objectives**

   The decision maker must be aware of the organisation's objectives so as to ensure that the decision being made falls within them.

2   **Considering alternatives**

   The decision maker should consider all possible courses of action to achieve the objective.

3   **Evaluating alternatives**

   As all courses of action are considered, each must then be evaluated and each ranked in preference.

4   **Selecting the best course of action**

   This is the final stage in the process where the most favourable course of action is chosen and implemented.

2   Relevant cost terminology used in decision making

2.1 Introduction

The terminology below relates to one-off short-term decisions which is the only type of decision within your syllabus. In later studies you will consider the use of this terminology to long-term decisions.

2.2 Relevant cost

Although an existing structure of costs, analysed between fixed and activity-variable items, will remain valid over a defined range of existing activities, the purpose of decision-making will normally be to alter some aspect of the business. When this is done, then the pre-existing levels of variable cost per unit or relevant fixed costs will cease to be applicable.

It will become necessary, therefore, to define for each decision which items of cost or revenue will be changed as a result of taking the decision.

Therefore we are moving away from a formal structure of fixed and variable costs, back to the economist's concept of truly 'marginal' changes.

The concept of relevant costs will be elaborated in the following paragraphs.

Historical cost

Every decision deals with the future. The function of the decision-maker is to select courses of action for the future and this decision must by its nature be based on predictions. Historical costs in themselves are therefore irrelevant to decisions, though they may be the best available basis for predicting future costs.

Variable costs

Costs which have been classified as variable by convention or on the basis of past experience, may not in fact vary under the circumstances of a particular volume decision. Accepting a special sales order, for example, may not involve incurring additional selling costs.

Relevant costs are only those expected **future costs** that will differ under alternative courses of action.

Fixed costs

Costs which have been classified as fixed by convention or on the basis of past experience may in fact be affected by a particular decision. This may be for two reasons:

- The costs are fixed in relation to the levels of activity previously experienced, but a decision may extend the range of activity and thus cause certain fixed costs to be stepped up to a new level.
- The costs are fixed in relation to the normal time horizon for forecasting; but if the time span of an action exceeds the normal period, then fixed costs may change.

2.3 Sunk costs

Costs incurred in the past ('sunk costs') will always be irrelevant. The decision-maker has no opportunity to alter what has already happened. Some specific examples of this are:

- **Obsolete stock** – the cost of stock already held, and now proved to be obsolete, has no relevance to a decision regarding its disposal or other use; even though the decision may result in a book loss being reported.
- **Old equipment** – the cost of new equipment and the disposal value of old equipment are relevant future transactions. The book value of old equipment is irrelevant to any decision-making technique.

2.4 Opportunity cost

This is the maximum alternative benefit that might have been obtained from the use of the resource in question.

In other words we are looking into the future to determine our cost and not back to the original (or historic) cost.

Note this only applies to resources that are 'scarce' – ie further supplies cannot be bought, or only at an uneconomic cost.

2.5 Example

Robin owns some plastic which cost £1,000 two years ago.

He could sell it for £750.

Alternatively, he could use it to produce product X. This would save him purchasing other materials to make X which would have cost £1,250.

Required

What is the relevant cost of using the plastic to produce a new product Y?

2.6 Solution

Having the plastic means that Robin has a choice of:

- receiving £750
- saving £1,250

Clearly he would choose to save £1,250.

The maximum alternative benefit is therefore £1,250.

Therefore, the opportunity cost of using the plastic in product Y is £1,250.

Note how the historic cost is ignored as it has no influence on the future benefits of owning the plastic.

Consider how these principles apply to Louise below before looking at the solution.

2.7 Example

Louise owns a barrel of acid which cost £1,700.

She could use it in product A which is a 'one-off' product for an overseas customer.

If she does not use it in product A, it will have to be neutralised at a cost of £500.

Required

What is the relevant cost of using the acid in product A?

2.8 Solution

Use of the acid gives rise to a SAVING not a cost at all (saving = £500). Therefore it will be treated as additional revenue from making product A.

2.9 Incremental cost

The incremental cost is the difference in total cost between alternatives.

Consider the following.

2.10 Example

Kathryn is about to buy machine Q for her factory. It will cost £15,000.

She is offered a contract that will require her to buy a larger machine for £20,000.

What is the marginal cost of taking the contract?

Chapter 10 Introduction to decision making and the limiting factor decision

2.11 Solution

	£
Cost with the contract	20,000
Cost without the contract	15,000
Therefore cost of the contract	5,000

2.12 Common, fixed or unavoidable costs

Where costs would be incurred regardless of the course of action chosen, the cost is NOT a relevant cost and should be excluded for the purposes of decision making.

Consider the case of Dick Limited below.

2.13 Example

The component division of Dick Ltd has been offered a contract to supply ten components at a price of £6,000.

The relevant cost of the contract is £3,500.

Head Office charges all contracts with £3,000 to recognise the fact that fixed costs have to be covered. (Head Office costs are unaltered by the acceptance or rejection of this contract.)

Should the contract be accepted?

2.14 Solution

If the contract is accepted, the company will be £2,500 better off.

	£
Revenue	6,000
Costs	3,500
	2,500

Therefore the company should accept it.

Note: The Head Office fixed overheads will be the same whether or not the contract is accepted and thus should be ignored.

Another way of putting this is that they are not incremental costs but common costs.

Remember: marginal costs are the *changes* in cash costs that arise as a result of the decision.

Practice question 1 *(The answer is in the final chapter of this book)*

Materials

Y plc needs the following materials for a potential contract.

	Required for contract	Stock available	Current cost per kg	Original cost per kg of stock
Material A	100 kg	100 kg	£5.00	£4
Material B	200 kg	150 kg	£15.50	£15
Material C	50 kg	20 kg	£12.00	£10

Material A is used on current production.

Current stock of Material B can be used but is obsolete and has a net realisable value of £13 per kg.

Current stock of Material C can be safely used but if not used on this contract will become toxic and will be disposed of at a cost of £3 per kg.

Required

Determine the relevant cost of material for use on the contract.

3 Relevant costs of labour

3.1 Example

X plc needs 1,000 hours of direct labour for a potential new contract. Labour is paid at £6 per hour.

Required

Determine the relevant cost of labour for use on the contract.

3.2 Solution

Unless told otherwise, we assume the 1,000 hours are additional hours that must be hired in the market place. The contract is simply charged at current wage rates.

Relevant cost of labour 1,000 hours × £6 = £6,000

3.3 Example (continued)

The situation is the same, except that the company expects to have 100 hours spare.

Required

Determine the relevant cost of labour for use on the contract.

3.4 Solution

We will assume that the 100 hours spare would have been paid at the normal wage rate. This means that if we use them on the new contract there is no additional cost so they are free of charge.

Relevant cost of labour:

	£
900 hours × £6	5,400
100 hours × NIL	NIL
	5,400

3.5 Example (continued)

To supervise work on the new contract we will need 100 hours of supervisory labour. We will use existing supervisors who are paid £20,000 per year which equates to £7 per hour.

Required

Determine the relevant cost of supervisory labour for use on the contract.

3.6 Solution

The supervisors are salaried. There is no indication that they receive additional pay for supervising the new contract, so there is no incremental cost involved. The relevant cost is therefore NIL.

3.7 Example (continued)

The situation is as before, except that additional direct labour workers cannot be recruited. Overtime hours are available at £3 per hour overtime premium.

Required

Determine the relevant cost of labour for use on the new contract.

3.8 Solution

All the required labour must be obtained in overtime working. Therefore labour is charged at overtime rates.

Relevant cost of labour:

1,000 hours × (£6 + £3) = £9,000

A common mistake by students is to charge at £3, just the premium. However, these are all *additional* hours so will be paid at £9.

3.9 Example (continued)

Now suppose that there is a shortage of direct labour in the market place and no overtime can be worked. If the contract proceeds labour will have to be moved from a different production line where the product earns a contribution of £4 per labour hour.

Required

Determine the relevant labour cost for use on the new contract.

3.10 Solution

We are back to opportunity costs. Every labour hour moved off alternative production lines loses the company £4 per hour. This must be charged to the new contract to assess it's true profitability for the company.

Relevant cost of labour:

	£
1,000 hours × £6 =	6,000
1,000 hours × £4 =	4,000
	10,000

Students often forget to include the basic cost of labour at £6, as well as the opportunity cost. The workers must still be paid £6 per hour by the new project.

Practice question 2 *(The answer is in the final chapter of this book)*
Labour

X plc needs 2,500 skilled labour hours and 1,150 unskilled labour hours for use on a new contract. 500 skilled labour hours are expected to be spare over the forthcoming period, but 600 of the unskilled hours will require overtime working at double time. Basic wage rates are £8 per hour for skilled labour and £5 per hour for unskilled.

Required

Determine the relevant cost of labour for use on the contract.

4 Overheads

4.1 Example

1,000 hours will be required for a potential new contract. The overhead absorption rate is £6 per hour. This is 40% for variable overhead and 60% for fixed overhead.

Required

Determine the relevant cost of overheads for use on the contract.

4.2 Solution

We assume that the variable overhead rate is accurate and, as variable overheads will vary with activity, we charge them as a relevant cost. The fixed overhead absorption rate is ignored. Fixed overheads are time based, so the existing cost will not change because of any change in production activity. Fixed overhead absorption rates are an invention of absorption costing.

Relevant cost of overhead

1,000 hours × £6 × 40% = £2,400

4.3 Example

1,000 labour hours will be required for a potential new contract. The fixed overhead absorption rate is £8 per hour. Owing to capacity problems the project would require a new factory unit to be rented at a cost of £3,000 for the duration of the contract.

Required

Determine the relevant cost of overheads for use on the contract.

4.4 Solution

Again we ignore the fixed overhead absorption rate as this simply relates to existing overheads. The additional factory rent is a step up in fixed overheads. As it is a direct result of the contract it is relevant.

Relevant cost of overhead step up in factory rent = £3,000

Practice question 3 *(The answer is in the final chapter of this book)*

Overheads

X plc needs 1,600 labour hours for a new contract. The overhead absorption rates are £3 per hour for fixed overhead and £5 per hour for variable overhead. The contract will last two months and a new foreman will be hired for this period at a salary of £1,500 per month.

Required

Determine the relevant overhead cost for use on the new contract.

5 Plant and machinery

5.1 Example

X plc will buy a new machine for use on the contract. It will cost £9,000 but will have a resale value of £4,000 at the end of the contract. X plc depreciates plant and machinery at 20% on a reducing balance basis.

Required

Determine the relevant cost of the machine for use on the contract.

5.2 Solution

Firstly, we ignore the depreciation rate. This is a financial accounting concept and as it is a percentage of a cost already expended it is effectively a sunk cost for our purposes.

The charges are the original purchase cost and the resale value.

Relevant cost of machine

	£
Purchase cost	9,000
Resale value	4,000
Relevant cost	5,000

5.3 Example

X plc will require the use of a machine for a new contract. A suitable machine is available already as it is not in use. It cost £15,000 and has a net book value of £10,000. It is depreciated at 25% per annum straight line. It could be sold now for £6,000 or after use on the contract for £3,500.

Required

Determine the relevant cost of the machine for use on the contract.

5.4 Solution

Firstly, we ignore original purchase price, net book value and depreciation rate as these are all sunk costs.

The machine is obsolete as it is not used at present. As with obsolete materials stock, we assume that the company was just about to sell the machine so the income forgone is an opportunity cost. However, in this case we can still sell it for a reduced fee at the end of the contract so this represents a further charge.

Relevant cost of machine

	£
Revenue forgone at start of contract	6,000
Revenue received at end of contract	3,500
Relevant cost of machine	2,500

The £2,500 effectively represents the true economic depreciation of the machine's use on the contract.

Practice question 4 *(The answer is in the final chapter of this book)*

Machine

X plc need the use of a machine on a contract. A suitable machine is available with an original cost of £15,000 and net book value of £6,000. As X plc does not need the machine for existing contracts it is currently on hire to another firm at £1,000 per month. The new contract is expected to last three months.

Required

Determine the relevant cost of the machine for use on the contract.

6 Exam technique

The above examples show the various relevant costs that appear in exam questions. Workings should be shown for more tricky areas, but it is good exam technique to tackle the easier relevant costs first to get any easy marks available.

When we make a decision using the relevant cost principles we accept as long as the benefits are greater than the relevant costs incurred. Whilst this is often a sound approach for one off decision making it can cause problems in some applications.

If the firm has spare capacity it is tempting to produce a special order for a customer if the revenue just exceeds the relevant costs. However, other customers may be disgruntled if they find out that rivals are obtaining better prices than they are.

If relevant cost principles are used for routine product pricing decisions, problems may arise. Fixed overheads are normally dismissed as non relevant. Thus the selling price set may indeed cover the relevant costs, but leave the fixed cost high and dry, resulting in a large loss.

Practice questions 5 and 6 *(The answers are in the final chapter of this book)*

5   **Research project**

A research project, which to date has cost the company £150,000, is under review.

If the project is allowed to proceed, it will be completed in approximately one year, when the results would be sold to a government agency for £300,000.

Shown below are the additional expenses which the managing director estimates will be necessary to complete the work.

Materials

This material was purchased some time ago at a cost of £60,000. It is toxic, and if not used in this project, must be disposed of at a cost of £5,000. The material is not used on other projects.

Labour

Skilled labour is hard to recruit. The workers concerned will be transferred to the project from a production department, and at a recent meeting the production manager claimed that if the men were returned to him they could generate sales of £150,000 in the next year, where the variable costs would be £100,000, including £40,000 for the labour cost itself.

Research staff

It has already been decided that, when work on this project ceases, the research department will be closed. Research wages for the year are £60,000, and redundancy and severance pay has been estimated at £15,000 now, or £35,000 in one year's time.

Equipment

The project utilises a special microscope which cost £18,000 three years ago. It has a residual value of £3,000 in another two years, and a current disposal value of £8,000. If used in the project it is estimated that the disposal value in a year's time will be £6,000. The microscope is not used at present.

Share of general building services

The project is charged with £35,000 per annum to cover general building expenses. Immediately the project is discontinued, the space occupied could be sub-let for an annual rental of £7,000.

Required

Recommend whether or not the project should be allowed to proceed.

6   **Finale**

Finale (Lake District) plc has received an enquiry from a customer for the supply of 500 units of a new product, the 'phell'. Negotiations on the final price to charge the customer are in progress and the sales manager has asked you, as the management accountant, to supply her with the most up-to-date relevant cost information. If the price were to be acceptable to the customer, production of the phell would start shortly and would be completed within ten to twelve weeks.

The following information is available.

(1)   Each unit of phell requires the following raw materials.

Raw material type

| Jey | 4kg |
| Kay | 6kg |

(2)   The company has 5,000 kgs of Jey currently in stock. This material was purchased last year at a cost of £7 per kg. If not used in the manufacture of phells, the stock of Jey could either be sold for £7.50 per kg or converted at a cost of £1.50 per kg, so that it could be used as a substitute for another raw material called Lig, which the company requires for other production. Lig can be purchased at a current price of £9.50 per kg and Jey for £8.25 per kg.

(3) There are 10,000 kgs of raw material Kay in stock valued on a FIFO basis at a total cost of £142,750. 3,000 kgs of the current stock were purchased six months ago at a cost of £13.75 per kg and the balance of the stock was purchased last month. Kay is a material that is used regularly by the company on normal production work. Since the last purchase of Kay a month ago the company has been advised by the supplier that the price per kg it charges for Kay has been increased by 4%.

(4) Each unit of phell requires the following number of labour hours in its manufacture.

Type of labour
Skilled   5 hours
Unskilled   3 hours

Skilled labour is paid £8 per hour and unskilled labour £6 per hour.

(5) There is a shortage of skilled labour, so that if production of phells goes ahead it will be necessary to transfer skilled operatives from other work to undertake it. The other work on which skilled operatives are engaged at present is the manufacture of thirls. The selling price and cost information of thirls are as follows.

	£ per unit	£ per unit
Selling price	100	
Less: variable costs of production		
Skilled labour	24	
Other variable costs	31	
	(55)	
		45

(6) The company has a surplus of unskilled labour operatives currently employed and paid. It is estimated that there are 900 hours available during the period of the contract. The balance of the unskilled labour requirements could be met by working overtime, which is paid at time and a half.

(7) The company absorbs production overheads by a machine hour rate which is currently £22.50 per hour, of which £8.75 is for variable overheads and the balance for fixed overheads. If production of phells is undertaken, it is estimated that fixed costs will increase by £4,000 in total for the duration of the work. Spare machining capacity is available and each unit of phell will require two hours of machining time in its manufacture using the existing equipment. In addition, special finishing machinery will be required to complete the phells in their final two weeks only of manufacture. This machinery will be hired at a cost of £2,650 per week.

(8) £3,250 has been spent already on the development work for the production of phells. It is estimated that before production of the phell is started a further £1,750 will need to be spent, making a total development cost of £5,000.

Required

Prepare a report for the sales manager which includes a statement that clearly identifies the relevant costs associated with the production of 500 units of the phell. Explain briefly but clearly for each figure incorporated into the statement the reason and basis for its inclusion. State in the report the absolute minimum price that the company should be prepared to accept for the 500 phells (ie the price that would just equal the total relevant costs of production).

7 Limiting factors

7.1 Introduction

This is where a firm has a choice between various types of products where there is a single, binding constraint, which will limit production. Limiting factors include materials, labour hours and machine hours. In addition, the firm may be limited by sales demand.

There are two main principles employed in these decisions:

- The benefit derived from each product is measured in terms of *contribution* (sales price – variable costs). Changing the volumes/mix of products is assumed not to affect overall fixed costs, which are therefore irrelevant to the decision. Any profit per unit figure given, which includes an arbitrary fixed overhead absorption, should be *ignored*, and contribution per unit used instead.

- Where the limiting factor is a common input resource such as materials or labour, we need to ensure that *each unit of that resource is used to maximum advantage in generating contribution.* Giving priority to a product with a high contribution *per unit* may not maximise contribution, if that product uses a relatively high amount of the scarce resource.

In order to decide on which mix of products yields the highest contribution we therefore calculate contribution per unit of limiting factor used, rank the products on this basis and from there make a decision.

7.2 Example

Products	X	Y	Z
Materials per unit (Kg)	24	18	10
Labour hours per unit	17	7	10
Variable overheads per unit (£)	20	48	32
Selling price per unit (£)	235	178	146
Maximum demand per month (units)	200	300	500

Materials cost £2 per Kg. The labour rate is £7 per hour.

Required

Calculate the optimum production plan if materials are limited to 6,000 kgs per month, and comment on your answer.

7.3 Solution

To determine the optimal production plan:

(1) Calculate the required Kg of materials to satisfy the maximum demand.

	X	Y	Z	Total
Total materials needed to satisfy demand	24 × 200 4,800	18 × 300 5,400	10 × 500 5,000	15,200

Materials are thus a limiting factor, as we only have 6,000 kg available.

(2) Calculate the contribution per unit for each product.

	X	Y	Z
Selling price	235	178	146
Variable costs:			
Materials	(48)	(36)	(20)
Labour	(119)	(49)	(70)
Variable overhead	(20)	(48)	(32)
	48	45	24

(3) As materials are the limiting factor, we need to make the best use of materials. Consequently, we calculate the contribution per KG of material for each product.

(In general this is known as the contribution per limiting factor).

	X	Y	Z
Contribution per Kg	$\frac{48}{24}$	$\frac{45}{18}$	$\frac{24}{10}$
=	£2 per Kg	£2.50 per Kg	£2.40 per Kg

(4) Rank the products in order of contribution per limiting factor.

	X	Y	Z
Rank (1 = best)	3	1	2

(5) Allocate the scarce resource to those products with highest contribution per limiting factor up to their maximum demand until all of the scarce resource is used.

Product	Units produced	Materials used	Materials left	Contribution per unit	Total contribution
Y	300	5,400	600	£45	13,500
Z	60	600	0	£24	1,440
					£14,940

There are three common pitfalls with this technique:

(1) Ensure the products are ranked according to contribution per limiting factor, not contribution per unit.

(2) Use contribution, not profit. This means ignore any absorbed fixed overheads.

(3) Remember that it is not worth producing more than the maximum demand for the product - which is why product Y's production was restricted to 300 units.

Comment

There are no units of product X being produced. This effectively reduces the company's product range from 3 to 2. They may lose customers through this policy, so it may be better to specify a minimum 9 Kg of each product to be produced.

Chapter 10 Introduction to decision making and the limiting factor decision

Practice question 7 *(The answer is in the final chapter of this book)*

A company produces and sells four products: A, B, C and D. Selling prices, costs of manufacture and maximum sales demand are given below.

	A	B	C	D
	£	£	£	£
Selling price	50	42	45	55
Material cost (£5 per unit)	15	5	15	20
Labour cost (£8 per hour)	8	12	4	12
Overhead cost	5	7	6	4
Total variable cost	28	24	25	36
Allocated fixed costs	6	7	5	2
Total cost of manufacture	(34)	(31)	(30)	(38)
Profit per item	16	11	15	17
Maximum sales demand per annum	50,000	40,000	60,000	30,000

Both materials and labour are in short supply.

Materials are restricted to 500,000 units and labour is restricted to 150,000 hours per annum.

Required

Calculate the optimum productions schedule and the maximum contribution per annum.

8 Limiting factors - make or buy decision

8.1 Example

X Plc makes three components internally for inclusion in its final products. The cost structures of the three components are as follows:

Component	A	B	C
	£	£	£
Materials @ £5 per Kg	10	20	25
Labour @ £6 per hour	12	18	24
Variable overhead @ £2 per hour	4	6	8
Fixed overhead @ £3 per hour	6	9	12
Total cost	32	53	69

The fixed overheads are not specific to the components.

An outside supplier has offered components at the following prices:

A - £28   B - £50   C - £62

Only 6,000 labour hours will be available over the forthcoming period and at least 1,000 of each component is required to meet contractual obligations.

Required

Determine the optimal production plan to minimise the cost of providing the components.

8.2 Solution

The company will not now be able to manufacture all the required components internally because of the shortage of labour hours but must buy from an outside source.

We need to calculate the most efficient use of the labour hours available using the limiting factor technique.

Component	A	B	C
	£	£	£
Variable costs of internal manufacture	26	44	57
External suppliers price	28	50	62
Saving on internal manufacture	2	6	5
Labour hours per unit	2	3	4
Saving per hour	1	2	1.25
Ranking	3	1	2

In order to make best use of the hours available we concentrate on making components that give the greatest saving per hour over the external purchase.

Now we produce a table to determine the optional plan.

Decision		Cost £	Hours
			6,000
1)	Make 1,000 B's internally	44,000	(3,000)
2)	Make $\frac{3,000}{4}$ = 750 C's with remaining hours	42,750	(3,000)
			NIL
3)	Buy 250 C's externally	15,500	
4)	Buy 1,000 A's externally	28,000	
Minimum cost		130,250	

The above plan will help keep the cost of acquiring 1,000 of each of the components to a minimum.

Practice question 8 *(The answer is in the final chapter of this book)*

Components

Q plc makes four components for inclusion in its final products. The cost profiles are as follows.

Component	W	X	Y	Z
	£	£	£	£
Materials @ £8 per kg	8	12	4	16
Labour @ £5 per hour	10	15	10	20
Variable overhead @ £2 per hour	4	6	4	8
Fixed overhead @ £3 per hour	6	9	6	12
Total cost	28	42	24	56

Q plc has been offered comparable quality components at the following prices.

W	£20
X	£36
Y	£24
Z	£50

Required

(a) Calculate whether the products should be bought or manufactured internally on purely cost grounds.

(b) It now becomes apparent that materials will be restricted to 10,000kg over the next period. X plc needs the following numbers of components next period.

W	1,000 units
X	2,000 units
Y	7,000 units
Z	4,000 units

Required

Calculate the optimal plan for acquiring the required components.

9 Summary

You should now be able to:

- Define a decision
- Explain the decision making process
- Explain and discuss the application of relevant cost terminology used in decision making
- Discuss and make recommendations regarding limiting factor decisions

Multiple choice questions *(The answers are in the final chapter of this book)*

1   The most relevant costs to be used in decision making are:

    A   costs already incurred which are known with certainty

    B   current costs

    ✓C   estimated future costs

    D   notional costs

2   BB Ltd makes three components - S, T and W. The following costs have been recorded:

	Component S £	Component T £	Component W £
Variable cost	2.50	8.00	5.00
Fixed cost	2.00	8.30	3.75
Total cost	4.50	16.30	8.75

Another company has offered to supply the components to BB Ltd at the following prices:

	Component S	Component T	Component W
Price each	£4	£7	£5.50

Which component(s), if any, should BB Ltd consider buying in?

A   Buy in all three components

B   Do not buy any

C   Buy in S and W

D   Buy in T only

3   Q Ltd has in stock 10,000 kg of V, a raw material which it bought for £5/kg five years ago. This was bought for a product line which was discontinued four years ago. At present, V has no use in its existing state but could be sold as scrap for £1.50 per kg. One of the company's current products (QX) requires 2 kg of a raw material which is available for £4.50 per kg. V can be modified at a cost of £1 per kg so that it may be used as a substitute for this material. However, after modification, 3 kg of V is required for every unit of QX to be produced.

Q Ltd has now received an invitation to tender for a product which could use V in its present state.

The relevant cost per kg of V to be included in the cost estimate for the tender is:

A   £1.00

B   £1.50

C   £2.00

D   £5.00

4   The following details relate to three products made by F Ltd:

	H £	J £	K £
Selling price per unit	60	85	88
Direct materials per unit	15	20	30
Direct labour per unit	10	15	10
Variable overhead per unit	5	8	10
Fixed overhead per unit	10	16	20
	40	59	70
Profit per unit	20	26	18

All three products use the same direct labour and direct materials, but in different quantities.

In a period when the labour used on these products is in short supply, the most and least profitable use of the labour is:

	Most profitable	Least profitable
A	K	J
B	H	J
C	J	K
D	H	K

CHAPTER 11

Cost volume profit analysis

EXAM FOCUS

In this chapter we again look at the application of marginal costing and how contribution aids in the running of a business. Apart from computational and graphical questions you may be asked to produce written work on explaining a contribution/sales ratio or explaining break even concepts. A thorough understanding of marginal costing is needed.

LEARNING OUTCOMES

This chapter covers the following Learning Outcomes of the CIMA Syllabus.

> Calculate and interpret the break even point, profit target, margin of safety and profit/volume ratio for a single product
>
> Prepare break even charts and profit/volume graphs for a single product
>
> Discuss CVP analysis

In order to cover these Learning Outcomes the following topics are included.

> Discuss and calculate break even related measures
>
> Demonstrate the break even point graphically
>
> Discuss the limitations of CVP analysis
>
> Explain the difference between the accountant's and the economist's model of cost volume profit analysis

1 Introduction to cost volume profit analysis

1.1 Break even analysis

Cost volume profit analysis is the term used to describe the inter-relationship between costs, volume and profit at various levels of activity. Break even analysis is a particular form of cost volume profit analysis, concerned with levels of activity where profit = 0.

In order to determine the break even part graphs or formulae can be used. These will be considered later in the chapter.

1.2 Contribution and profit

Under marginal costing we calculate the **contribution per item** by taking the sales price and deducting all variable production and selling costs. As we have seen, this procedure is a useful starting point for a wide variety of calculations used in management decision making.

1.3 Illustration

We illustrate the relevance of contribution with the example of a product selling at a unit price of £15, with variable materials cost of £4 per unit and other variable costs of £2 per unit. Contribution is therefore £9 per unit (£15 − £4 − £2). Suppose that fixed costs are £40,000 per period.

- If 5,000 units are produced and sold what is the total contribution and the net profit?

Contribution	=	5,000 x £9	=	£45,000
Profit	=	£45,000 − £40,000	=	£5,000

- What is the total contribution and profit if 7,000 units are produced and sold?

Contribution	=	7,000 x £9	=	£63,000
Profit	=	£63,000 − £40,000	=	£23,000

- What is total contribution and profit if 3,000 units are sold?

Contribution	=	3,000 x £9	=	£27,000
Profit	=	£27,000 − £40,000	=	£(13,000), ie a loss of £13,000

1.4 Contribution and profit graph

These results can be plotted on a graph as follows.

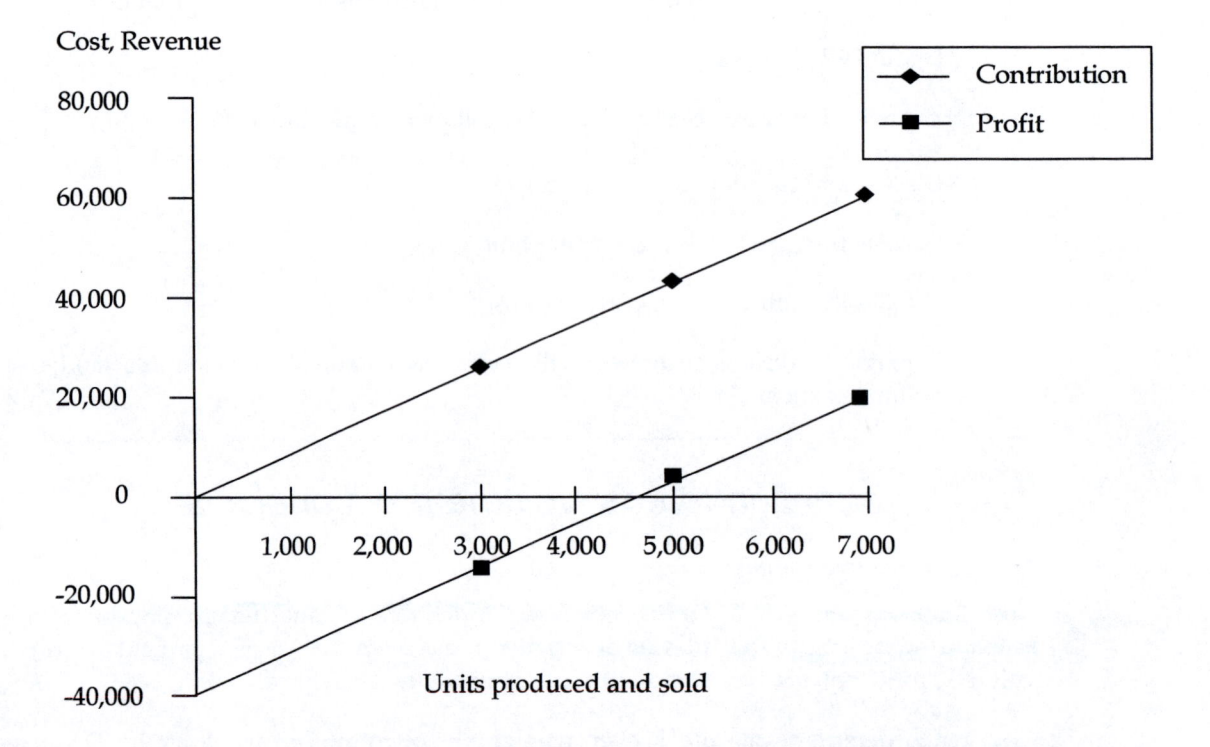

Notice that the two lines are **parallel** to one another. The **steepness** of the line represents the **contribution per item**; the **vertical distance** between the two lines represents the **fixed costs**. In other words if you know the total contribution, subtract £40,000 to arrive at the net profit. If zero units are made then no contribution is earned, but all the fixed costs must still be paid, resulting in a loss of £40,000.

This reinforces another concept that we looked at in the previous chapter, the idea that contribution is a more useful measure to a management accountant than profit.

If you look at the chart above, you will see that as the output doubles, so does the total contribution. Since this relationship is not true of profit, contribution is a more useful indicator. In this chapter we will look at some of the uses to which contribution can be put.

2 Break even analysis

2.1 Break even point

The break even point (sometimes abbreviated to BEP) is the amount of sales (in units or in revenue) that a business must achieve in order to break even, to make £0 profit or loss.

At first glance you might ask why is this useful: no company wants to make £0 profit. The answer is that if a company knows how many units they need to sell to break even, then if they sell any additional units they are making a profit.

2.2 Graphical approach

From the graph above if we look at the point at which the profit line crosses zero we could read this as approximately 4,500 units. Therefore if the company can sell more than about 4,500 units, they will make a profit.

2.3 Formula

In addition to graphing the contribution and profit, the break even point can also be calculated as follows.

At break even : Total contribution − Fixed costs = 0

⇨ Units × Contribution per unit = Fixed costs

⇨ Break even (units) = $\dfrac{\text{Fixed costs}}{\text{Contribution per unit}}$

2.4 Example

In our example remember that contribution is £9 per item and fixed costs were £40,000. The break even point can then be calculated as follows.

$$\text{BEP} = \dfrac{£40,000}{£9} = 4,444 \text{ units}$$

This calculation confirms our earlier approximation derived from inspection of the graph.

2.5 Revenue break even

Notice that this gives the break even point in units. In some cases it will be more useful to give the break even point in terms of sales revenue (the company knows that if they have revenue over a certain amount they will have made a profit).

In the above example, we know the BEP is 4,444 units. This is equivalent to sales revenue of 4,444 × £15 = £66,660 (remember that the sales price was £15 per unit).

The company now knows that if it sells more than 4,444 units or receives more than £66,660 in sales revenue it will be making a profit.

2.6 Target profit

Most companies will have a budgeted profit level that they are aiming for. CVP analysis can also tell the company what sales level they will need to achieve to reach this.

2.7 Example

If the company above wants to make a profit of £14,000, how many units will they have to sell?

2.8 Solution

Again, we could take a reading from the graph. Find the required profit on the scale going up the left hand side, draw a horizontal line along to the profit line and move down to read off the number of units. In our example, to earn £14,000 profit shows sales of about 6,000 units. Once again, we can calculate the required units more exactly using the following formula.

Units × Contribution per unit – Fixed costs = Target profit

$$\Rightarrow \text{Units to make target profit} = \frac{\text{Fixed costs} + \text{Target profit}}{\text{Contribution per unit}}$$

In the case of the example this is $\frac{£40,000 + £14,000}{£9} = 6,000$ units

Notice that break even is just a special version of this formula (where target profit is £0) so there is only one formula to remember.

3 CVP charts

3.1 Break even chart

The following table shows the level of revenue, variable costs, fixed costs and total costs for various levels of output in the above example. These can then be plotted on a graph, called a break even chart.

(Recap: Selling price = £15 per unit, Variable costs = £6 per unit)

Fixed costs = £40,000 per period

Units	Revenue £	Variable costs £	Fixed costs £	Total costs £	Profit/(Loss) £
0	0	0	40,000	40,000	(40,000)
3,000	45,000	18,000	40,000	58,000	(13,000)
5,000	75,000	30,000	40,000	70,000	5,000
7,000	105,000	42,000	40,000	82,000	23,000

Break even chart

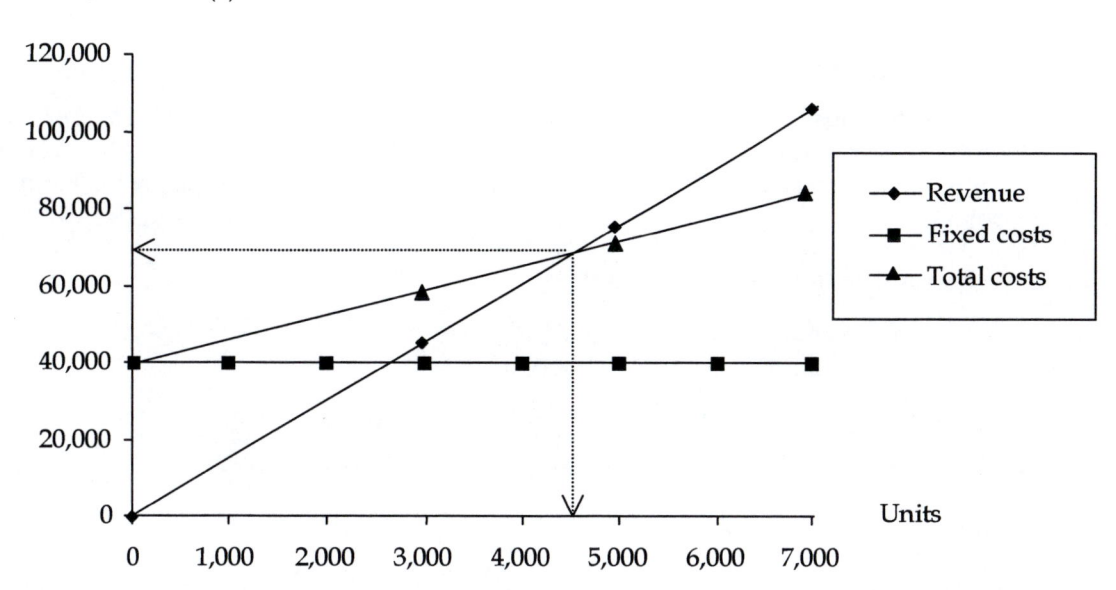

Cost, Revenue (£)

[Break even chart showing Revenue, Fixed costs and Total costs lines plotted against Units from 0 to 7,000. Fixed costs are horizontal at £40,000. Break even point indicated at approximately 4,500 units / £66,000.]

A break even chart shows total revenue, fixed costs and total costs. Along the bottom is the number of units, with the revenue and costs in £ plotted up the side.

Plot the fixed costs as a horizontal line and then plot the total cost line (note that it will start at £40,000). Notice that where the total costs line crosses the total revenue line is the **break even point**. If you draw a vertical line down to the units, this will tell you the **break even point in terms of units**. Similarly if you draw a horizontal line from the intersection of the revenue and cost lines this will give you **break even revenue**.

From this chart we can see that the break even point is about 4,500 units or £66,000.

3.2 Reading profit

We can also read off the amount of profit or loss at any point by looking at the difference between the total revenue and total cost lines.

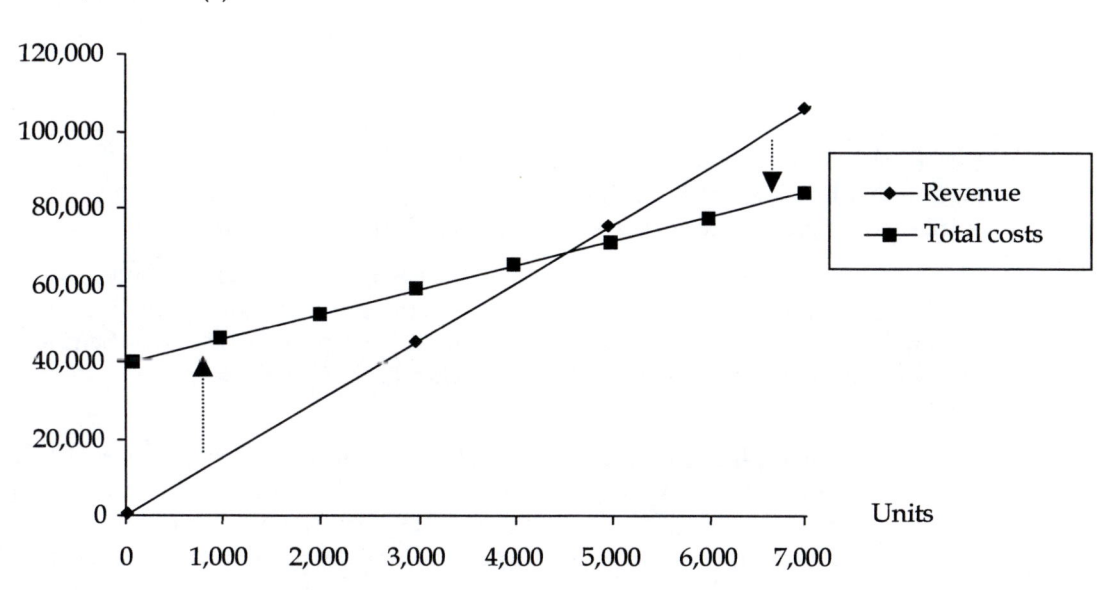

Cost, Revenue (£)

[Chart showing Revenue and Total costs lines plotted against Units from 0 to 7,000, with arrows indicating loss at around 1,000 units and profit at around 6,500 units.]

The dotted arrows show the amount of profit or loss. The first arrow (pointing upwards) indicates a loss, whilst the second (pointing downwards) indicates a profit. The actual amount of profit or loss can be read using this graph.

3.3 Profit/volume chart

Perhaps the most useful graph is called the profit/volume (PV) chart. This simply shows the profit at each level of production and sales. The best way to draw it is to calculate total contribution at various production levels and then subtract fixed costs to get total profit at each point.

Using the data from our example, we had:

Units	Profit
0	(40,000)
3,000	(13,000)
5,000	5,000
7,000	23,000

Plotting these gives the following PV chart:

Profit/volume chart

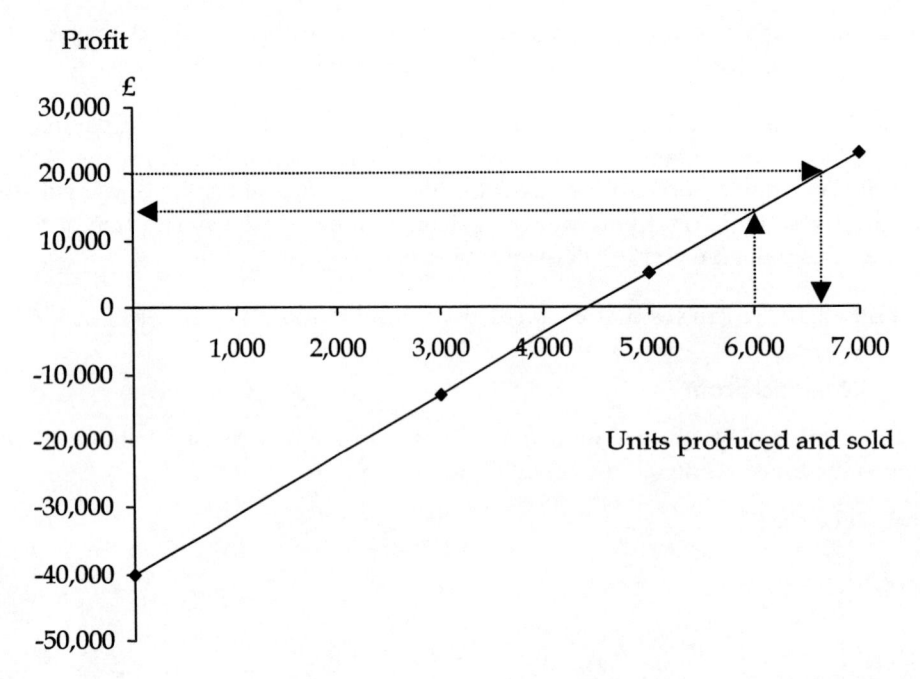

This is exactly the same graph as we started this chapter with (in 1.4) except that the contribution line has not been drawn in. At any point we can read off the exact amount of profit or loss which the company will make if it sells that many units

To find the profit at any particular production level, go up from the units produced to the profit line (upward arrow) and along to read off the profit (arrow pointing left). For example we could read off how much profit will be made if we produce 6,000 units. Start at 6,000 units, go up to the profit line and then draw a horizontal line along to read off the profit (about £14,000).

Similarly we could calculate the units required to make a certain level of profit. On the graph it has been shown how many units are required to make a profit of £20,000. Start with the required profit level and go along to the profit line (arrow pointing right) and then down to read the required number of units (downward pointing arrow). In this case the required level of sales can be read as about 6,700 units.

3.4 Example

JH Ltd plans to sell a new product in the coming year. Details are as follows.

	£
Materials	5
Labour	7
Variable overheads	2

Annual fixed costs are expected to be £60,000. JH Ltd is expecting to sell this product for £29.

Required

(a) Calculate the break even point in units.

(b) Calculate the break even point in revenue.

(c) Calculate the sales volume required to make a profit of £6,000.

(d) Draw a break even chart showing units along the horizontal axis.

(e) Draw a profit volume chart showing revenue along the horizontal axis.

(f) Calculate profit if sales are 5,000 units.

3.5 Solution

(a) Contribution = £29 − £5 − £7 − £2 = £15 per unit

Fixed costs = £60,000

$$\text{Break even point in units} = \frac{£60,000}{£15} = 4,000 \text{ units}$$

(b) Break even point in revenue = 4,000 × £29 = £116,000

(c) Required sales to make profit of £6,000 = (60,000 + 6,000)/15 = 4,400 units

(d) Chart workings

Units	Revenue £	Variable costs £	Fixed cost £	Total costs £	Profit/(Loss) £
0	0	0	60,000	60,000	(60,000)
3,000	87,000	42,000	60,000	102,000	(15,000)
6,000	174,000	84,000	60,000	144,000	30,000

Break even chart

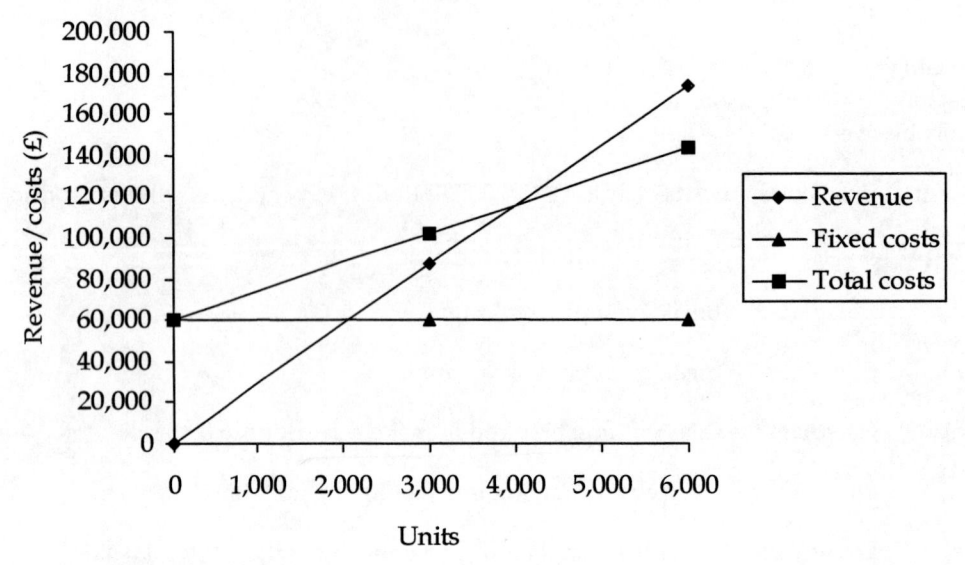

[Break even chart showing Revenue, Fixed costs, and Total costs plotted against Units from 0 to 6,000]

(e) **Profit volume chart**

[Profit volume chart showing Profit/loss (£) against Revenue (£)]

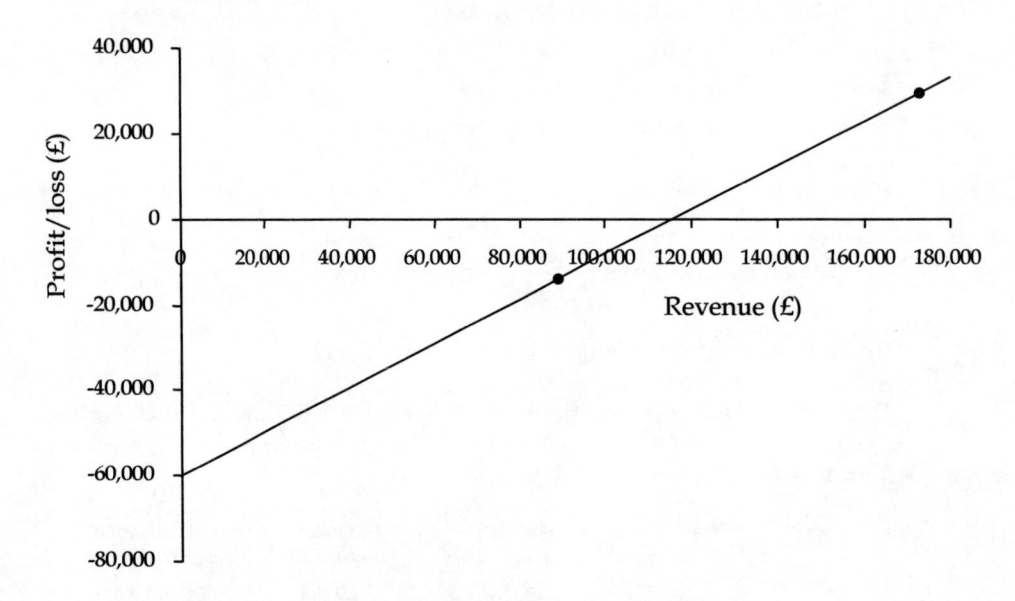

⚠️ Note: Did you read the question properly? It asked for **revenue** along the horizontal axis (in place of units). Ensure you always plot what is required.

(f) Contribution   = 5,000 × £15 = £75,000

Fixed costs   = £60,000

Profit   = £75,000 − £60,000 = £15,000

3.6 Margin of safety

Continuing with this example, suppose that JH Ltd expects to sell 6,000 units. How far is this above the break even point?

$$\text{Extra sales} = \frac{(6,000 - 4,000)}{4,000} = 50\%$$

This is known as the **margin of safety**. It represents how much sales can fall short of budget before the company is at break even point. In this case, JH know that their sales can fall by up to 50% and they will still be making a profit.

4 Contribution/Sales ratio (C/S ratio)

4.1 Introduction

The contribution/sales ratio shows how contribution is generated **per £ of sales revenue** rather than per unit.

The calculation can be done as either contribution per unit divided by selling price per unit or total contribution divided by total sales revenue (used when more than one product is being sold).

$$\text{Contribution/Sales ratio} = \frac{\text{Contribution/unit}}{\text{Selling price/unit}} \quad \text{OR} \quad \frac{\text{Total contribution}}{\text{Total sales revenue}}$$

4.2 Use in break even

The C/S ratio can be used in place of contribution per unit in the break even formula to give the answer directly in terms of sales revenue.

$$\text{Break even revenue} = \frac{\text{Fixed costs}}{\text{C/S ratio}}$$

4.3 Example

In the previous example (JH Ltd), sales price = £29, contribution = £15, and fixed costs = £60,000.

$$\text{C/S ratio} = \frac{£15}{£29} = 0.517$$

$$\text{Break even revenue} = \frac{£60,000}{0.517} = £116,000$$

The advantage of the C/S ratio is that we do not need contribution per unit.

4.4 Target profit

$$\text{Level of sales revenue to achieve a target profit (£)} = \frac{\text{Fixed costs + Target profit}}{\text{C/S ratio}}$$

In the example above (JH Ltd), if target profit is £20,000

$$\text{Level of sales revenue} = \frac{£60,000 + 20,000}{0.517} = £154,739 \text{ (or 154,667 depending on rounding)}$$

5 Assumptions underlying CVP analysis

5.1 The accountant's assumptions

A group of assumptions, only one of which deals with linearity, underlies our approach to break even and cost-volume-profit analysis. These assumptions are so important we list them fully below.

- Fixed costs remain fixed throughout the range charted.
- Variable costs fluctuate proportionally with volume.
- Selling prices do not change.
- Efficiency and productivity do not change.
- Cost factor prices do not change.
- A single product or static mix of products is dealt with.
- Volume is the only factor affecting cost.
- Stock levels do not change significantly (sales = production).
- Cost and revenue behaviour is reliably determined over the relevant range.
- Linearity is appropriate.

✓ It is highly likely that a question on this area will require students to discuss the assumptions of break even.

5.2 The economist's model of cost volume profit analysis

The economist would claim that break even or P/V charts should look like the chart examples below.

As a general model these are quite useful. They show that costs will tend to rise quickly as production commences; become more regular after a certain level then, as production is squeezed out of existing resources, cost per unit rises. Revenues are fairly regular but, as more and more sales are sought, unit price must be dropped until the total return begins to drop. This all seems logical but, for each individual company, the precise functions will be difficult to derive.

Over a limited range the cost accountant's charts are likely to be fairly similar to that of the economist and give a reasonable working model of the real situation for short-term decision-making; neither will be exact.

Break even chart

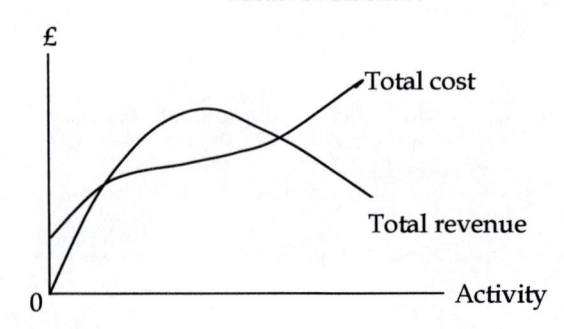

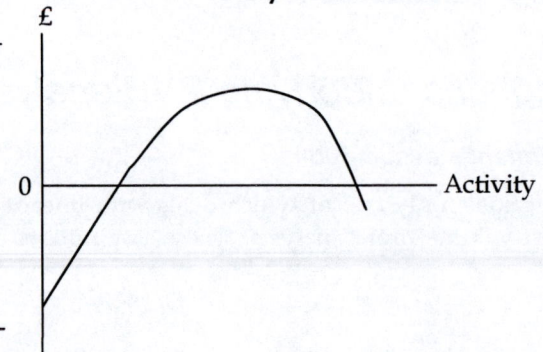

Profit/volume chart

Practice questions 1 and 2 *(The answers are in the final chapter of this book)*

1 CVP analysis

A company has provided the following information.

Budgeted sales and production volume	20,000 units
Variable cost per unit	£12
Fixed cost per unit	£6
Selling price per unit	£20

Required

(a) Calculate the break even point (unit sales)

$\frac{6 \times 20000}{20-12} = 15000$

(b) Calculate the break even point (sales revenue)

$15000 \times 20 = £300000$

(c) Calculate the sales (units) to earn a profit of £45,000

$\frac{120000 + 45000}{8} = 20625$

(d) Calculate the change in sales (revenue) from the budget needed to earn a profit of £45,000

$\frac{165000}{.4} - 400000 = 12,500$

(e) Calculate the margin of safety and the margin of safety ratio   £100,000

(f) Prepare a break even chart

(g) Prepare a profit/volume chart

2 Polyvinylchloride

The estimated variable production cost for the manufacture of plastic traffic cones is as follows.

	£
Materials	1.50
Labour	0.50
Variable production in overhead	1.00
	3.00

The variable selling cost is 20p per unit.

Fixed production overheads are £47,000 per month. Fixed selling and administration overheads are expected to be £25,000 per month.

A selling price of £8 per cone has been set and an anticipated level of production and sales of 20,000 cones per month has been budgeted.

Required

(a) Find the profit at the budgeted level of activity and also the profit figures if that activity level falls by 10% and alternatively increases by 10%.

(b) Find the break even point in terms of cones sold and in terms of sales revenue; hence find the margin of safety and the margin of safety ratio.

(c) What level of activity must be achieved to ensure that a profit of £20,000 is made?

(d) In the belief that the workforce are capable of producing more and that sales are likely to increase despite a general economic gloom, the firm considers changing the conditions of employment from piece rate to a fixed wage (based on 20,000 units per month).

What effect would replacing a variable cost with a fixed cost have on the three profit figures in (a) and on the break even point in (b)?

(e) Assuming now that both labour and variable overheads could be changed from a variable to a fixed cost as described in (d), draw a break even chart and a profit volume chart to show the original position from (a) and this revised position.

6 Summary

You should now be able to:

♦ Discuss and calculate the CVP formulae as below:

a) Break even point (in units) = $\dfrac{\text{Fixed costs}}{\text{Contribution/unit}}$

b) Break even point (in £ sales) = $\dfrac{\text{Fixed costs}}{\text{Contribution/unit}} \times \text{sales price/unit}$

or $\dfrac{\text{Fixed costs}}{\text{C/S ratio}}$

c) Contribution/sales ratio = $\dfrac{\text{Contribution/unit}}{\text{Sales/unit}} \times 100$

d) Level of sales to achieve a target profit (in units) = $\dfrac{\text{Fixed costs} + \text{Target profit}}{\text{Contribution/unit}}$

e) Level of sales to achieve a target profit (in £) = $\dfrac{\text{Fixed costs} + \text{Target profit}}{\text{c/s ratio}}$

f) Margin of safety = Break even sales units

♦ Demonstrate the break even point graphically
♦ Discuss the limitations of CVP analysis
♦ Explain the difference between the accountant's and the economist's model of cost volume profit analysis

Multiple choice questions *(The answers are in the final chapter of this book)*

1. A Ltd has fixed costs of £60,000 per annum. It manufactures a single product which it sells for £20 per unit. Its contribution to sales ratio is 40%.

    A Ltd's break even point in units is:

    A   1,800

    B   3,000

    C   5,000

    ✓ D   7,500

2. A Ltd makes a single product which it sells for £10 per unit. Fixed costs are £48,000 per month and the product has a contribution to sales ratio of 40%.

    In a period when actual sales were £140,000, A Ltd's margin of safety, in units, was:

    ✓ A   2,000

    B   6,000

    C   8,000

    D   12,000

3. B Ltd makes a single product which sells for £50 per unit. Fixed costs are £25,000 per month and marginal costs are £30 per unit. What sales level will produce a profit of £5,000?

    A   833 units

    B   1,000 units

    C   1,250 units

    ✓ D   1,500 units

CHAPTER 12

Budgeting

EXAM FOCUS

In this chapter we look at budgeting. This is a relatively straightforward topic which can appear in all three sections of the paper integrated with other aspects of the syllabus. You can expect both computational and written questions in this area. The written questions will focus on the stages in budget preparation whilst the computational questions will be concerned with the calculation of the departmental budgets.

LEARNING OUTCOMES

This chapter covers the following Learning Outcomes of the CIMA Syllabus.

- Explain why organisations prepare budgets
- Explain how organisations prepare budgets
- Explain the use of IT in the budget process
- Prepare functional budgets, profit and loss account, balance sheet and a simple cash budget

In order to cover these Learning Outcomes the following topics are included.

- Define a budget and discuss its objectives
- Distinguish between the incremental and zero-based methods of budgeting
- Describe the budgeting process
- Prepare and explain the functional budgets
- Prepare and explain the elements of the master budget: cash budget, profit and loss account and balance sheet budgets
- Consider the impact of IT in the budgeting process

1 Why budget?

1.1 Definition

The budget is defined as

> "A quantitative statement, for a defined period of time, which may include planned revenues, expenses, assets, liabilities and cashflows. A budget provides a focus for the organisation, aids the coordination of activities and facilitates control. Planning is achieved by means of a **fixed master budget**, whereas control is generally exercised through the comparison of actual costs with a **flexible budget**."
>
> CIMA Official Terminology

1.2 Objectives of budgeting

The budget process has many objectives and written parts of examination questions often address these.

The objectives of budgeting are as follows:

- Planning
- Control
- Communication
- Coordination
- Performance appraisal
- Resource utilisation
- Motivation

We examine each of these in turn.

1.3 Planning

A budget is not supposed to be a prediction of where a company will be in a period's time if it meanders along doing what it normally does. On the contrary, budgeting is part of the dynamic strategic planning process.

A strategic plan is normally prepared for several years ahead and hence is often a fairly general plan of where the organisation is aiming to be placed at the end of this period. Budgets are prepared for shorter periods of time, often a year. They are normally more detailed than strategic plans and aim to break the plan down into shorter more achievable parts. Thus budgeting is a planning device.

1.4 Control

Once a period has elapsed we can compare the actual results of the company for the period with budgeted results to see how close we came to achieving the plan. This will enable the company potentially to bring about improvements for the future.

This style of control is known as *feedback control* as it is carried out after the event on a reactive basis. Standard costing and variances form the main feedback control device.

Earlier we stated that budgeting is the short-run aspect of the long-run planning process. The strategic planning process will define the corporate objectives. If the budget prepared does not satisfy these objectives then steps can be taken to amend the budgeted plan of action. The taking of corrective action before the event on a pro-active basis is known as *feedforward control*.

1.5 Communication

In large organisations, particularly if they are organised along divisional lines, it is often difficult to communicate to people the objectives and plans of the entire organisation. The budget is a plan of action expressed in quantitative terms. By providing people within the organisation with such a plan it helps communicate the wishes and objectives of the entire organisation.

1.6 Co-ordination

In large organisations it is often difficult to co-ordinate the activities of the various components to work for the common good of the entire organisation. By establishing a budget committee under the control of a principal budget officer it should be possible to co-ordinate the plans and objectives of the component parts of the organisation to ensure they complement one another and work towards organisational aims.

1.7 Performance appraisal

If the budget is set on a disaggregated basis, so that each area of responsibility provides a budget which is added to others to produce the overall company budget, then this improves the appraisal of the various components of the organisation and the people responsible for these components. The feedback control mentioned earlier can be accurately directed to aid performance appraisal.

1.8 Resource utilisation

The business will have a variety of resources at its command: people, machinery and cash for instance. The budgeting process can greatly aid the use to which those resources are directed so that they produce the greatest added value for the organisation. Techniques such as limiting factor analysis greatly aid this, as does the zero based approach discussed later in this chapter.

1.9 Motivation

We are now approaching the 'people' part of management accounting. Whether budgets motivate staff to increased effort on behalf of the firm depends on a number of factors. As soon as people are involved there are no easy answers. The following points could be made.

Some budget is better than no budget

Various studies have found that in many organisations the complete absence of budgets and formalised plans confuses many people. They feel insecure and do not know what they are expected to achieve. Management may say 'do a good job' but this is so woolly that staff have no idea what is meant by a 'good job'. This has led to a belief that some system of budgetary control is better than none at all; at least staff then have an idea what is required of them no matter how preposterous the requirement may be.

The degree of inherent difficulty

This is probably the most important influence on budgets as a tool for motivating staff. Let us consider the extremes and their likely impact on motivation of staff.

- *Budget target is ridiculously difficult*

    This is unlikely to produce a positive motivating effect in the long run.

    In the short run staff may strive to meet the overdemanding target. However they will quickly realise the impossibility being demanded of them and give up, leading to a loss of motivating effort.

    A by-product of this approach to target setting is likely to be antagonism between staff and management leading to high and unsettling staff turnover.

- *Budget target is ridiculously easy*

    This is also unlikely to lead to a positive motivating effect on staff.

    If the target is too easy staff will simply achieve it or beat it slightly to make themselves look good but no more effort is likely to be forthcoming – it is human nature unfortunately. Anybody breaking ranks and working hard is likely to be pressurised by their colleagues into a go slow in case the target is made more difficult for the next period.

A by-product of this approach tends to be friendly relations between staff and management. However this style of management (known as 'country club management') despite resulting in a happy workforce tends to lead to insolvency for the company.

We have seen that the extremes of difficulty tend to have adverse motivational consequences most of the time. Therefore a compromise is needed. The generally held belief these days is that the budget should be 'tough but attainable'. This should produce good effort from staff plus the added benefit of staff respecting management for their expertise in this manner. However there is no formula for finding the 'tough but attainable' situation. In practice it usually comes down to management skill. Good managers who know their staff and are experienced in their jobs will find this target intuitively – bad managers never will no matter how many textbooks they read or courses they attend.

1.10 The extent of participation allowed

Many organisations run an authoritarian 'top down' approach to budget setting. Senior people set the targets and then 'impose' these targets on the people below them who have no say in the degree of difficulty inherent in the targets. This imposed budget situation may cause resentment and a lack of budget acceptance. This is particularly true with white collar workers although many blue collar workers have come to expect this.

The alternative extreme is to run a 'bottom up' or participative style of budget setting. Meetings are held where the people expected to meet budgetary targets have a say in what that target should be. Some texts regard participation as the panacea to all budgeting problems, leading to acceptance and improved motivation.

However, the truth is not so simple. We are dealing with people here. When people are asked by managers how long a job should take this is normally followed by a sharp intake of breath and a ridiculously lenient reply is likely to be forthcoming. This is known as 'budgetary slack' or 'padding' and describes the situation where participators try to set themselves very easy targets to give themselves an easy life.

Perhaps again a compromise is needed. Participation not only leads to greater acceptance of targets but also potentially to better budgets as the experience of the participators can be very valuable. To avoid padding perhaps a participative bottom up style coupled with a system of budget challenging is the best answer. Challenging is a situation where managers do not accept the word of the staff but call into question its credibility and demand changes as necessary.

However once again we are back to management policy – good managers know when to challenge, bad managers do not.

So in conclusion:

Q: Are budgets good for motivation?

A: It depends!

2 Methods of budget preparation

2.1 Introduction

Here we will look at how budgets are prepared and other budgeting terms. All are likely written areas for exam questions.

2.2 Incremental budgeting

Incremental budgeting is the most common way of setting a budget. The starting point is last year's budget. This is taken and 'tweaked' to form the budget for the current period by adjusting for such things as inflation, volume changes and efficiency changes.

Advantages of the incremental approach

- It is quick to prepare the budget for the forthcoming period.
- It is cheap to prepare the budget as all we are doing is adjusting previous work.

Disadvantages of incremental approach

- In the search for speed and cost effectiveness the required adjustments for the current period may not be effectively made.
- The starting point is last year's budget. If this contains areas of waste or inefficiency this will be perpetuated in the forthcoming period.

2.3 Zero-based budgeting

A more modern approach to budget setting is known as zero based budgeting (ZBB). In its simplest form the start point is a clean sheet of paper. The budget is built up from scratch each period.

Advantages of zero based approach

- Previous period's waste or inefficiency is not automatically incorporated in the current target.
- As the previous period is no longer the yardstick management are more likely to challenge the plan resulting in a more cost effective budget.

Disadvantages of zero based approach

- Compared to the incremental approach it will be more time consuming.
- As it is more time consuming it will also be more costly to prepare.

2.4 Zero-based budgeting in practice

Many firms and government departments do use ZBB nowadays. Other firms like to combine the two approaches to get the best of both worlds. They run an incremental system for three to or four years then introduce ZBB, for a period, then go back to incremental.

Experience has also shown that ZBB is a very useful resource allocation tool for support departments (sometimes called discretionary cost centres). The 'decision package' system is used. For example, take a machine maintenance department. The manager puts forward several 'decision packages' on budgets as follows.

Decision package number 1	Machines routinely inspected and overhauled every month.
	Annual cost £100,000
Decision package number 2	Machines routinely inspected and overhauled every fortnight.
	Annual cost £220,000
Decision package number 3	Machines routinely inspected and overhauled every week.
	Annual cost £500,000

These proposals will be sent to management who will challenge the accuracy of the figures and adjust as necessary. Management will then decide which proposal gives the best value for money in terms of cost versus machinery breakdown avoided and allocate cash accordingly.

3 Budgeting process

3.1 Stages in budget preparation

The stages in budget preparation can be summarised as:

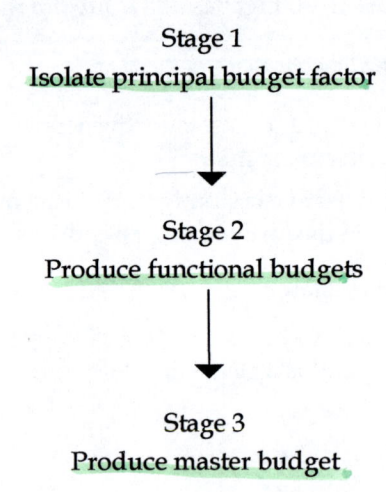

Stage 1
Isolate principal budget factor

↓

Stage 2
Produce functional budgets

↓

Stage 3
Produce master budget

3.2 The principal budget factor

The *principal budget factor* is the factor that restricts the company's level of activity. It is a limiting factor. The principal budget factor could relate to material or labour availability but is more likely to represent sales demand. Sales demand is a limiting factor because there is no point in producing more than customers are willing to buy.

In the examination you will usually be told what the limiting factor is.

3.3 The functional budgets

The *functional budgets* (ie the budgets for each functional area in the business) build up the various costs to arrive at the figures for inclusion in the profit and loss account. A logical order is followed along the lines of:

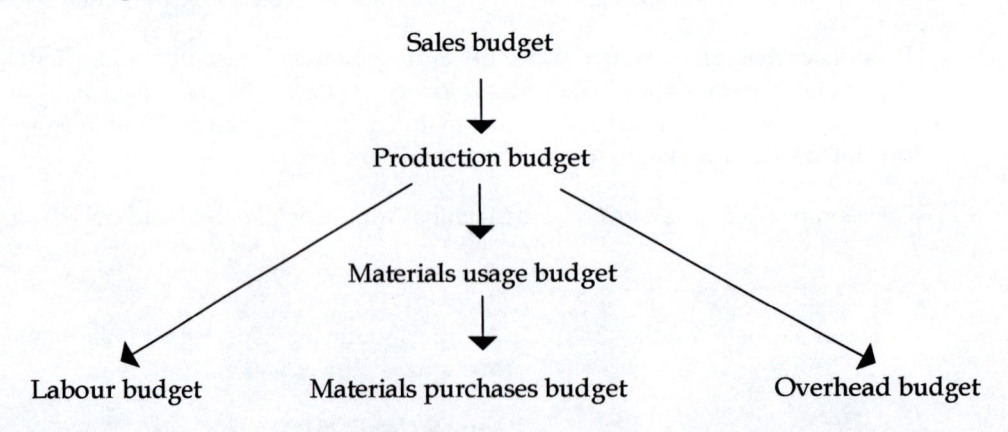

Sales budget
↓
Production budget
↓
Materials usage budget
↓
Labour budget   Materials purchases budget   Overhead budget

Note the logical order.

- We begin with the sales budget because sales in this case is assumed to be the principal budget factor.

172

- Achieving a given sales level has implications for our required production levels, so the production budget comes next.
- This in turn has implications for the amount of production resources we will use. The next stage is therefore the labour materials and overheads usage budgets, and so we proceed.

3.4 The master budget

The *master budget* incorporates:

- The budgeted profit and loss account
- The budgeted cashflow forecast
- The budgeted balance sheet

A series of examples now follow showing the build up of a budget.

4 Preparation of functional budgets

4.1 Sales budget - example

A plc estimates that its sales of Product X in the coming period will be 10,000 units and of Product Y 15,000 units. At these volumes Product X is likely to sell for £30 per unit and Product Y for £25 per unit.

Required

Produce a sales budget.

4.2 Solution

Product	X	Y	Total
Budgeted sales (units)	10,000	15,000	
Selling price	£30	£25	
Sales budget	£300,000	£375,000	£675,000

Practice question 1 *(The answer is in the final chapter of this book)*

Sales budget

B plc estimates its sales for next month as Product Q 10,000 units, Product R 8,000 units and Product S 11,000 units. Selling prices are expected to be £40 per unit for Product Q, £36 for Product R and £20 for Product S.

Required

Produce a sales budget.

4.3 Production budget

A production budget will be compiled next. Note that production volumes will be different from sales volumes if stocks of finished goods change over the period. The formula is:

Budgeted production = Budgeted sales - opening stock + closing stock

4.4 Example

A plc (see earlier example) has 1,000 units of Product X and 5,000 units of Product Y in stock. At the end of the coming period it wants to increase stocks of X by 10% and decrease stocks of Y by 50%.

Required

Prepare a production budget.

4.5 Solution

Product	X	Y
	Units	Units
Budgeted sales	10,000	15,000
Opening stock	(1,000)	(5,000)
Closing stock		
1,000 × 110%	1,100	
5,000 × 50%		2,500
Budgeted production	10,100	12,500

Practice question 2 *(The answer is in the final chapter of this book)*

Production budget

B plc (see Question 1 above) has 5,000 units of Product Q, 3,000 units of R and 6,000 units of S in stock at present. By the end of next month it wants to increase stocks of Q by 20% of next month's sales of Q, reduce stocks of R by 20% of the existing figure and reduce stocks of S by 50% of next month's sales of S.

Required

Prepare a production budget.

4.6 Materials usage budget

Once production volume is known we can produce a materials usage budget. This is material usage per unit × number of units produced. This can then be multiplied by the unit cost of materials converted to a value.

4.7 Example

Each unit of Product X (see earlier examples of A Plc) requires 2kg of material M and 1kg of material N. Each unit of Product Y requires 2½ kg of M. M costs £5 per kg and N £4 per kg. Production quantities were 10,100 units (X) and 12,500 units (Y).

Required

Prepare a materials usage budget.

4.8 Solution

Material	M kg	N kg	
Used in production of:			
Product X 10,100 × 2	20,200		
10,100 × 1		10,100	
Product Y 12,500 × 2½	31,250		
Budgeted materials usage (kg)	51,450	10,100	
Price per kg	£5	£4	
Materials usage (£)	£257,250	£40,400	Total £297,650

Practice question 3 *(The answer is in the final chapter of this book)*

Materials usage budget

Each unit of Product Q (see Questions 1 and 2) takes 4kg of material E, 2kg of material F and 1kg of material G. Each unit of Product R takes 3½ kg of material E, 1kg of material F and 2kg of material H. Each unit of Product S takes 4kg of material H. Materials prices in £ per kg are as follows: E - £3, F - £2.50, G - £4, H - £3.

Required

Prepare a materials usage budget.

4.9 Materials purchases budget

If opening stocks of raw materials are different from closing stocks then materials usage and materials purchases are not the same.

Material purchases (units) = material usage - opening stock + closing stock

4.10 Example

In A plc, opening stocks of Material M are 6,000kg and of Material N 5,000kg. Desired closing stocks are 50% higher for both materials. Usages were 51,450 kg (M) and 10,100 kg (N).

Required

Prepare a materials purchases budget.

4.11 Solution

Material	M kg	N kg	
Materials usage	51,450	10,100	
Opening stock	(6,000)	(5,000)	
Closing stock:			
6,000 × 150%	9,000		
5,000 × 150%		7,500	
Materials purchases	54,450	12,600	
Price per kg	£5	£4	
Materials purchases (£)	£272,250	£50,400	Total £322,650

Practice question 4 *(The answer is in the final chapter of this book)*

Materials purchases budget

B Plc again. Stocks of Materials E, F, G and H are 20,000kg, 18,000kg, 6,000kg and 4,000kg. Over the period stocks of Material E are to be halved, stocks of Material F to reduce to 20% of that period's usage, stocks of Material G to remain static and stocks of Material H to increase by 20%.

Required

Prepare a raw materials purchases budget.

4.12 Labour budget

The labour budget can only be prepared after the production budget. It is calculated in the same way as the material usage budget.

Labour hours = hours per unit × number of units
Labour cost = total hours × rate per hour

4.13 Example

In A plc the production budget was 10,100 units X and 12,500 units Y (4.5). Each unit of Product X requires ½ hour of skilled labour and 1 hour of unskilled labour. A unit of Product Y takes ¼ hour of skilled labour and 1 hour of unskilled labour. Skilled labour is paid at £6 per hour and unskilled at £4 per hour.

Required

Prepare a labour budget.

4.14 Solution

Labour Type	Skilled hrs	Unskilled hrs	
Worked on production of:			
X 10,100 × ½	5,050		
10,100 × 1		10,100	
Y 12,500 × ¼	3,125		
12,500 × 1		12,500	
Labour hours	8,175	22,600	
Labour rate per hour	£6	£4	
Labour costs	£49,050	£90,400	Total £139,450

Practice question 5 *(The answer is in the final chapter of this book)*

Labour budget

In B Plc, to make a unit of Product Q (budget production 12,000 units) takes ¼ hour of Grade I labour and 10 minutes of Grade II. A unit of Product R (7,400 units) takes 12 minutes of Grade I and 24 minutes of Grade II. A unit of Product S (5,500 units) takes 30 minutes of Grade I labour only. Labour rates are £5 per hour for Grade I and £8 per hour for Grade II.

Required

Prepare a labour budget.

4.15 Overheads budget

If absorption rates are used these are normally calculated *after* the labour budgets as labour hours are often used for the calculation.

4.16 Example

A plc absorbs variable production overhead at £2 per skilled labour hour. Marginal costing is used and fixed overheads are expected to be £25,000 for the period.

Required

With reference to the data in 4.14, produce an overheads budget.

4.17 Solution

Variable overheads	£
8,175 hrs × £2 =	16,350
Fixed overheads	25,000
Total overheads	41,350

As marginal costing is used fixed overhead absorption rates are not used.

Practice question 6 *(The answer is in the final chapter of this book)*

Overheads budget

B plc absorbs variable overhead at 50p per Grade I labour hour and £1 per Grade II labour hour. Fixed overheads are £150,000 per period and marginal costing is used.

Required

Prepare an overhead budget.

---

5 Preparation of the master budget

5.1 Compiling the master budget

Now we have done the functional budgets we can put the information together in a master budget. Remember this comprises:

- budgeted profit and loss account
- budgeted cashflow statement
- budgeted balance sheet.

The work done on functional budgets leads mainly to the first of these.

5.2 Example – budgeted profit and loss account

Produce a budgeted profit and loss account for A plc as far as the information given throughout section 4 permits.

5.3 Solution

We will need to value stocks of finished goods so this is calculated first.

Product X	£
Material M 2kg × £5	10
Material N 1kg × £4	4
Skilled labour ½ hr × £6	3
Unskilled labour 1 hr × £4	4
Variable overhead ½ hr × £2	1
Stock valuation per unit	22

Product Y	£
Material M 2½ kg × £5	12.50
Material N	Nil
Skilled labour ¼ hr × £6	1.50
Unskilled labour 1 hr × £4	4.00
Variable overhead ¼ hr × £2	0.50
Stock valuation per unit	18.50

As marginal costing is used fixed overheads are not included in stock values.

Product	X	Y	Total
	£	£	£
Opening stock value			
1,000 × £22	22,000		
5,000 × £18.50		92,500	114,500
Closing stock value			
1,100 × £22	24,200		
2,500 × £18.50		46,250	70,450

Now we assemble the information into profit and loss account format.

A plc budgeted profit and loss account for period 1

	£	£
Sales		675,000
Opening stock	114,500	
Materials usage	297,650	
Labour	139,450	
Variable overheads	16,350	
	567,950	
Less: closing stock	(70,450)	
Variable cost of sales		(497,500)
Contribution		177,500
Fixed overhead		25,000
Profit		152,500

Because A plc uses a marginal costing system we highlight the figure for contribution.

Note the cost of sales figure could also be derived as follows:

X - 10,000 × £22	£220,000
Y - 15,000 × £18.50	£277,500
Total variable cost of sale	£497,500

Practice question 7 *(The answer is in the final chapter of this book)*

Profit and loss account

Required

Prepare a budgeted profit and loss account for B plc, using the data given and derived in the previous practice questions.

5.4 Cash budgets

Now we have dealt with functional budgets and budgeted profit and loss accounts we turn our attention to cash budgets (or cashflow forecasts).

A cash budget is one of the most important budgets prepared in an organisation. It shows the expected cash receipts and expected cash payments during the budget period. Liquidity and cash flow management are key factors in the successful operation of any organisation.

A cash budget must contain every type of cash inflow or receipt and every type of cash outflow or payment. In addition to the amounts, the timings of receipts and payments must also be forecast.

5.5 Cash not income and expenditure

It is important to realise that cash receipts and payments are not the same as sales and the costs of sales found in a firm's profit and loss account because:

(i) Not all cash receipts affect profit and loss account income eg the issue of new shares results in a cash inflow but would not be shown on the profit and loss account.

(ii) Not all cash payments affect the costs shown in the profit and loss account eg the purchase of a fixed asset.

(iii) Some profit and loss items are derived from accounting conventions and are not cashflows eg depreciation.

(iv) The timing of cash receipts and payments does not coincide with the profit and loss accounting period eg a sale is recognised in the profit and loss account when the invoice is raised yet the cash payment from the debtor may not be received until the following period or later.

5.6 Approach to cash budget exam questions

Your approach to cash budget questions in the examination should be as follows.

- Use a sensible recognised format. A suitable proforma is shown below.
- Try to insert the easy cashflows onto the schedule first to gain easy marks. The easier cashflows may include rent and rates, dividends and tax paid, purchase and sale of fixed assets, and capital raised and redeemed.
- Do a back up working for the more difficult cashflows. These tend to be cash received from sales and cash paid to suppliers.
- Never include depreciation or profit/loss on asset sales because these are non-cash items.

5.7 Proforma cash budget

	January	February	March
Inflows			
Cash received from customers			
Proceeds of asset sales			
Proceeds of share issue			
	——	——	——
	——	——	——
Outflows			
Cash paid to suppliers			
Wages			
Expenses			
Dividends			
Purchase of fixed assets			
	——	——	——
	——	——	——
Net inflow (outflow)			
Balance b/f	X	X	X
	——	——	——
Balance c/f	X	X	X
	——	——	——

5.8 Example

J plc is setting up a new business. Its sales for the first three months are expected to be £10,000, £15,000 and £30,000. 20% of sales are for cash and 80% on credit terms. Of the credit sales, 50% will pay within a month, 30% within two months and 10% within three months. Any debts not paid after three months are considered bad.

Required

Calculate the cashflows resulting from these sales.

5.9 Solution

To get a better picture of the cashflows it helps to select a nominal value of sales – say £100 – and to analyse when the cash is received.

	£	
Cash sales (20%)	20	
Credit sales (80%)	80	
	100	

	£	
Credit sales:		
1 month lag	40	40% of total
(50% × £80)		
2 month lag	24	24% of total
(30% × £80)		
3 month lag	8	8% of total
(10% × £80)		
	72	
Bad debts	8	8% of total
(Balance)	80	

When the question says that 50% are paid within the month it has been interpreted as one month after the month of sale. Cash budget questions are notoriously badly worded. Make an assumption rather than wasting time worrying about it.

The percentages for credit sales do not add up to 100%. The difference must therefore relate to bad debts. In this question you were given a hint that bad debts might be an issue. Sometimes you are expected to make this inference without any specific reference in the question.

With the percentages from the workings we can now calculate cashflows from these sales.

Month	1	2	3	4	5	6
	£	£	£	£	£	£
Received in month of sale						
£10,000 × 20%	2,000					
£15,000 × 20%		3,000				
£30,000 × 20%			6,000			

Received one month after month of sale
 £10,000 × 40%   4,000
 £15,000 × 40%   6,000
 £30,000 × 40%   12,000

Received two months after month of sale
 £10,000 × 24%   2,400
 £15,000 × 24%   3,600
 £30,000 × 24%   7,200

Received three months after month of sale
 £10,000 × 8%   800
 £15,000 × 8%   1,200
 £30,000 × 8%   2,400

Cashflow   2,000   7,000   14,400   16,400   8,400   2,400

Practice question 8 *(The answer is in the final chapter of this book)*

Cash budget

K plc, a long established business, wants to prepare a cash budget for the months of January, February and March. 10% of its sales are cash sales and a 15% cash discount is given on these. 40% of credit customers pay within one month and are allowed a 5% settlement discount, 45% pay after two months and 10% after three months.

Actual and budgeted sales are as follows.

	Oct	Nov	Dec	Jan	Feb	Mar
Sales	£8,000	£10,000	£5,000	£15,000	£12,000	£10,000
	Actual	Actual	Actual	Budget	Budget	Budget

Required

Calculate cashflows from these sales for January, February and March.

5.10 Cash paid to suppliers

When calculating cashflows paid to suppliers of materials the calculations can be complicated by introducing a sizeable element of functional budgeting into the equation.

5.11 Example

T plc manufactures a product which requires 3kg of Material V per unit. The timing of production is such that stocks of finished goods represent the next two months worth of sales. Stocks of raw materials represent the next month's raw material usage. T plc is allowed one month's credit by its suppliers. Actual and budgeted sales are as follows (in units).

	Oct	Nov	Dec	Jan	Feb	Mar	Apr
Sales (units)	5,000	10,000	8,000	12,000	15,000	6,000	8,000
	Actual	Actual	Actual	Budget	Budget	Budget	Budget

Each unit of Material V costs £10.

Required

Calculate cash paid to suppliers in January and February.

5.12 Solution

	Oct Units	Nov Units	Dec Units	Jan Units	Feb Units	Mar Units	Apr Units
Sales	5,000	10,000	8,000	12,000	15,000	6,000	8,000
Closing stock	18,000	20,000	27,000	21,000	14,000		
Opening stock		(18,000)	(20,000)	(27,000)	(21,000)		
Production		12,000	15,000	6,000	8,000		
Materials usage (kg)		36,000	45,000	18,000	24,000		
Closing stock (kg)		45,000	18,000	24,000			
Opening stock (kg)			(45,000)	(18,000)			
Purchases (kg)			18,000	24,000			
Cashflow (£)				180,000	240,000		

> Having calculated the purchases, do not forget to include the one month's credit so that payment will be delayed by one month.

This is as complicated as it gets. Ultimately we want a cash budget but in order to achieve this we first need to do a functional budgeting exercise following the approach studied earlier.

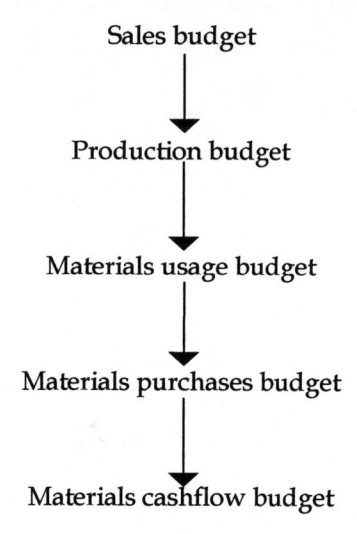

Sales budget
↓
Production budget
↓
Materials usage budget
↓
Materials purchases budget
↓
Materials cashflow budget

If T plc were not a manufacturing company but a wholesaler then the production and usage budget would not be required and we could jump directly to the purchases budget.

5.13 Budgeted balance sheet

The figures for a budgeted balance sheet, if required in an examination question, will come from three sources:

- the question itself (re fixed assets, depreciation, loans, share capital, etc)
- your functional budget workings (closing stock)
- your cash budget workings (debtors, creditors, cash).

For example, looking back to the example of J plc in 5.8, the budgeted balance sheet at the end of the first three months would show debtors of:

£55,000 (total sales) - £23,400 (cash received per cash budget) = £31,600

(before any provision for bad debts).

The following example illustrates how to tackle a question that requires all three elements of the master budget.

5.14 Example of a complete master budget

On January 1 the summary balance sheet of CH Ltd was as follows:

	£	£	£
Fixed asset at cost			80,000
Depreciation			(19,200)
			60,800
Current assets:			
Stock		24,200	
Debtors		25,000	
		49,200	
Current liabilities:			
Proposed dividends	1,000		
Overdraft	9,000		
		(10,000)	
Net current assets			39,200
			100,000
Long term liabilities			
Loan 15%			(40,000)
Net assets			60,000
Share capital			40,000
Accumulated profit			20,000
			60,000

The following are expected during the next three months:

	Sales £	Purchases £	Expenses £
January	150,000	100,000	20,000
February	200,000	150,000	25,000
March	300,000	280,000	30,000

All sales are on credit and the collections have the following pattern:

During the month of sale	80% (a 4% discount is given for payment in this period)
In the subsequent month	20%

Payment for purchase is made in the month of purchase in order to take advantage of a 10% prompt settlement discount, calculated on the gross purchase figures shown above. Stock levels are expected to remain constant throughout the period. Depreciation of machinery is calculated at a rate of 12% pa on cost. The appropriate portion for each month January to March is included in the expenses figures above. Expenses are paid for in the month in which they are incurred. The proposed dividend will be paid in January. Loan interest for the three months will be paid in March.

Required

(a) Prepare a cash budget for each of the three months January to March

(b) Prepare a forecast profit and loss account for the period

(c) Prepare a forecast balance sheet as at 31 March

5.15 Solution

(a) **Cash Budget: January - March**

	January £	February £	March £
Receipts of Cash			
Current month' sales	120,000	160,000	240,000
Less discounts given	(4,800)	(6,400)	(9,600)
Previous month's sales	25,000	30,000	40,000
	140,200	183,600	270,400
Cash payments			
Purchases	100,000	150,000	280,000
Less discounts received	(10,000)	(15,000)	(28,000)
Expenses (W1)	19,200	24,200	29,200
Dividend	1,000		
Interest (W2)			1,500
	110,200	159,200	282,700
Net cashflow for month	30,000	24,400	(12,300)
Opening balance	(9,000)[1]	21,000	45,400
Closing balance	21,000	45,400	33,100

[1] From the balance sheet

Workings

W1 Monthly depreciation = 12% x 80,000 x 1/12 = £800
Deduct this from the monthly expense figures to obtain the cash flow

W2 Loan interest per annum = 15% x £40,000 = £6,000
Loan interest per quarter = ¼ x £6,000 = £1,500

(b) **Budgeted Profit and Loss account for January – March**

	£	£
Sales		650,000
Cost of Sales (= purchases since stocks constant)		530,000
Gross Profit		120,000
Add: Discounts received		53,000
		173,000
Less:		
Expenses (including depreciation)	75,000	
Interest	1,500	
Discounts allowed	20,800	
		(97,300)
Net Profit		75,700

(c) **Budgeted Balance Sheet for the period ended 31 March**

	£	£	£
Fixed Asset at cost			80,000
Depreciation (19,200 + 800 × 3)			(21,600)
			58,400
Current Assets:			
Stock		24,200	
Debtors (300,000 × 20%)		60,000	
Cash		33,100	
		117,300	
Current Liabilities:		Nil	
Net Current Assets			117,300
			175,700
Long-term Liabilities:			
Loan 15%			(40,000)
Net Assets			135,700
Share Capital			40,000
Accumulated Profit (20,000 + 75,700)			95,700
			135,700

Practice questions 9 and 10 *(The answers are in the final chapter of this book)*

9 Cash paid to suppliers

W plc manufactures Product P which requires 4Kg of Material Z at a cost of £3 per kg. It is W's policy to keep finished goods stock sufficient for the next month and a half's sales and raw material stocks sufficient for the next two months production. W plc is allowed two months credit on supplies of Material Z.

The sales of Product P are as follows (in units).

	Sept	Oct	Nov	Dec	Jan	Feb	Mar	Apr	May
Sales (units)	20,000	25,000	22,000	15,000	16,000	20,000	22,000	27,000	30,000

Required

Calculate the cash paid to suppliers in January, February and March.

10 ABC Ltd

The following data and estimates are available for ABC Ltd for June, July and August:

	June £	July £	August £
Sales	45,000	50,000	60,000
Wages	12,000	13,000	14,500
Overheads	8,500	9,500	9,000

The following information is available regarding direct materials:

	June £	July £	August £	September £
Opening stock	5,000	3,500	6,000	4,000
Material usage	8,000	9,000	10,000	

Notes

1. 10% of sales are for cash, the balance is received the following month. The amount received in June for May's sales is £29,500.

2. Wages are paid in the month they are incurred.

3. Overheads include £1,500 per month for depreciation. Overheads are settled the month following. £6,500 is to be paid in June for May's overheads.

4. Purchases of direct materials are paid for in the month purchased.

5. The opening cash balance in June is £11,750.

6. A tax bill of £25,000 is to be paid in July.

Required

(a) Calculate the amount of direct material purchases in EACH of the months of June, July and August. **(3 marks)**

(b) Prepare cash budgets for June, July and August. **(9 marks)**

(c) Describe briefly the advantages of preparing cash budgets. **(3 marks)**

(Total : 15 marks)

6 IT and the budgeting process

The introduction of the spreadsheet has allowed flexibility and versatility in budget preparation.

A spreadsheet is an electronic worksheet arranged as a grid with each column labelled alphabetically and each row numerically. The intersection of a column and row is known as a cell. In the cell data a formula is held and the nature of the worksheet allows the data in the cell to be manipulated in any way.

The key feature of the spreadsheet is its ability to change all elements in the worksheet automatically when one or more assumptions are changed. This makes it particularly useful for budgeting. This is because the budgeting process involves preparation of data based on certain assumptions but if these assumptions change the ability to see the effect of the change is essential. The spreadsheet allows this process.

Students are advised to familiarise themselves with spreadsheets as preparation for their examination.

7 Summary

You should now be able to:

- Define a budget
- Discuss the reasons for preparing budgets
- Distinguish between the incremental budgeting and zero based budgeting

- Describe the budgeting process
- Prepare the functional budgets, budgeted profit and loss account, budgeted balance sheet and budgeted cash flow.
- Consider the impact of IT in the budgeting process.

Multiple choice questions *(The answers are in the final chapter of this book)*

1   A master budget comprises:

    A   the budgeted profit and loss account

    B   the budgeted cashflow, budgeted profit and loss account and budgeted balance sheet

    C   the budgeted cashflow

    D   the capital expenditure budget

2   The following details have been extracted from the debtor collection records of C Ltd:

Invoices paid in the month after sale	60%
Invoices paid in the second month after sale	25%
Invoices paid in the third month after sale	12%
Bad debts	3%

Invoices are issued on the last day of each month.

Customers paying in the month after sale are entitled to deduct a 2% settlement discount.

Credit sales values for June to September 20X5 are budgeted as follows:

June	July	August	September
£35,000	£40,000	£60,000	£45,000

The amount budgeted to be received from credit sales in September 20X5 is:

    A   £47,680

    B   £48,850

    C   £49,480

    D   £50,200

CHAPTER 13

Budgetary control

EXAM FOCUS

✓ This chapter focuses on how the budget is used from a control point of view. Your understanding of cost behaviour is imperative to this chapter as you will be required in the exam to prepare flexible budgets. Questions in this area tend to be both computational and written. The computational element concentrating on the calculation of a flexible budget and variances arising from actual. The written aspect may involve questions requiring you to explain how knowledge of cost behaviour is vital in budgetary control.

LEARNING OUTCOMES

This chapter covers the following Learning Outcomes of the CIMA Syllabus.

    Calculate simple cost estimates using high-low method and line of best fit

    Prepare simple reports showing actual and budgeted results

    Explain the differences between fixed and flexible budgets

    Prepare a fixed and flexible budget

    Calculate expenditure, volume and total budget variances

In order to cover these Learning Outcomes the following topics are included.

    Identify the control cycle

    Distinguish between feedback and feedforward controls

    Distinguish between fixed and flexible budgets

    Prepare flexible budgets for a range of activity levels

    Prepare reports which compare flexible budget with actual results identifying variances in relation to:

- Income
- Expenditure
- Volume
- Total

1 The control cycle

1.1 Introduction

Budgetary control involves the comparison of actual results to planned results and reporting on deviations so that corrective action can be taken.

There are three stages in the control cycle.

1 *Record*

The actual results for the organisation are recorded on a period by period basis.

2 *Compare*

The actual results are then compared to the plans and deviations are identified.

3 *Correct*

The deviations are investigated and action is taken to either modify the budget in line with current conditions or to adjust future performance so that the discrepancies will be eliminated in the longer run.

1.2 Feedback

The reporting of actual results and of variances from plan is sometimes referred to as the *feedback* arising from the budgetary control system.

Feedback is the process of continuous self-adjustment of a system. It requires some predetermined standards against which to compare actual results. Any differences between the actual results and standard targets which are outside tolerance limits will indicate the need for action to be taken in an attempt to bring about consistency between actual and target.

Feedback is therefore a fundamental part of any system of control including financial control systems such as budgetary control.

1.3 Feedforward

Where feedback involves the reporting of actual results against planned results, feedforward involves the forecasting of differences between actual and planned outcomes, and the implementation of actions, before the event, to avoid such differences.

2 Fixed and flexible budgets

2.1 Introduction

A **fixed budget** is a budget which is normally set prior to the start of an accounting period, and which is not changed in response to subsequent changes in activity or costs/revenues.

A **flexible budget** is a budget which, by recognising different cost behaviour patterns, is designed to change as volume of activity changes.

CIMA Official Terminology

When determining whether the company has achieved its objective on profit target a fixed budget is used as this contains the target volume for the period.

When determining whether the company has operated efficiently at the actual volume achieved the flexible budget is best as this adjusts the costs in accordance with cost behaviour.

2.2 Flexible budget preparation

This involves taking the fixed budget and 'flexing' it on the basis of cost behaviour to illustrate what the budget should have been **for the actual level of activity achieved.**

Steps

1. Determine the cost behaviour patterns of each cost element. This may be achieved by using the high low method.
2. If the cost is fixed it will remain fixed regardless of the change in activity.
3. If the cost is variable it will change in direct proportion to changes in activity.
4. If the cost is semi-variable ie an element of fixed and variable cost, the fixed element will remain constant and the variable element will change in direct proportion to changes in activity.
5. Prepare the flexible budget.
6. The operating statement is then prepared. This shows the fixed budget, flexible budget, actual costs and deviations ie variances.

You should learn the above steps and apply them to examination questions in this area.

The above steps are illustrated in the example below.

2.3 Example

RJD is in an industry sector which is recovering from a recent recession. The directors of the company hope next year to be operating at 85% of capacity, although currently the company is operating at only 65% of capacity. 65% of capacity represents output of 10,000 units of the single product which is produced and sold.

The budgets for a range of possible capacities, based upon results from the current year are:

Capacity level	55% £	65% £	75% £
Direct materials	846,200	1,000,000	1,153,800
Direct wages	1,480,850	1,750,000	2,019,150
Production overhead	596,170	650,000	703,830
Selling and distribution overhead	192,310	200,000	207,690
Administration overhead	120,000	120,000	120,000
Total costs	3,235,530	3,720,000	4,204,470

Required

Prepare a flexible budget on the assumption that the company operates at 85% of capacity.

2.4 Solution

It is first necessary to identify the behavioural aspects of each item of cost – this is done using the high - low method studied in Chapter 1.

(i) Direct materials

	£	Activity %
High capacity	1,153,800	75
Low capacity	846,200	55
	307,600	20

Variable cost = $\frac{£307,600}{20}$ = £15,380 per 1%

By substitution:

	£
Total variable cost at 55% = £15,380 × 55	845,900
Therefore fixed cost	300
Total as above	846,200

Materials budget at 85% is therefore: (85 × £15,380) + £300 = **£1,307,600**

(ii) Direct wages

	£	Activity %
High	2,019,150	75
Low	1,480,850	55
	538,300	20

Variable cost = $\frac{£538,300}{20}$ = £26,915 per 1%

By substitution:

	£
Total variable cost at 55% = £26,915 × 55	1,480,325
Therefore fixed cost	525
Total as above	1,480,850

Direct wages budget at 85% is therefore: (85 × £26,915) + £525 = **£2,288,300**

(iii) Production overhead

	£	Activity %
High	703,830	75
Low	596,170	55
	107,660	20

Variable cost = $\frac{£107,660}{20}$ = £5,383 per 1%

By substitution:

	£
Total variable cost at 55% = £5,383 × 55	296,065
Therefore fixed cost	300,105
Total as above	596,170

Production overhead budget at 85% is therefore: (85 × £5,383) + £300,105 = **£757,660**

(iv) Selling and distribution overhead

	£	Activity %
High	207,690	75
Low	192,310	55
	15,380	20

Variable cost = $\dfrac{£15,380}{20}$ = £769 per 1%

By substitution:

	£
Total variable cost at 55% = £769 × 55	42,295
Therefore fixed cost	150,015
Total as above	192,310

Selling and distribution overhead budget at 85% is therefore:

(85 × £769) + £150,015 = **£215,380**

(v) Administration overhead

This cost is constant at all activity levels so it is a fixed cost of £120,000 at all capacities.

	Flexed Budget 85%
Direct materials	£1,307,600
Direct wages	£2,288,300
Production overhead	£757,660
Selling and distribution overhead	£215,380
Administration overhead	£120,000
	£4,688,940

3 Budgetary control reports

3.1 Introduction

A budgetary control report/statement compares the actual costs with the flexed budgeted costs to determine how well the company has performed. The variances are labelled as Favourable – which means the actual costs were less than the flexed budget costs or Adverse – the actual costs were greater than the flexed budget costs.

3.2 Example

Wye Ltd manufactures one product and when operating at 100% capacity can produce 5,000 units per period, but for the last few periods has been operating below capacity.

Below is the flexible budget prepared at the start of last period, for 3 levels of activity at below capacity:

	Level of activity		
	70%	80%	90%
	£	£	£
Direct Materials	7,000	8,000	9,000
Direct Labour	28,000	32,000	36,000
Production Overheads	34,000	36,000	38,000
Administration, selling and distribution overheads	15,000	15,000	15,000
Total Cost	84,000	91,000	98,000

In the event, last period turned out to be even worse than expected, with production of only 2,500 units. The following costs were incurred:

	£
Direct Materials	4,500
Direct Labour	22,000
Production Overheads	28,000
Administration, selling and distribution overheads	16,500
Total Cost	71,000

Required

(a) Prepare a flexed budget for 2,500 units

(b) Use this budget to prepare a budgetary control statement showing differences between budgeted and actual costs incurred, and whether these are favourable or adverse.

3.3 Solution

(a) Determine the cost behaviour for each cost element and use this to produce a budget for 2,500 units.

Note: Using the high low method, 70% capacity represents 3,500 units and 90% capacity represents 4,500 units.

Direct Materials:	Units	£
High activity level	4,500	9,000
Low activity level	3,500	7,000
	1,000	2,000

Variable cost = $\frac{£2,000}{1,000}$ = £2 per unit

At high activity level:

		£
Total cost	=	9,000
Variable cost = 4,500 × £2	=	9,000
Fixed cost	=	0

Flexed budget for 2,500 units = 2,500 × £2 = **£5,000**

Direct Labour:	Units	£
High activity level	4,500	36,000
Low activity level	3,500	28,000
	1,000	8,000

Variable cost = $\dfrac{£8,000}{1,000}$ = £8 per unit

At high activity level:

		£
Total cost	=	36,000
Variable cost = 4,500 × £8	=	36,000
Fixed cost	=	0

Flexed budget for 2,500 units = 2,500 × £8 = **£20,000**

Note: For each of these costs, since they are direct, you would expect them to be purely variable. You can check for this by dividing two total cost levels by the relevant activities. If the cost per unit is constant, there is no fixed element.

eg – Direct materials

At 90% : $\dfrac{£9,000}{4,500}$ = £2/unit

At 70% : $\dfrac{£7,000}{3,500}$ = £2/unit

Production Overheads:	Units	£
High activity level	4,500	38,000
Low activity level	3,500	34,000
	1,000	4,000

Variable cost = $\dfrac{£4,000}{1,000}$ = £4 per unit

At high activity level:

		£
Total cost	=	38,000
Variable cost = 4,500 × £4	=	18,000
Fixed cost	=	20,000

Flexed Budget for 2,500 units = 2,500 × £4 + £20,000 = **£30,000**

Administration, selling and distribution overheads are fixed, so that the budget for 2,500 units is **£15,000**.

(b) **Budgetary Control Report**

	Budgeted costs for 2,500 units	Actual costs for 2,500 units	Variance
	£	£	£
Direct Materials	5,000	4,500	500 (Fav)
Direct Labour	20,000	22,000	2,000 (Adv)
Production Overheads	30,000	28,000	2,000 (Fav)
Administration, selling and distribution overheads	15,000	16,500	1,500 (Adv)
Total Cost	70,000	71,000	1,000 (Adv)

Note: Fav means favourable variance and Adv means adverse variance. These are standard terms that you should learn.

Practice question 1 *(The answer is in the final chapter of this book)*

Restaurant

A conference centre has a newly appointed management accountant who has sent the following report to the supervisor of the restaurant. Prior to the receipt of this report the restaurant supervisor has been congratulating herself on a good start to the year, with a substantial increase in the use of the restaurant.

MEMORANDUM

To: Restaurant supervisor

From: Management accountant

Subject: Performance report

Date: 5 April

As part of the campaign to improve efficiency within the conference centre, quarterly budgets have been prepared for each department.

I attach a performance report for your department for the three months to the end of March, showing all discrepancies between budgeted and actual expenditure.

A indicates an adverse variance and F a favourable variance.

Operating statement

	Fixed Budget £	Actual £	Variances £	
Food and other consumables	97,500	111,540	14,040	A
Labour – hourly paid	15,000	16,500	1,500	A
– supervisor	3,750	3,700	50	F
Power	8,500	9,250	750	A
Breakages	1,000	800	200	F
Allocated overheads	21,000	24,000	3,000	A
	146,750	165,790	19,040	A
No of meals served	32,500	39,000	6,500	F

You have apparently incurred costs which exceed the budget by £19,040.

Please explain this to me at the meeting of the management committee on 15 April.

Required

Redraft the operating statement and supporting memorandum in a way which, in your opinion, would make them more effective management tools.

4 Summary

You should now be able to:

- Identify the control cycle
- Distinguish between feedback and feedforward controls

Chapter 13 Budgetary control

- Distinguish between fixed and flexible budgets
- Prepare flexible budgets for a range of activity levels
- Prepare reports which compare the flexible budget with actual results identifying variances

Multiple choice questions *(The answers are in the final chapter of this book)*

1. A flexible budget is:

    A   a budget of variable production costs only

    B   a budget which is updated with actual costs and revenues as they occur during the budget period

    C ✓   a budget which shows the costs and revenues at different levels of activity

    D   a budget which is prepared using a computer spreadsheet model

2. The actual output of 162,500 units and actual fixed costs of £87,000 were exactly as budgeted. However, the actual total expenditure of £300,000 was £18,000 over budget.

    What was the budgeted variable cost per unit?

    A ✓   £1.20

    B   £1.85

    C   £1.31

    D   It cannot be calculated without more information.

3. The following data has been extracted from the budget working papers of BL Ltd:

Production volume	1,000	2,000
	£/unit	£/unit
Direct materials	4.00	4.00
Direct labour	3.50	3.50
Production overhead - department 1	6.00	4.20
Production overhead - department 2	4.00	2.00

    The total fixed cost and variable cost per unit are:

	Total fixed cost £	Variable cost per unit £
A	3,600	7.50
B	3,600	9.90
C	7,600	7.50
D ✓	7,600	9.90

CHAPTER 14

Standards and standard setting

EXAM FOCUS

This chapter and the next cover one of the most examinable areas of the syllabus, standard costing (including variance analysis). You can expect this topic on every examination paper and it is therefore vital that you gain a thorough understanding of it. Both computational and written questions can be expected in this area. Computational questions focusing on the calculation of the different cost variances and their presentation in the operating statement. Written questions will tend to focus on the explanation of the different types of standards, how standard costing and variance analysis differs to budgets and budgetary control along with possible explanations why any variances calculated have occurred.

LEARNING OUTCOMES

This chapter covers the following Learning Outcomes of the CIMA Syllabus.

> Explain the principles of standard costing
>
> Prepare the standard cost for a product/service

In order to cover these Learning Outcomes the following topics are included.

> Explain standard costing
>
> Identify the types of industries in which standard costing is relevant and why
>
> Distinguish between standard cost/revenues and budgeted cost/revenues
>
> Identify the different types of standards – basic, ideal and attainable
>
> Establish how a standard cost/revenue is established

1 Standard costing

1.1 Introduction

A standard cost is a planned unit cost of products, components or services produced in a period.

The main uses of standard costs are in performance measurement, control, stock valuation and in the establishment of selling prices.

CIMA Official Terminology

Whenever identical operations are performed or identical products are manufactured time and time again, it should be possible to decide in advance not merely what they are likely to cost but, more positively, what they ought to cost. In other words, it is possible to set a standard cost for each operation or product unit.

A standard cost will comprise two elements:

a) **Technical standards** for the quantities of material to be used and the working time required; and

b) **Cost standards** for the material prices and hourly rates that should be paid.

1.2 Standard cost -v- budgeted cost

Standard costs and budgeted costs both involve setting performance and cost levels for control purposes. However their application is somewhat different:

- **Standards are a unit concept** ie the cost is applied to individual products or operations.
- **Budgets are concerned with totals** ie they are costs which are determined for functions, departments and organisations as a whole.

However the standard cost of a unit can be used to develop budgeted costs for production of a number of units.

Standard costing is an acceptable method of cost bookkeeping (see Chapter 9) whereas budgets do not enter the double-entry system, they are merely memorandum figures.

This is a very topical examination area.

2 Types of standard

2.1 Setting standards

The way in which control is exercised and the interpretation and use of variances from standards will depend on the manner in which those standards are set.

2.2 Ideal standards

In some cases standards are established on the assumption that machines and employees will work with **optimal efficiency** at all times, and that there will be no stoppages and no losses of material or services.

Such standards would represent an ideal state of affairs and therefore the objectives they set are never achieved.

Managers who are responsible for the costs can hardly approve of targets which they can never reach and which, therefore, result in large adverse variances from the standards.

2.3 Attainable (expected) standards

In other cases the standards set will be those which are **reasonably attainable**, consideration being given to the state of efficiency which can be achieved from the existing facilities. There is no question of assuming, as for ideal standard costs, that production resources will be used at maximum efficiency.

A positive effort is still made to achieve a high level of efficiency, but there is no question of going beyond what is attainable.

2.4 Basic standards

A basic standard is one which, having been fixed, is not generally revised with changing conditions, but **remains in force for a long period of time**. It may be set originally having regard to either ideal or expected conditions. Under circumstances of rapid technological change or of significant price changes, basic standards are of limited value in relation to the achievement of the benefits outlined above.

2.5 Which to use?

There may be variations on these methods, but the aim should be to select the standard cost which is likely to be the most realistic for the business concerned. It should be remembered that standards are the yardstick against which efficiency is measured and therefore, if they are unrealistic then the variances will be of little meaning.

In general, attainable standards will be for the purpose of meaningful cost control.

You should be familiar with these three types of standards along with their advantages and disadvantages. They may form a written part of a larger question on standard costing and variance analysis.

3 Methods of developing standards

3.1 Standards from past records

Past data can be used to predict future costs if operating conditions are fairly constant between past and future time periods. The main disadvantage with this method is that past data may contain inefficiencies which would then be built into the standards, thus not encouraging improvements.

3.2 Engineering standards

This involves engineers developing standards for materials, direct labour and variable overheads by studying the product and the production process, possibly with the help of time and motion studies. This method is particularly useful when managers are evaluating new products as the historical records are only of value where they can be related to operations needed to make the new product.

The main disadvantage is that engineering standards may be too tight as they may not allow for the behaviour of the workers.

3.3 Setting technical standards

Standard material usage

In setting material usage standards, the first stage is to define what quantity of material input is theoretically required to achieve one unit of measured output.

In most manufacturing operations the quantity or volume of product emerging will be less than the quantity of materials introduced. In machining operations, for example, this waste will be due to cutting losses. This type of waste is normal to the type of operation and the usage figure would be increased by an allowance for this normal waste.

Standard time allowed

The standard or allowed time for an operation is a realistic estimate of the amount of productive time required to perform that operation based on work study methods. It is normally expressed in standard hours.

Various allowances may be added to the theoretical operating time, to take account of operator fatigue and personal needs and periodical activities such as machine setting, clearing up, regrinding tools and on-line quality inspection. An allowance may also be made for spoilt work as indicated under material usage above, or for rectification of defects appearing in the course of processing.

3.4 Setting cost standards

Basic approach

When setting cost standards at a point in time, there are two basic approaches:

(a) To use the prices or rates which are current at the time the standards are set.

This has the advantage that each standard is clearly identifiable with a known fact. On the other hand, if prices are likely to change then the standards based on them will have a limited value for planning purposes.

The standards would have to be revised in detail from time to time to ensure that they are up to date. If this is not done, then any differences between standard and actual costs are likely to be largely due to invalid standards.

(b) To use a forecast of average prices or rates over the period for which the standard is to be used.

This can postpone the need for revision, but has the disadvantages that the standard may never correspond with observed fact (so there will be a price variance on all transactions) and that the forecast may be subject to significant error.

Neither method, therefore, will be ideal for all purposes and in deciding between them it will be necessary to consider whether the cost standards are being set principally to put a consistent value on technical variances, or as a help in budgeting, or as a means of exercising cost control, or merely to simplify bookkeeping.

Material price standards

In setting material price standards, it will often be found that a particular item of material is purchased from several suppliers at slightly different prices and the question arises which price shall be adopted as standard. There are three possible approaches:

(a) To identify the major supplier and to use his price as the standard.

This is particularly appropriate where there is no intention of buying large quantities from the alternative suppliers, but merely to use them as a means of ensuring continuity of supply should there be any delay or failure by the principal supplier.

(b) To use the lower quoted price as the standard.

This method can be used if it is wished to put pressure on the buyer to obtain price reductions from other suppliers.

(c) To forecast the proportion of supplies to be bought from each supplier and to calculate a weighted average price as the costing standard.

This is the most satisfactory method for control purposes if the required forecast can be made with reasonable accuracy.

Another question in relation to material price standards is whether to include the cost of carriage inwards and other costs such as non-returnable packing and transit insurance. The object always will be to price incoming goods at their total delivered cost, so the costs such as those instanced above should be included in the standards.

Standard labour rates

A decision to be made when setting standard labour rates, is whether to use basic pay rates only, or to incorporate overtime premiums. The answer will depend on the nature of the overtime work and the approach to cost control adopted by management.

(a) If a normal level of overtime work can be identified and is accepted as necessary, or if overtime is planned for the company's convenience, then the relative overtime premium payments will normally be included in the standard labour rate.

(b) If it is a management objective to reduce or eliminate overtime working, the standard rate may be restricted to basic pay.

(c) Where overtime is worked at the request of particular customers, then the related premium payments are a direct cost of the work done and would not be included in a standard rate which was applied generally to other work.

(d) Where part of employee remuneration takes the form of incentive bonuses, then it will be necessary to forecast the level of efficiency to be achieved and the bonus payments appropriate to that performance. These bonuses will then be included in the calculation of the standard rate.

4 Standard cost card

A standard cost card is built up using the technical specification for one unit.

A simple standard cost card is as follows:

Standard Cost Card

	£
Direct material: 1.5 sq m @ £28 per sq m	42.00
Direct labour: 4 hours @ £5.25 per hour	21.00
Variable overheads: 4 hours @ £0.75 per hour	3.00
Fixed overheads: 4 hours @ £7 per hour	28.00
Total standard cost	94.00

You can see that:

Standard direct material cost = Standard quantity of material × standard material price

Standard direct labour cost = Standard direct labour hours × standard labour rate

Standard overhead cost = Standard direct labour hours × standard overhead absorption rate

This, of course, assumes a direct labour hour overhead absorption rate. Other OARs may be used and applied where relevant.

If a marginal costing system is used, the standard cost will exclude fixed overheads.

Practice question 1 *(The answer is in the final chapter of this book)*

1   **K Ltd**

    (a)   K Ltd makes 2 products. From the information given below about one of its products you are required to prepare a standard cost card for one unit and enter on the standard cost card the costs to show subtotals for:

        (i)   prime cost

        (ii)   variable production cost

        (iii)   total production cost

        (iv)   total cost.

The following data are given:

Budgeted output for the year: 900 units

Standard details for one unit:

Direct materials: 50 square metres at £3.20 per square metre

Direct wages: Department A: 24 hours at £5.10 per hour

        Department B   18 hours at £4.80 per hour

Budgeted costs and hours per annum:

	£	*Direct labour hours*
Variable overhead:		
Department A	45,000	30,000
Department B	25,000	25,000
Fixed Overhead Apportioned to this product:		
Production	36,000	
Selling, distribution and administration	27,000	

Note: Variable overheads are recovered (absorbed) using hours, fixed overheads are recovered on a unit basis.

    (b)   Calculate the selling price per unit allowing for a profit of 20% of the selling price

5 Summary

You should now be able to:

- Explain standard costing
- Distinguish between standard cost and budgeted cost
- Identify the different types of standards
  - Basic standard
  - Ideal standard
  - Attainable standard
- Establish how standard cost is established
- Prepare standard cost card for a product

CHAPTER 15

Variance analysis

EXAM FOCUS

Variance analysis is perhaps one of the most examinable areas of the syllabus. You can expect this topic on every examination paper and it is therefore vital that you gain a thorough understanding of it. Both computational and written questions can be expected in this area as discussed at the start of the previous chapter. We will start by looking at principles and computations of the different types of variances. These may then be used to reconcile actual and budget profit figures. At the end of this chapter we revisit the area of cost bookkeeping under an integrated system except this time with the complication of standard costing and variance analysis. Questions in this area normally form part of a larger question on variances and therefore you need to have a general knowledge of the treatment of the variances in the accounts but you would not be required to do a full question on standard integrated cost bookkeeping.

LEARNING OUTCOMES

This chapter covers the following Learning Outcomes of the CIMA Syllabus.

Calculate and interpret variances for sales, materials; labour; variable overheads and fixed overheads

Prepare a report reconciling budget gross profit/contribution with actual profit

Prepare accounting entries for an integrated accounting system using standard costs

In order to cover these Learning Outcomes the following topics are included.

Explain variance analysis and responsibility accounting

Explain and calculate the variances in relation to

- Material variances
- Labour variances
- Variable overhead variances
- Fixed overhead variances
- Sales variances

Identify and discuss possible reasons for variances occurring

Prepare an operating statement which reconciles budgeted profit and actual profit under an absorption and marginal costing system

Prepare accounting entries using an integrated accounting system within a standard costing system

1 Introduction

1.1 Definitions

A **variance** is the difference between a planned, budgeted or standard cost and the actual cost incurred. The same comparison can be made for revenues.

Variance analysis involves the evaluation of performance by means of variances, whose timely reporting should maximise the opportunity for managerial action.

CIMA Official Terminology

Variances may be **adverse** (A) or **favourable** (F), adverse representing a situation where actual cost is greater than standard cost and favourable representing a situation where actual cost is less than standard cost.

1.2 Responsibility accounting

Variances should be quantified and identified with the manager responsible so that corrective action can be taken, this is known as responsibility accounting. Whilst this is ideal it is sometimes difficult to achieve as it is quite usual for there to be interrelationships between different variances. This is discussed in detail later in this chapter.

1.3 The basic principles

Before we embark on the computations of individual cost variances, it is important that you first understand the following underlying principles.

1. The **total cost variance** for any particular type of cost is derived by a comparison of:

   ♦ actual cost incurred

   against

   ♦ standard cost **for actual level of production** (ie a *flexed* budget figure).

   The use of a flexed budget figure, instead of the original budget, ensures that the variances will relate directly to the efficiency or otherwise of buying/production activities rather than being distorted by 'volume' variances arising from operating at a different activity level than expected.

   Look back at the budgetary control report in Chapter 13 (3.3) – the variances were computed on exactly this principle, by budgeted costs for the actual activity level of 2,500 units.

2. In general, each **total cost variance** can be sub-analysed between:

   ♦ differences in total cost due to a *different price/rate per unit of resource* (**a price/rate variance**)

   and

   ♦ differences in total cost due to *different amounts of resource used per unit of output* (**a usage/efficiency variance**).

   The impact of the price/rate variance on total cost is generally evaluated over the **actual** amount of resource used/purchased.

   The impact of the wage/efficiency variance is evaluated at the **standard** cost per unit of resource.

2 Materials cost variances

2.1 Standard material cost

The standard cost of a unit will be prepared by estimating the **quantity** of material expected to be used and the **price** that each individual item of material is likely to cost.

As an example, one unit of Product X may be expected to require 3kg of aluminium at an expected price of £6 per kg. The standard cost of Product X will then contain an amount of £18 in respect of this raw material.

If we introduce actual results for a period we can start to calculate variances.

2.2 Total material cost variance

For example, suppose that in January A plc budgeted to provide 1,000 units of Product X. It actually produced 1,200 units, using 3,500kg of aluminium at an average cost per kg of £6.05. The following comparison *could* then be made.

	£	
Actual materials cost of 1,200 units of X (3,500kg @ £6.05)	21,175	
Budgeted materials cost of 1,000 units of X (1,000 @ £18)	18,000	
Difference (variance) – overspend (adverse)	3,175	A

However, this comparison is not very useful. This is because £21,175 is the *actual cost* of producing 1,200 units whereas £18,000 is the *standard or budgeted cost* of 1,000 units. Thus the apparent overspend is misleading: we have produced more than we budgeted, so naturally costs are higher than planned.

This illustrates the first principle of reporting variable cost variances discussed earlier: the budget should always be *flexed*, that is adjusted onto a production volume that takes into account the *actual* volume of production.

Failure to do this is a very common mistake in examinations!

The following comparison would be more useful to management.

	£	
Actual materials cost of 1,200 units	21,175	
Standard materials cost of 1,200 units (flexed budget: 1,200 @ £18)	21,600	
Variance (underspend - favourable)	425	F

2.3 Sub-analysing the total cost variance

Now we know how to calculate a materials total variance (or materials cost variance as it is sometimes known) we can try to increase the information it provides by subdividing it into its component parts.

In our example we are expecting to use 3kg of aluminium per unit of X and each kg is expected to cost £6. If either the actual usage differs from the standard usage or the actual price differs from the standard price, or both, this will contribute to the total variance.

We can therefore split the total variances into a **price variance** and a **usage** variance.

2.4 Material price variance

Working from first principles we can calculate the price variance as follows.

	£	
Actual price paid per kg	6.05	
Standard price per kg	6.00	
Variance per kg (overspend – adverse)	0.05	A
Actual kg used	3,500	
Price variance (3,500 × £0.05)	£175	A

As an overspend is indicated an adverse sign is used.

2.5 Material usage variance

Working from first principles we can also calculate the usage variance.

	kg	
Actual usage	3,500	
Standard usage **for actual production** – 1,200 units at 3kg	3,600	
Saving in material usage (favourable variance)	100	F
Standard price per kg	£6	
Usage variance (100kg @ £6)	£600	F

A usage variance is costed at standard price to avoid double counting the price effects.

We can now see how the variances come together to form the total variance.

	£	
Price variance	175	A
Usage variance	600	F
Total variance	425	F

2.6 Example layout – 'line-by-line'

✓ Whilst variances can be calculated using any working the student wishes the following grid system is probably quickest in exams, and helps you to understand exactly what is being computed:

	£	
Actual expenditure (actual usage at actual price)		
3,500kg × £6.05	21,175	
Price variance 175 A		Total
Actual usage at **standard** price		variance
3,500kg × £6	21,000	£425 F
Usage variance 600 F		
Flexed budget expenditure	21,600	

(**Standard** usage for actual production at standard price)
   3 × 1,200 × £6
(or number of units × standard cost/unit)
   12,000 units × £18

This system can be used for all variable cost variances. **The principle of variances is to compare what has happened with what should have happened.** Therefore the rules are as follows.

- Put actual expenditure on the top (everything at actual)
- Put flexed budget expenditure on the bottom (everything at standard)
- Design extra lines to subdivide the total variance in as meaningful a manner as possible, by changing one element at a time from actual to standard. Conventionally, we extract the **price** variance **first** by changing actual price to standard price.

To get the signs of the above variances correct without too much effort we can use the following approach.

- The bottom line represents the true value of our production (in standard costing systems stock is valued at standard cost, as explained later).
- We start at the top and work down considering if we have underspent or overspent as we go.

'We have spent £21,175 to obtain something worth £21,000 by that stage = Overspend = Adverse'.

Then

'We have spent £21,000 to obtain something worth ultimately £21,600 = Underspend = Favourable'.

If you can remember the grid and the quick method of selecting the signs it will greatly speed up the calculation of materials variances.

Practice question 1 *(The answer is in the final chapter of this book)*

Materials costs

The standard cost card for Product A includes the following details in respect of raw materials.

Standard cost of Chemical X = 4 litres @ £15 per litre = £60

Budgeted output of Product A for the month of June is 800 units.

Actual output of Product A in June is 700 units.

Actual litres used in June = 2,860 litres at a total cost of £41,756.

Required

Calculate all materials cost variances for the month of June in respect of Chemical X.

2.7 The causes of materials cost variances

Once materials variances have been calculated management would need to establish their exact cause prior to taking corrective action. Below are some possible causes.

Price variances	Usage variances
Inaccurately set budgets or standards	Inaccurately set budgets or standards
Purchase of different quality materials	Exceptionally efficient or inefficient working by production workers
Very competitive or uncompetitive actions by the buying department	Different usage from standard due to condition of production machines
Materials price movements in the market	

Once the exact cause of a variance is understood responsibility can be allocated and the appropriate control action taken.

There may be interdependencies between the variances. For example, if the buying department buy cheaper substandard materials resulting in favourable price variances this could result in a higher incidence of rejects than standard and therefore adverse usage variances.

3 Labour cost variances

3.1 Standard labour cost

The standard labour cost of producing a product is prepared by estimating the labour time required to make it and estimating the labour rate of pay prevailing over the forthcoming period.

As an example, one unit of Product X may be expected to require five labour hours at an expected rate of £8 per hour. The standard cost of Product X will then contain an amount of £40 per unit in respect of labour.

If we introduce actual results for a period we can start to calculate variances. These follow the same principles as those for materials.

3.2 Total labour cost variance

For example, suppose that in January A plc budgeted to produce 1,000 units of Product X. It actually produced 1,200 units, using 6,150 labour hours at an average pay rate of £7.80 per hour.

Firstly we will calculate direct labour total variance or cost variance as follows.

	£
Actual labour cost of 1,200 units of X (6,150 hours @ £7.80)	47,970
Budgeted labour cost of 1,200 units of X (flexed budget: 1,200 @ £40)	48,000
Variance (favourable – underspend)	30 F

3.3 Sub-analysis

As with materials the total variance can be sub-divided to produce more useful control information.

If we look at the standard labour cost we see that the total variance could be due to the labour hours taken being different from standard, the labour rate being different from standard, or both.

Thus we can split the total variance into a **rate variance** (similar to the price variance on direct materials) and an **efficiency variance** (similar to the usage variance on direct materials).

3.4 Labour rate variance

Working from first principles we can calculate the rate variance as follows.

	£	
Actual labour rate per hour	7.80	
Standard labour rate per hour	8.00	
Variance per hour (underspend – favourable)	0.20	F
Actual hours worked	6,150	
Rate variance (6,150 hours @ £0.20)	£1,230	F

3.5 Labour efficiency variance

Working from first principles we can also calculate the efficiency variance.

	£	
Actual hours worked	6,150	
Standard hours for actual production – 1,200 × 5	6,000	
Extra hours worked	150	
Standard wage rate per hour	£8	
Efficiency variance	£1,200	A

Again, the efficiency variance is costed at standard rate to avoid double counting the rate effects.

We can now see how the variances come together to form the total variance.

	£	
Rate variance	1,230	F
Efficiency variance	1,200	A
Total variance	30	F

3.6 Alternative layout

As for materials variances labour variances can be calculated most quickly using a line-by-line grid system.

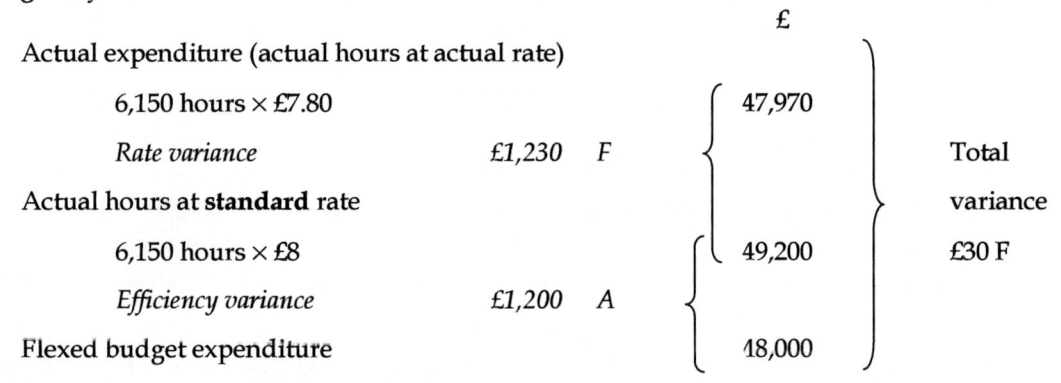

			£		
Actual expenditure (actual hours at actual rate)					
6,150 hours × £7.80			47,970		
Rate variance	£1,230	F			Total
Actual hours at **standard** rate					variance
6,150 hours × £8			49,200		£30 F
Efficiency variance	£1,200	A			
Flexed budget expenditure			48,000		

(Standard hours for actual production at standard rate)
    5 × 1,200 × £8
(or number of units × standard cost/unit)
    1,200 units × £40

The same logic is used to achieve the signs (F or A) of the variances as for materials.

Practice question 2 *(The answer is in the final chapter of this book)*

Labour costs

The standard cost card for Product B includes the following details in respect of labour costs.

Standard labour cost: 6 hours @ £5 per hour	=	£30
Budgeted production for February	=	5,000 units of B
Actual production for February	=	6,200 units of B
Actual labour hours worked	=	40,000 at a total cost of £210,000

Required

Calculate the labour cost variances for the month of February.

3.7 The causes of labour cost variances

Again, further investigation of the subvariances must be carried out before responsibility can be allocated and the appropriate control action can be exercised. Below are some possible causes.

Rate variances	*Efficiency variances*
Inaccurate standards	Inaccurate standards
Different grade of labour used from standard by workforce	Exceptionally efficient or inefficient working
Overtime premiums may have been paid	Machine breakdowns leading to lost hours
Mistakes by the wages department	Different hours from standard owing to condition of machines
Re-negotiation of wage rate	

Again, there may be interdependencies between the variances. If we decide to use a cheaper grade of labour than standard (which should result in a favourable rate variance) then we would expect an adverse efficiency variance as inexperienced workers should take longer. This may in turn lead to adverse material usage as workers' inefficiency leads to more materials being wasted than budgeted for.

4 Variable production overhead cost variances

4.1 Standard variable production overhead cost

The standard cost of variable production overheads may simply be estimated directly, on a unit basis. Alternatively, hourly absorption rates may be used: the standard cost of variable production overheads is then the hourly absorption rate absorbed according to the standard number of hours for producing a unit.

As an example, the variable production overhead cost of one unit of Product X in the earlier example may be absorbed at the rate of £2 per labour hour. Since each unit of Product X requires a standard labour input of 5 hours, this means a standard variable overhead production cost of £10 per unit of Product X.

The standard or budgeted variable production overhead cost of Product X is £10 per unit.

If we introduce actual results for a period we can start to calculate variances.

4.2 Example

Suppose that in January A plc budgeted to produce 1,000 units of Product X. It actually produced 1,200 units taking 6,150 labour hours. A plc paid £11,600 for variable production overhead.

You are required to calculate the cost variances in respect of variable production overheads.

4.3 Solution

Firstly we will calculate the variable production overhead total variance. If absorption rates are not used this is all that is required.

	£
Actual variable production overhead cost of 1,200 units of X	11,600
Budgeted variable production overhead cost of 1,200 units of X (Flexed budget: 1,200 @ £10)	12,000
Variance – underspend	400 F

4.4 Expenditure and efficiency variances

If absorption rates are used the total variance can be subdivided. Many overheads, such as the electricity cost of powering machines, are very closely related to the labour hours worked on the machines. Thus an **efficiency** variance is calculated to show how the efficiency of the workforce is affecting the cost of overhead. Any remaining variance shows how the spending on overhead has differed from standard and is called an **expenditure** variance.

Variable overhead variances are best calculated using a line-by-line grid, which is very similar to that used for labour.

		£	
Actual hours at actual rate		11,600	
Expenditure variance	£700 F		Total
Actual hours worked at standard absorption rate (6,150 hours × £2 per hour)		12,300	variance
Efficiency variance	£300 A		£400 F
Flexed budget expenditure		12,000	

(Standard hours for actual production at standard rate per hour)
    1,200 × 5 × £2
(or number of units produced × standard cost/unit)
    1,200 units × £10

4.5 Interpretation

The variable overhead efficiency variance is related to the labour efficiency variance and always has the same sign (A or F).

| Labour efficiency variance | £1,200 | A |
| Variable overhead efficiency variances | £300 | A |

The difference in monetary amount arises because the labour variance is costed at the labour rate of £8 per hour, while the variable overhead variance is costed at the absorption rate of £2 per hour. Thus the labour efficiency variance is four times larger.

The expenditure variance shows that after adjusting for the number of labour hours worked the company still made cost savings of £700 on overheads.

Practice question 3 *(The answer is in the final chapter of this book)*

Variable overheads

The standard cost card for Product C includes the following details in respect of variable production overheads.

Four labour hours absorbing variable overhead at £3 per hour = 4 × £3 = £12

The budgeted production for March was 11,000 units.

In March 9,400 units were made in 39,000 hours at a cost of £107,500.

Required

Calculate the variable production overhead cost variances for the month of March.

5 Worked example of all variable cost variances

5.1 Introduction

We have now studied the variable production cost variances. As previously mentioned, the main mistake students make is to compare actual expenditure with the *original budgeted expenditure*. Remember that variable costs must always be flexed for a meaningful comparison. Work through the following example as much as you can before looking at the answer.

5.2 Example

The standard variable production cost for one unit of Product Y is as follows.

	£
Materials 10kg @ £3 per kg	30
Labour 6 hours @ £6 per hour	36
Variable overhead 6 hours @ £2 per hour	12
Standard variable cost	78

Budgeted production in period 1 is 12,500 units

Actual results in period 1 were as follows.

Production volume	15,100 units
Materials used	145,000 kg
Price per kg	£2.95
Labour hours worked	93,000 hours
Labour rate per hour	£6.10
Variable overhead cost	£190,000

You are required to calculate variances in respect of all the above variable costs.

5.3 Solution

Materials variances

		£
Actual expenditure (145,000kg × £2.95)		427,750
Price variance	£7,250 F	
Actual usage × standard price (145,000 × £3)		435,000
Usage variance	£18,000 F	
Flexed budget expenditure (15,100 × 10kg × £3)		453,000

Labour variances

		£
Actual expenditure (93,000 × £6.10)		567,300
Rate variance	£9,300 A	
Actual hours × standard rate (93,000 × £6)		558,000
Efficiency variance	£14,400 A	
Flexed budget expenditure 15,100 × 6 hours × £6		543,600

Variable overhead variances

		£
Actual expenditure (given)		190,000
Expenditure variance	£4,000 A	
Actual hours worked × standard absorption rate per hour (93,000 × £2)		186,000
Efficiency variance	£4,800 A	
Flexed budget expenditure 15,100 × 6 hours × £2		181,200

5.4 Operating cost statement

Now we can present the variances in a statement for management, reconciling the **standard** cost of units produced to the **actual** cost. Note the layout.

		F £	A £	£
Standard variable cost of goods produced (15,100 × £78)				1,177,800
Variable cost variances				
Materials:	Price	7,250		
	Usage	18,000		
Labour:	Rate		9,300	
	Efficiency		14,400	
Variable overhead:	Expenditure		4,000	
	Efficiency		4,800	
		25,250	32,500	7,250 A
Actual variable costs				1,185,050

This final figure can be checked as follows.

Actual cost of materials	427,750
Actual cost of labour	567,300
Actual cost of variable overhead	190,000
	1,185,050

Practice question 4 *(The answer is in the final chapter of this book)*

Product D

Standard variable production costs for Product D are as follows:

	£
Materials 12 litres @ 50p/litre	6
Labour 2 hours @ £7 per hour	14
Variable overhead	3
Standard variable production cost	23

Budgeted production in Period 11 is 26,000 units

Actual results in Period 11:

Actual production		23,200	units
Materials	£136,000	295,000	litres used
Labour	£340,000	46,000	hours
Variable overhead	£75,000		

Required

Prepare an appropriate statement for management analysing the results for the period.

6 Fixed overhead variances

6.1 The nature of fixed overheads

As the name suggests, variable production costs are higher or lower (in total) depending on the level of production. By contrast, fixed production overheads (such as factory rental) are assumed not to be affected by the level of production within the relevant range. Instead, they are said to be *time-based*: the rent for six months is higher than the rent for three months, but it is irrelevant how much production is carried out in the period.

You would expect, therefore, that the computation of the fixed overhead cost variance would not involve a 'flexed budget'. Whilst this is true where a marginal costing approach is taken, it is not true for an absorption costing system, as explained below.

6.2 Fixed overhead variances – marginal costing

We shall start with the easiest situation, where fixed overheads are treated as a period cost and not absorbed into cost units.

In this case, the only fixed overhead variance is an **expenditure variance** – the difference between the actual cost and the original budgeted cost (it is not appropriate to flex here – the 'standard cost for actual production' is simply the original budget cost).

6.3 Fixed overhead variances – absorption costing

Under absorption costing, fixed overheads are effectively treated as if they were variable – units are charged with (ie absorb) a pre-determined fixed cost, and the more units that are produced, the more fixed cost is absorbed.

We have already seen the problem this can give rise to – even if the actual period fixed overheads are as budgeted (ie there is no expenditure variance), if actual production is not as budgeted, fixed overheads will be **under/over absorbed into production**. We saw that this would need to be adjusted in the profit and loss account to ensure the right amount of fixed costs are charged.

This volume adjustment is now treated as a variance – the **fixed overhead volume variance** – although it is not actually an extra cost/cost saving like the other variances, it is simply the result of flexing a cost that should be treated as fixed.

This is then combined with any expenditure variance to get the total fixed overhead cost variance, as follows:

	£	£
Actual expenditure		X
Expenditure variance	X	
Budgeted expenditure (**what we *expected* to absorb**)		X
Volume variance	X	*(what we over/under absorbed)*
Flexed budget expenditure:		
Standard cost of actual expenditure (**what we *did* absorb**)		X
Total cost variance	X	

So you see that we end up with the same basic computation of the total cost variance as all the variable costs – comparing actual and flexed budget cost – although you should appreciate that this is in fact a combination of the 'true' fixed overhead variance – the expenditure – and a necessary adjustment to eliminate over/under absorption due to a change in activity level.

6.4 Example

Suppose that the standard fixed production overhead cost for Product X is calculated as five labour hours at an absorption rate of £2 per labour hour: £5 × 2 = £10.

The standard fixed production overhead cost per unit of X is £10.

Data for January is as follows.

Original budgeted production (in units of X)	=	1,000 units
Actual production	=	1,200 units
Actual labour hours worked	=	6,150 hours
Actual fixed overhead spent	=	£10,400

You are required to calculate cost variances in respect of fixed production overheads.

6.5 Solution

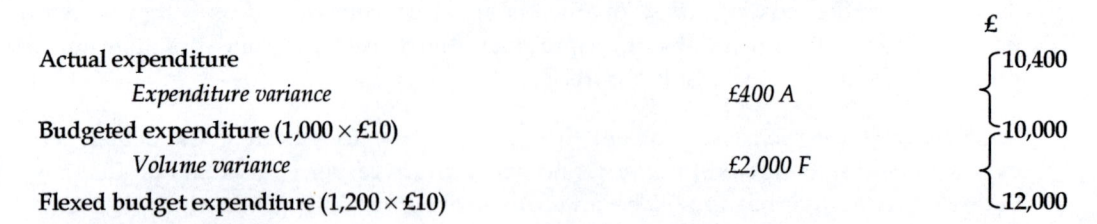

		£
Actual expenditure		10,400
Expenditure variance	£400 A	
Budgeted expenditure (1,000 × £10)		10,000
Volume variance	£2,000 F	
Flexed budget expenditure (1,200 × £10)		12,000

6.6 Interpretation

The **expenditure variance** shows that the company has spent £400 more than the original variance expected.

The **volume variance** shows that as 200 more units were made than the budget expected, the company has absorbed 200 × £10 = £2,000 more fixed overhead than expected. Thus, this needs to be **added back** to profit (or deducted from cost) via the **favourable** variance.

6.7 Standard marginal costing

As mentioned earlier, under a standard marginal costing system only the fixed production expenditure variance is calculated as with this system fixed production costs are not absorbed into units of production. Therefore the volume variance is not appropriate in a standard marginal costing system and the only variance will be the fixed overhead expenditure variance of £400 A as seen above.

Practice question 5 *(The answer is in the final chapter of this book)*

Fixed

Standard fixed production overhead cost of Product E = £45 per unit.

The budgeted production for period 3 was 800 units but only 500 were produced. The fixed overhead cost for the period was £38,000.

Required

Calculate the fixed production overhead cost variances for the period.

---

7 Sales variance

7.1 Introduction

In the previous sections we have considered how standard costing and variance analysis is used to control costs. To achieve planned profits it is also necessary to control the profit on sales. This is why we calculate the total sales margin variance.

Note that the term 'margin' can mean different things depending upon whether a marginal or absorption costing system is in place.

- Under marginal costing, margin is *contribution*
- Under absorption costing, margin is *profit*

7.2 The total sales profit margin variance

The total sales margin volume variance is used to complete the reconciliation between budgeted margin (profit or contribution) and actual margin. It will reflect two things:

- the effect on margin of having a **different unit selling price** from that budgeted
- the effect on margin of **selling a different volume** from that budgeted.

It is important to note that throughout the computation we **keep costs at standard** (variable or total, depending upon the margin being used).

The computation is thus as follows:

Budgeted total margin (contribution/profit) = *budgeted sales volume at standard margin (standard price – standard cost)*	X
Actual sales volume at 'actual' margin *(actual price – standard cost)*	(X)
Total sales margin volume variance	X

7.3 Example

A company has a budgeted profit of £200,000 for 10,000 units. The actual sales volume was 9,000 units at a selling price of £40. The standard production cost was £22/unit. Calculate the total sales margin variance.

Budgeted profit from sales (10,000 × £20)				£200,000
Actual profit from sales when cost of sales is valued at standard cost:				
Actual sales	9,000 × £40	=	£360,000	
Standard cost of sales	9,000 × £22	=	(£198,000)	
	9,000 × £18			£162,000
Sales margin variance				£38,000 A

Sales margin variance may be subdivided into price and volume, but that is beyond the scope of this syllabus.

8 Operating statements

Now the basic variances have all been learned we can start to consider their presentation to management.

In order to communicate the feedback efficiently to management we normally present the variances in the form of an **operating statement**.

The following proforma represents a fairly traditional operating statement (under absorption costing) and you should learn its format.

To:	The management	
From:	The management accountant	
Date:	–	
Subject:	Variance operating statement for the period – to –	

	£
Budgeted profit	X
Total sales margin variance	X
Actual revenue less standard costs for actual activity level	X

219

Cost variances:

	F	A	
Materials price	X		
Materials usage	X		
Labour rate		X	
Labour efficiency	X		
Variable overhead expenditure		X	
Variable overhead efficiency	X		
Fixed overhead expenditure	X		
Fixed overhead volume		X	
	X	X	X

Actual profit X

Note how the statement reconciles budget profit to actual profit using variances alone.

✓ You must learn the above proforma as it is the method used for presenting variance information.

Considerable variations in the presentation of operating statements apply in practice but the above proforma is satisfactory.

Practice questions 6 and 7 *(The answers are in the final chapter of this book)*

6 Columbus Ltd

Columbus Ltd prepared the following budget.

Output/sales		40,000 units
Selling price per unit		£1.50
Costs		£
Materials	10,000kgs	8,000
Labour	500 hours	10,000
Variable overhead		5,000
Fixed overhead		30,000

Actual results were as follows:

		£	£
Sales	42,000 units @ £1.52		63,840
Materials	11,000kgs @ 70p	7,700	
Labour	530 hours	10,950	
Variable overhead		5,350	
Fixed overhead		36,000	
			(60,000)
Profit			3,840

Required

You are required to prepare an operating statement.

7 Flashbulb

Flashbulb Ltd commenced business on 1 January 20X0, in order to manufacture torches. It is going to operate a standard costing system.

A profit of £125,000 based on producing and selling 500,000 torches @ £2.50 was budgeted for the year to 31 December 20X0 as follows.

	£
Materials – 1 case @ £0.50	0.50
Labour – ¼ hour @ £5.00 per hour	1.25
Variable overhead – ¼ hour @ £1.00 per hour	0.25
Fixed overhead – ¼ hour @ £1.00 per hour	0.25
	2.25

Actual production and sales of torches in the year to 31 December 20X0 were 452,000 torches at £3.00 and the following costs were incurred.

	£
Materials – 480,000 cases	180,000
Labour – paid for 100,000 hours @ £5.50 (Hours worked – 95,000)	550,000
Variable overhead	120,000
Fixed overhead	120,000

Required

Analyse the variances and present your answer in the form of an operating statement prepared for the directors.

---

9 Standard cost bookkeeping

9.1 Introduction

The incorporation of standard costs into the cost accounting system greatly simplifies the task of tracing costs for stock valuation and saves a considerable amount of time.

Standard cost bookkeeping can be used in either an interlocking or integrated cost accounting system. Remember integrated is where a single set of accounts is held for both cost and financial accounting purposes whereas interlocking involves a separate set of accounts for cost and financial accounting purposes.

The syllabus requires you to be familiar with standard integrated accounting systems. Standard interlocking accounting systems are beyond the scope of the syllabus.

9.2 Standard integrated cost accounting procedure

Actual cost information is recorded as normal in the accounts.

If 10,000kg of materials are purchased on credit for £10,000 the double entry will be as follows:

DR Raw materials	£10,000	
CR Creditors		£10,000

The transfer of materials, labour or production overheads to the work in progress account is recorded at **standard** cost.

For example, if we transfer 5,000kgs of material to work in progress, we transfer at standard cost. Let us assume the standard price is 75p/kg. The double entry will be as follows:

CR	Raw materials 5,000 × 75p	£3,750	
DR	Work in progress	£3,750	

9.3 Recording price variances

The variances for price, rate and expenditure are recorded in the **relevant cost account** and these represent the difference between the actual price, rate or cost and the standard price, rate or cost for the actual purchases or hours used.

For example, the price variance for materials in our raw material account will be as follows:

	£/kg
Standard price	0.75
Actual price	1.00
	0.25
	× 10,000 kg
	= £2,500 A

The double entry will be as follows:

CR	Raw materials	£2,500
DR	Variances	£2,500

Our T account will be as follows:

Raw materials

Creditors	£10,000	WIP	£3,750
		Material price variance	£2,500
		Closing stock 5,000 × 75p	£3,750
	£10,000		£10,000

9.4 Recording usage variances

The variances for usage and efficiency are recorded in the **work in progress account** as it is only when the work is being undertaken that we realise our inefficiencies in material usage and labour.

For example, let us assume the standard usage per unit was 0.8kg. We would therefore expect 5,000kg to be used when producing 6,250 units. However due to inefficient handling of materials only 5,000 units were produced. Therefore this will give rise to a usage variance as follows:

Standard usage 0.8kg × 5,000	=	4,000kg
Actual usage	=	5,000kg
Usage variance (kg)		1,000kg A
× std price/kg 75p	=	£750 A

The double entry will be as follows:

CR	Work in progress	£750
DR	Variances	£750

The work in progress account will be as follows:

WIP materials (extract)

Materials a/c	£3,750	Transfer to finished goods	
		5,000 × 0.8kg × 75p	£3,000
		Materials usage variance	£750
	£3,750		£3,750

9.5 Closing off the variances account

The balance on the variance account is debited ie written off or credited ie written back in the profit and loss account.

9.6 Other variances

The above procedure is also applied to **labour and variable overheads**.

The **fixed overhead variances** are recorded in the fixed overhead account.

The **total sales margin variance** is not recorded in the ledger as the sales values are recorded at actual amounts.

By recording the variances in different accounts it highlights the efficiency/inefficiency of the managers responsible.

10 Summary

You should now be able to:

- Explain variance analysis and responsibility accounting
- Explain and calculate the variances in relation to materials, labour, variable overhead, fixed overhead and sales margin.
- Identify and discuss possible reasons for variances occurring
- Prepare an operating statement which reconciles budgeted profit and actual profit under an absorption and marginal costing system
- Prepare accounting entries using an integrated accounting system within a standard costing system

Multiple choice questions *(The answers are in the final chapter of this book)*

1   During a period 17,500 labour hours were worked at a standard cost of £6.50 per hour. The labour efficiency variance was £7,800 favourable.

    How many standard hours were produced?

    A   1,200

    B   16,300

    C   17,500

    D   18,700

2   XY Ltd purchased 6,850 kgs of material at a total cost of £21,920. The material price variance was £1,370 favourable. The standard price per kg was:

    A   20p

    B   £3.00

    C   £3.20

    D   £3.40

3   Z plc uses a standard costing system and has the following labour cost standard in relation to one of its products:

        4 hours skilled labour @ £6.00 per hour   £24.00

    During October 20X5, 3,350 of these products were made which was 150 units less than budgeted. The labour cost incurred was £79,893 and the number of direct labour hours worked was 13,450.

    The direct labour variances for the month were:

	Rate	Efficiency
A	£804 (F)	£300 (A)
B	£804 (F)	£300 (F)
C	£807 (F)	£297 (A)
D	£807 (F)	£300 (A)

4   F Ltd has the following budget and actual data:

Budget fixed overhead cost	£100,000
Budget production (units)	20,000
Actual fixed overhead cost	£110,000
Actual production (units)	19,500

The fixed overhead volume variance is:

A £500 adverse

B ✓ £2,500 adverse

C £10,000 adverse

D £17,500 adverse

5 The following details relate to product T, which has a selling price of £4.00:

	£/unit
Direct materials	15.00
Direct labour (3 hours)	12.00
Variable overhead	6.00
Fixed overhead	4.00
	37.00

During April 20X6, the actual production of T was 800 units, which was 100 units fewer than budgeted. The budget shows an annual production target of 10,800, with fixed costs accruing at a constant rate throughout the year. Actual total overhead expenditure totalled £8,500 for April 20X6.

The fixed overhead variances for April 20X6 were:

	Expenditure £	Volume £
A	367 A	1,000 A
B	100 A	1,000 A
C	367 A	400 A
D ✓	100 A	400 A

6 When a standard cost bookkeeping system is used and the actual price paid for raw materials exceeds the standard price, the double entry to record this is:

A debit raw material control account, credit raw material price variance account

B debit work-in-progress control account, credit raw material price variance account

C debit creditor for raw materials, credit raw material price variance account

D ✓ debit raw material price variance account, credit raw material control account

CHAPTER 16

Solutions to practice questions

Chapter 1 Solutions

MULTIPLE CHOICE SOLUTIONS

1 D

2 C

3 D

		£
50,000 units		34,000
Less: "Step"		4,000
		30,000
Less: 20,000 units		21,000
Variable cost for additional 30,000 units		9,000 ie 30p each

Fixed cost = 21,000 – (20,000 × .3) = 15,000
Total cost for 30,000

Variable	9,000
Fixed	15,000
Step	4,000
	28,000

∴ Cost per unit $\dfrac{28{,}000}{30{,}000} = £0.93$

4 B

W : At 100 units, unit cost = £80
At 140 units, unit cost = £75.43
∴ W is a semi-variable cost

X : As total cost is the same at both activity levels, X is a fixed cost

Y : At 100 units, unit cost is £65
At 140 units, unit cost is £65
∴ Y is a variable cost

Z : At 100 units, unit cost is £67
At 140 units, unit cost is £61.29
∴ Z is a semi-variable cost

Chapter 2 Solutions

1 Stores records

The term "perpetual inventory" refers to records of the movements of materials in and out of the stores. A perpetual inventory may be in the form of bin cards or stores ledger accounts. Details of receipts are referenced to the relevant goods received notes and details of issues are referenced to the relevant stores requisitions. (In the case of finished products, the corresponding documents may be termed **factory delivery notes** and **warehouse delivery notes** respectively.) Providing the balance column of a bin card or stores ledger account is completed immediately after every issue or receipt, the recorded balance should correspond with the physical quantity of the materials on hand.

The term "continuous stocktaking" refers to the checking of the physical quantities of materials with the corresponding perpetual inventory records on a daily, rather than periodic, basis. If sufficient items are checked each day, it is possible to check every item stored at least once during the course of a year, and high value items more frequently. In some cases it may then be considered unnecessary to carry out a complete annual stocktaking, but to obtain the year-end stock figure from the stock records.

2 FIFO and LIFO

(a) Under the FIFO method, issues to production are priced at the cost price of the material in the order in which it was taken into stock. When the units originally taken into stock have been exhausted, the next price is used and so on.

Under LIFO, the issue price is the cost price of the material most recently taken into the stock from which the issue could have been drawn, until the units are exhausted, then the next most recent price is used.

(b) The main advantage claimed for the LIFO method of pricing material issues is that production costs tend to reflect current values of materials. In an environment of rising prices, the method results in conservative valuation of material stocks and conservative profits.

Disadvantages of the LIFO method are:

(i) when an issue exceeds the quantity of recent receipts, part of the issue will be charged to production at out of date prices, thereby defeating the object described above;

(ii) the method involves possibly complicated arithmetical calculations when frequent stock movements occur and cost prices vary;

(iii) it does not follow the physical treatment of materials – normally, the storekeeper would issue the stock held longest;

(iv) because of the conservative evaluation of profit it is not acceptable by the Inland Revenue for taxation purposes.

(c) Stores ledger account (weighted average pricing).

No. 1234

Date	Quantity (litres)	Receipts per unit £	Value £	Quantity	Issues per unit £	Value £	Quantity	Balance per unit £	Value £
20X1									
1 Sept							100	1.00	100.00
18 Sept				60	1.00	60.0	40	1.00	40.00
30 Sept	40	1.20	48.00				80 (a)	1.10	88.00
12 Oct				60	1.10	66.00	20	1.10	22.00
31 Oct	80	1.30	104.00				100 (b)	1.26	126.00
4 Nov	20	1.50	30.00				120 (c)	1.30	156.00
19 Nov				70	1.30	91.00	50	1.30	65.00

Calculation of weighted average prices:

(a) 40 in hand at £1.00   £40.00
     40 received at £1.20   £48.00
                             ──────
     80   £88.00   therefore average   £1.10

(b) 20 in hand at £1.10   £22.00
     80 received at £1.30   £104.00
                             ───────
     100   £126.00   therefore average   £1.26

(c) 100 in hand at £1.26   £126.00
     20 received at £1.50   £30.00
                             ──────
     120   £156.00   therefore average   £1.30

3 Component ABC

Weighted average cost

		Units	Price		Purchase cost	(i) Cost of production	(ii) Closing stock
			£	£	£	£	£
1/5	Purchase	100	41.000	4,100	4,100		
10/5	Purchase	75	42.000	3,150	3,150		
		175	41.429	7,250			
15/5	Issue	(50)		(2,071)		2,071	
		125		5,179			
20/5	Issue	(65)		(2,693)		2,693	
		60		2,486			
23/5	Purchase	40	45.000	1,800	1,800		
		100	42.860	4,286			
30/5	Issue	(50)		(2,143)		2,143	
		50		2,143			2,143
					9,050	6,907	2,143

4 Stock accounting methods

The statement quoted is based on the contention that "profit" can only arise after provision has been made for the replacement of any assets used up in earning that profit. When stocks are used therefore, there should be a charge in the profit and loss account for their replacement cost, ie their current cost at the time of use.

Unless stocks are used up very quickly neither FIFO nor the average cost method will normally give the required charge against profits, because both take account of historical purchase prices. The LIFO method will certainly result in stock usage being valued at a more recent price than the other methods, and from this point of view might be regarded as "preferable"; but it is not an ideal solution for two reasons:

(a) the LIFO price is also historical, and in many cases will not be identical with the current cost of replacing the stocks used;

(b) it will result in stock balances for balance sheet purposes being reported at those stock ledger prices which are most out of date.

5 Stock ordering

(a) Under the periodic review system, the quantity of stock in hand and the trend of sales demand are reviewed at regular intervals of time. As a result of that review a purchase order for stock replacement will be placed if necessary, the quantity ordered being that required to cover expected demand and to maintain a safety margin until the next review date.

Under the reorder level system, a fixed quantity of stock will be ordered whenever the stock holding falls to a predetermined order level. This order level would take account of the normal level of demand and the delivery delay between ordering and receipt of the goods. It should represent the average amount of stock held.

(b) The average amount of stock held will obviously be dependent on the size of each purchase order and in consequence on the frequency of ordering. The ideal order quantity will be that which involves the lowest annual total of the combined cost of:

(i) holding the stock – in terms of floor space occupancy costs and any interest charge on the amount of the money tied up in stock holdings;

(ii) placing orders – in terms of wage costs, stationery, etc.

The fixed order quantity at which this total is at a minimum is known as the 'economic order quantity'.

6 Component BCD

(a) (i) The reorder level = maximum lead time usage
= 1,100 × 4
= 4,400

(ii) Reorder quantity is the unknown X in the following formula:

Maximum level	=	Reorder level plus order quantity less minimum lead time usage
ie 5,500	=	4,400 + X − (900 × 2)
X	=	5,500 − 4,400 + 1,800
Reorder quantity	=	2,900

(iii)
The minimum level	=	Reorder level less average lead time usage
	=	4,400 − (1,000 × 3)
	=	1,400

(iv) The average stock held is minimum stock plus half the order quantity

$$1,400 + \frac{2,900}{2}$$

= 2,850

(An acceptable alternative is average of minimum and maximum levels

ie ½ × (5,500 + 1,400) = 3,450.)

(b) Some of the essential practices of efficient storekeeping are:

- provision of secure and suitable storage conditions;

- full identification of materials;

- correct location of all materials;

- economic use of storage space;

- efficient receipt and issue of materials;

- accurate recording of stock movements;

- maintain adequate stock levels;

- watching for slow moving or obsolete stocks

7 Mr G

(i) FIFO

Date	Receipts Qty	Amt £	Unit price £	Issues Qty	Amt £	Balance Qty	Amt £
13/1	200	7,200	36			200 @ 36	7,200
8/2	400	15,200	38			200 @ 36 400 @ 38	22,400
10/2				200 @ 36 300 @ 38	18,600	100 @ 38	3,800
11/3	600	24,000	40			100 @ 38 600 @ 40	27,800
12/4	400	14,000	35			100 @ 38 600 @ 40 400 @ 35	41,800
20/4				100 @ 38 500 @ 40	23,800	100 @ 40 400 @ 35	18,000
15/6	500	14,000	28			100 @ 40 400 @ 35 500 @ 28	32,000
25/6				100 @ 40 300 @ 35	14,500	100 @ 35 500 @ 28	17,500
		74,400			56,900		
30/6	Stock loss			100 @ 35	3,500	500 @ 28	14,000
		74,400			60,400		

232

(ii) LIFO

	Receipts			Issues		Balance	
Date	Qty	Amt £	Unit price £	Qty	Amt £	Qty	Amt £
13/1	200	7,200	36			200 @ 36	7,200
8/2	400	15,200	38			200 @ 36 400 @ 38	22,400
10/2				400 @ 38 100 @ 36	18,800	100 @ 36	3,600
11/3	600	24,000	40			100 @ 36 600 @ 40	27,600
12/4	400	14,000	35			100 @ 36 600 @ 40 400 @ 35	41,600
20/4				400 @ 35 200 @ 40	22,000	100 @ 36 400 @ 40	19,600
15/6	500	14,000	28			100 @ 36 400 @ 40 500 @ 28	33,600
25/6				400 @ 28	11,200	100 @ 36 400 @ 40 100 @ 28	22,400
		74,400			52,000		
30/6	Stock loss			100 @ 28	2,800	100 @ 36 400 @ 40	19,600
		74,400			54,800		

(iii) Weighted average

Date	Receipts Qty	Amt £	Issues Qty	Amt £	Balance Qty	Amt £	Weighted unit price at date of receipt
13/1	200	7,200			200	7,200	36.00
8/2	400	15,200			600	22,400	* 37.33
10/2			500 @ 37.33	18,665	100	3,735	
11/3	600	24,000			700	27,735	39.62
12/4	400	14,000			1,100	41,735	37.94
20/4			600 @ 37.94	22,764	500	18,971	
15/6	500	14,000			1,000	32,971	32.97
25/6			400 @ 32.97	13,188	600	19,783	
		74,400		54,617			
30/6	Stock loss		100 @ 32.97	3,297	500	16,486	
		74,000		57,914			

$$* \quad \frac{\text{Balance of amount}}{\text{Balance of stock}} = \frac{£22,400}{600} = £37.33$$

MULTIPLE CHOICE SOLUTIONS

1 Physical stock + outstanding order = customer orders + free stock

    Physical stock + 27,500 = 16,250 + 13,000

    Physical stock = 16,250 + 13,000 - 27,500

     = 1,750

∴ **Correct answer: A**

2 Re-order level = Maximum usage × maximum lead time

     = 175 × 16

     = 2,800

∴ **Correct answer: B**

3 Maximum stock level = Re-order level + Re-order quantity
    - (minimum usage × minimum lead time)

     = 2,800 + 3,000 - (90 × 10)

     = 4,900

∴ **Correct answer: C**

4 FIFO means that issues are valued at the oldest prices, so that closing stock is at the currents prices.

∴ **Correct answer: A**

Chapter 3 Solutions

1 Bonus payment

An incentive bonus payable to a tradesman's labourer is a necessity if the labourer is to be satisfied with his job, and willing to work hard at it. If an incentive bonus is restricted to the skilled worker, the labourer may well feel aggrieved that he is unable to participate. Such feeling will slow down his work, thus decreasing the output and remuneration of the skilled worker, and may also be shown by an unwillingness on the part of the labourer to learn more about the job in order to improve his performance.

Therefore, the introduction of some pecuniary incentive for the labourer is desirable, although it may be difficult to initiate because the work performed by unskilled assistants cannot be clearly measured. One practical solution to this problem is to treat the tradesman and his mate as a team and to regard their performance as being the product of their combined efforts.

If a bonus is paid on the basis of team effort the skilled worker will discourage slackness in his labourer because his own bonus is at stake, while the labourer will be glad of the opportunity to earn more from increased effort. In theory, both the tradesman and his mate will expedite the work, provided that relations between them are harmonious.

As with most bonus schemes the problem exists of fixing the time to be allowed for the performance of a particular task. Often the work of a tradesman's labourer cannot be divided into specific tasks for time and motion study. While standard times might readily be fixed for routine maintenance jobs, tasks of a non-routine nature would present more difficulty. A compromise would need to be achieved between a standard time which is too tight and one which is too generous. If the standard time is too tight, the work will either be rushed and badly performed or the incentive will be too remote to take effect. A standard time which is too generous will lessen the effect of the incentive. It is usual to calculate the bonus of the labourer at a lower percentage than for the skilled man; for example, the labourer may receive one-third of the time saved, as against 50% for the skilled man. The circumstances of each case will obviously dictate the rates laid down. If a bonus scheme is firmly geared to increased production or efficiency, the labourer will be encouraged to work harder to increase his remuneration so that the scheme will be effective.

A number of indirect incentives (such as a good attitude on the part of management, canteen and recreation facilities, a suggestion bonus scheme, and accident prevention bonuses) are effective in so far as they increase the status of the job in the eyes of the tradesman's labourer. However, such incentives do not have a direct bearing on the effort extended by the labourer to do his job. A system of merit pay, with an annual bonus or profit-sharing scheme (whereby extra remuneration is awarded in direct relation to the efficiency of the employee as gauged by the management) is more effective, but if favouritism is thought to influence the division, it can be the cause of dissatisfaction A timekeeping bonus will be most effective in ensuring that employees begin work at the appropriate time, though it can have no effect on the amount of effort which they put into the job. In cases where it is difficult to measure the work, a bonus may be paid in the form of a high time rate, but while this would be satisfactory to the employee it may not produce any extra effort. An extension of the team system is for a group of skilled men with their labourers to receive a group bonus based on production. Shares in the payment to the group are calculated by reference to basic time rates of each employee.

MULTIPLE CHOICE SOLUTIONS

1 20% of time worked is idle, 80% is productive

2,400 hours = 80% of worked hours

$\therefore$ worked hours = $\dfrac{2,400}{80\%}$ = 3,000 hours

Budgeted labour cost = 3,000 × £10 = £30,000

$\therefore$ **Correct answer: D**

2 Indirect labour is a costing concept. The double entry is:

Wages Control		Overhead Control	
	Indirect labour × (overheads)	Indirect labour × (wages)	

$\therefore$ **Correct answer: C**

Chapter 4 Solutions

1 Peter Radford

Cost apportionment schedule (to the nearest £000)

Cost	Basis	Total £000	Cutting £000	Assembly £000	Packing £000
Rent	Area	18	5	6	7
Light and heat	Area	38	10	13	15
Depreciation					
Premises	Area	15	4	5	6
Machine	NBV	41	30	10	1
Maintenance					
Premises	Area	30	8	10	12
Machines	50:50:0	30	15	15	-
Cleaning	Area	25	8	5	12
Supervisors	Number	80	32	32	16
Control	Hours	84	24	45	15
Warehousing	Usage	40	34	4	2
Insurance					
Premises	Area	12	3	4	5
Machines	NBV	12	9	3	-
Canteen	Staff	32	10	16	6
		457	192	168	97

2 Ensign

Department	Total £000	Machine £000	Assembly £000	S £000	M £000	C £000
Overheads	880	311	422	46	61	40
Split canteen (35:50:10:5)		14	20	4	2	(40)
Split stores (72:24:4)		36	12	(50)	2	
Split maintenance (60:40)		39	26		(65)	
Overheads	880	400	480			
Production hours (000)		40	60			
Hourly rates		£10	£8			

3   Pirie

Part (a)

Cost apportionment

Cost	Basis	Total £000	A £000	B £000	C £000	S £000	M £000
Overheads	Area	30	8.0	4.0	8.0	8.0	2.0
Canteen expenses	Employees*	52	17.8	13.5	15.1	2.8	2.8
Insurance							
Machine	Value	24	8.4	9.6	3.6	1.2	1.2
Building	Area	48	12.8	6.4	12.8	12.8	3.2
Cons stores	Materials	118	35.9	32.6	40.1	–	9.4
Supervisors	Number	152	60.8	30.4	30.4	15.2	15.2
Ind labour	Number	248	82.6	41.3	82.7	20.7	20.7
Rent and rates	Area	306	81.6	40.8	81.6	81.6	20.4
Depreciation							
Machine	Value	368	128.8	147.2	55.2	18.4	18.4
Building	Area	84	22.4	11.2	22.4	22.4	5.6
		1,430	459.1	337.0	351.9	183.1	98.9
Split stores	Materials	–	55.7	50.5	62.3	(183.1)	14.6
Split maintenance	Hours	–	35.5	52.5	25.5		(113.5)
Final apportionment		1,430	550.3	440.0	439.7		

Notes

(1) Some figures have required rounding; alternatives are possible.

(2) The basis of apportioning canteen expenses is by total employees: direct, indirect and supervisory.

(3) In view of the closeness of the final figures to round numbers the costs of the three departments are rounded in (b) below.

*   Employees include direct, indirect and supervisors.

Part (b)

Absorption of overheads

(i) *Fixed overhead rate per hour*

Department	A	B	C
Fixed overheads (£000)	550	440	440
Labour hours (000)	100	80	100
Rate per hour	£5.50	£5.50	£4.40

(ii) *Cost per unit for Gordon*

$(5 \times £5.50) + (6 \times £5.50) + (6 \times £4.40) = £86.90$

Part (c)

Absorption on a unit basis

Fixed overheads (£000)	1,430
Units produced (000)	20
Cost per unit	£71.50

Part (d)

Calculating a fixed overhead cost per unit figure is a somewhat arbitrary exercise. Nevertheless, some attempt should be made to produce a figure which is fair (reflects the "use" that a particular product has made of fixed resources). It should also be fair insofar as the total absorption cost bears a similar relationship to likely selling price for each product and does not result in one product showing a loss. This effectively means stock being valued in excess of net realisable value.

If a product passes through several departments one should apportion fixed costs between those departments on an equitable basis. Having done this, it is then important to ensure that different products are "charged" with an appropriate amount of fixed overhead cost. The hourly rate calculation would seem the most sensible method to use, though others are possible. Currently activity based costing is in vogue, which produces several fixed overhead cost per unit figures for each element of cost, or at least for each cost driver, which are then aggregated.

Difficulties arise with apportioning overheads to production departments when reciprocal service arrangements exist. For Pirie, stores held material for the maintenance department, but the maintenance team did not spend any time repairing equipment in the stores. Had they done so, the calculations in (a) would have been lengthy or complicated using a "direct" method, "stepped" method or possibly a "reciprocal" method using algebra or repeated reapportionment of overheads.

4   PQR

Part (a)

	Department P calculation	Department P £	Department Q £	Department R £
Repairs and maintenance	Given in question	42,000	10,000	10,000
Depreciation	$\frac{170,000}{400,000} \times £40,000$	17,000	14,000	9,000
Consumable supplies	$\frac{50,000}{100,000} \times £9,000$	4,500	2,700	1,800
Wage related costs	12½% × £386,000	48,250	26,250	12,500
Indirect labour	$\frac{50,000}{100,000} \times £90,000$	45,000	27,000	18,000
Canteen	$\frac{25}{50} \times £30,000$	15,000	9,000	6,000
Business rates and insurance	$\frac{5,000}{10,000} \times £26,000$	13,000	10,400	2,600
		184,750	99,350	59,900
Direct labour hours		50,000	30,000	20,000
Absorption rate		£3.70	£3.31	£3.00

Part (b)

Job 976: Sample quotation

		£	£
Direct materials			800.00
Direct labour	P (30 × £386,000/50,000)	231.60	
	Q (10 × £210,000/30,000)	70.00	
	R (5 × £100,000/20,000)	25.00	
			326.60
Overhead absorbed	P (30 × £3.70)	111.00	
	Q (10 × £3.31)	33.10	
	R (5 × £3.00)	15.00	
			159.10
Production cost			1,285.70
Selling, distribution and administration costs	20% of production costs		257.14
Total cost			1,542.84
Profit margin = 20% of selling price (= $\frac{20}{80}$ × cost) £1,542.84 × 20/80			385.71
Sales price			1,928.55

Quotation for Job 976 using auditor's system

	£
Direct materials	800.00
Direct labour	326.60
Prime cost	1,126.60
Overhead applied (125% of prime cost)	1,408.25
Sales price	2,534.85

Auditor's system results in higher cost for this quotation. Other quotations may work out cheaper under auditor's system.

MULTIPLE CHOICE SOLUTIONS

1

	£
Actual overheads	138,000
Over absorption	23,000
Absorbed overheads	161,000

Absorbed overheads = Actual hours × OAR

£161,000 = 11,500 × OAR

OAR = $\frac{£161,000}{11,500}$ = £14 per hour

∴ **Correct answer: D**

2    $\text{OAR} = \dfrac{\text{Budgeted overheads}}{\text{Budgeted hours}} = \dfrac{258{,}750}{11{,}250} = £23$

	£
Actual overheads	254,692
Absorbed overheads	
10,980 × 23	252,540
Under absorption	2,152

∴ **Correct answer: A**

3   Where common costs are split between cost centres on the basis of benefit received, the costs are apportioned between centres.

∴ **Correct answer: B**

Chapter 5 Solutions

1 Absorption costing

		£/unit	
(a)	Prime cost	35.70	(8.50 + 27.20)
(b)	Full production cost	61.00	(35.70 + 11.30 + 14.00)
(c)	Full cost of making and selling	68.15	(61 + 2.20 + 4.95)
(d)	Marginal cost of making and selling	49.20	(68.15 – 14 – 4.95)
(e)	Absorption cost stock value	61.00	(as (b))
(f)	Selling price (W1)	61.50	
(g)	Unit profit	(6.65)	(61.50 – 68.15)
(h)	Unit contribution	12.30	(61.50 – 49.20)

(W1) Contribution = 20% of revenue

∴ Marginal cost = 80% of revenue

∴ Revenue (Price) = $\dfrac{\text{Marginal Cost}}{0.8} = \dfrac{£49.20}{0.8}$ = £61.50

2 Marginal costing

Absorption cost profit = 9,600 × (£20 – £15) = £48,000

Marginal cost profit = 9,600 × (£20 – £12) – £30,600 (W) = £46,200

The difference of £1,800 is due to fixed production costs being carried forward with absorption costing as stock level rises, ie

Rise in stock × Fixed production cost per unit (OAR) = 600 × £3 = £1,800

Working

Actual fixed cost = OAR × budgeted production = (15 – 12) × 10,200 = £30,600

3 McTack

Part (a)

Standard cost cards

	Marginal costing		Absorption costing	
	£	£	£	£
Sales		500		500
Production costs				
Materials	100		100	
Labour	200		200	
Variable overhead	50		50	
Fixed overhead	–		50	
Cost of production		(350)		(400)
Contribution/profit		150		100

Part (b)

Budgeted profit and loss account: marginal costing

	Qtr 1 £	Qtr 2 £	Qtr 3 £	Qtr 4 £
Sales	50,000	55,000	60,000	65,000
Opening stock	–	7,000	10,500	10,500
Production costs (W2)	42,000	42,000	42,000	42,000
Closing stock (W1)	(7,000)	(10,500)	(10,500)	(7,000)
	35,000	38,500	42,000	45,500
Contribution	15,000	16,500	18,000	19,500
Fixed costs	(6,000)	(6,000)	(6,000)	(6,000)
Budgeted profit	9,000	10,500	12,000	13,500

Budgeted profit and loss account: absorption costing

Quarter	1 £	2 £	3 £	4 £
Sales	50,000	55,000	60,000	65,000
Opening stock	–	8,000	12,000	12,000
Production costs (W2)	48,000	48,000	48,000	48,000
Closing stock (W1)	(8,000)	(12,000)	(12,000)	(8,000)
	40,000	44,000	48,000	52,000
Budgeted profit	10,000	11,000	12,000	13,000

Part (c)

Reconciliation

The profit figures in Quarter 1 are different when using the two bases because the stock is valued differently.

Increase in stock in Quarter 1	20 units
	£/unit
Stock value using absorption costing	400
Stock value using marginal costing	350
Difference	50
20 units @ £50 per unit	£1,000

In other words, when using absorption costing £50 of fixed overheads is capitalised into each unit of stock and therefore carried forward to the next period in the closing stock.

When using marginal costing the fixed overheads are written off in the period.

Thus, when stock increases during a period the absorption costing profit will exceed the marginal costing profit; when stock decreases the absorption costing profit will be smaller than the marginal costing profit (eg in Quarter 4).

WORKINGS

(1)   Stock valuations

	Marginal costing £		Absorption costing £	
Production cost (part (a))		350		400
Closing stock value				
Quarter 1	£350 × 20 =	7,000	£400 × 20 =	8,000
Quarter 2	£350 × 30 =	10,500	£400 × 30 =	12,000
Quarter 3	£350 × 30 =	10,500	£400 × 30 =	12,000
Quarter 4	£350 × 20 =	7,000	£400 × 20 =	8,000

(2)   Production costs

		£
Marginal costing	120 units × £350	42,000
Total absorption costing	(per question)	48,000

MULTIPLE CHOICE SOLUTIONS

1   Fixed costs = ¼ × 16 = £4 per unit

Difference between marginal costing and absorption costing profit is:

(closing stock - opening stock) × fixed OAR

= (2,500 - 0) × £4 = £10,000

As stock has increased, absorption costing profit will be bigger.

∴ **Correct answer: B**

2   Profit: When stocks increase, some fixed costs incurred are carried through to next period (because of the accruals concept) in an absorption costing system. This means that the profit will be higher under absorption costing.

Closing stock: The absorption costing valuation of closing stock includes fixed cost, which the marginal costing system excludes, hence the valuation will be higher in the absorption costing system.

∴ **Correct answer: B**

3 Fixed OAR = $\dfrac{£60,000}{30,000}$ = £2 per unit

Total unit cost:

	£
Direct materials	3.50
Direct labour	4.00
Variable overhead	2.00
Fixed overhead	2.00
	11.50

Production	2,400 units
less	180 units
Sales	2,220 units

As production ≠ sales, there will be under or over absorption

	£
Overheads charged = $\dfrac{60,000}{12}$	= 5,000
Overheads absorbed = 2,400 × £2	= 4,800
Under absorption	200

Profit statement:

		£
Sales:	2,220 × 15	33,300
Cost of sales:	2,220 × 11.50	(25,530)
		7,770
less under absorption		(200)
Profit		7,570

∴ **Correct answer: B**

Chapter 6 Solutions

1   Jeremy Bilt

(a) **The contract account**

(i) The first step is to write up the contract account, leaving blanks where figures are not known.

Contract account – 91 Queens Gate

	£		£
Materials purchased	12,150	Stock of materials c/f	1,560
Materials from other sites	1,040	Cost of sales	?
Labour	8,460	Work in progress c/f	?
Plant hire	1,070		
Direct expenses	3,900		
Administration expenses	140		
	26,760		26,760

(ii) Now calculate the profit to be taken to profit and loss account for the year.

		£	£	£
Total contract price				50,000
Less:	Costs incurred to date (26,760 – 1,560)		25,200	
	Estimated costs to completion			
	Materials (5,940 + 1,560)	7,500		
	Labour	5,670		
	Plant hire	750		
	Other expenses	2,920		
		16,840		
				42,040
Total profit estimated on contract				7,960

Profit attributable to work performed to date = $£7,960 \times \dfrac{30,000}{50,000} = £4,776$

(iii) We can now complete the account (note that 'work in progress' is the balancing figure):

Contract account – 91 Queens Gate

	£		£
Materials purchased	12,150	Stock of materials c/f	1,560
Materials from other sites	1,040	Cost of sales (28,500 - 4,776)	23,724
Labour	8,460	Work in progress c/f	1,476
Plant hire	1,070		
Direct expenses	3,900		
Administration expenses	140		
	26,760		26,760
Stock of materials b/f	1,560		
Work in progress b/f	1,476		

(b) ### The work certified account

	£		£
Turnover to profit and loss account	28,500	Debtors account 30,000 × 95% (5% retention)	28,500

(c) ### Debtors' account

	£		£
Work certified account	28,500	Cash	28,500

(d) ### Profit and loss account - extract

	£		£
Cost of sales	23,724	Turnover (work certified a/c)	28,500
Profit to date	4,776		
	28,500		28,500

2   Contractors Ltd

Contract 59 account

20X0	£	20X0	£
Materials purchased	18,692		
Materials issued from store	1,496		
Wages	8,457		
Direct expenses	4,835	Plant c/f (W1)	8,820
Administration expenses	1,780	Stock of materials c/f	1,580
Plant purchased	10,800	Cost of sales (38,000 – 3,000) (W2)	35,000
Accrued wages c/f	640	WIP c/f	1,300
	46,700		46,700
1.1.20X1 Plant b/f	8,820	1.1.20X1 Accrued wages b/f	640
Stock of materials b/f	1,580		
Work in progress b/f	1,300		

WORKINGS

(1)   Depreciation of plant $= £\dfrac{10,800 - 5,760}{28}$ per month

$= £180$ per month

Value of plant on 31/12/X0 $= 10,800 - 11 @ £180$

$= £8,820$

(2)   Calculation of attributable profit

	£	£
Total contract price		98,250
Less: Estimated total costs		
Materials (18,692 + 1,496 + 25,250)	45,438	
Wages (8,457 + 14,420)	22,877	
Direct expenses (4,835 + 8,030)	12,865	
Administration expenses (1,780 + 2,750)	4,530	
Depreciation on plant (10,800 – 5,760)	5,040	
		90,750
Estimated total profit on contract		7,500

Costs incurred to 31 December 20X0		
Materials		
Purchased	18,692	
Issued from stores	1,496	
	20,188	
Less: stock of materials	(1,580)	
		18,608

Wages

Paid	8,457	
Accrued	640	
		9,097
Direct expenses		4,835
Administration expenses		1,780
Depreciation on plant $\frac{11}{28} \times (10{,}800 - 5{,}760)$		1,980
		36,300

Attributable profit = £7,500 × $\frac{36{,}300}{90{,}750}$ = £3,000

MULTIPLE CHOICE SOLUTIONS

1 The cost of a job is built up as for any other cost unit:

Direct materials (i)
+ Direct labour (iv)
+ Overheads - absorbed using an OAR (iii)

∴ **Correct answer: C**

2 OAR = $\frac{\text{Total Overheads}}{\text{Total Labour Cost}} = \frac{140{,}000}{12{,}500 + 23{,}000 + 4{,}500} = \frac{140{,}000}{40{,}000}$

= 3.5 or 350% of labour cost

	Job 1 £	Job 2 £
Opening work-in-progress	8,500	0
Material	17,150	29,050
Labour	12,500	23,000
Overheads = 350% of labour	43,750	80,500
Total value	81,900	132,550
Value of closing work-in-progress	= £81,900 + £132,550	
	= £214,450	

∴ **Correct answer: D**

3

	Job 3 £
Opening work-in-progress	46,000
Material	0
Labour	4,500
Overheads = 350% of labour	15,750
Total cost	66,250
Total profit = 50%	33,125
Total price	£99,375

Price per board = $\frac{£99{,}375}{2{,}400}$ = £41.41

∴ **Correct answer: C**

4 Profit on "certified" work is:

	£000
Value certified	1,300
Costs certified	1,000
	300

Cash has only been received for £1.2 million.

So profit should be reduced proportionately.

Attributed profit $= 300{,}000 \times \dfrac{1.2}{1.3}$

$= £277{,}000$ (to the nearest £000)

∴ **Correct answer: B**

Chapter 7 Solutions

1 Retail store

The costs of a departmental store would need to be analysed between:

(a) the various selling departments in the shop, such as clothing, hardware, furnishings and stationery;

(b) the administration departments of the business, including accounts and buying (if this was not decentralised);

(c) service departments such as warehousing and transport.

Apart from the cost of goods sold it is likely that most of the operating costs of the business would be "fixed", predominantly premises charges and salaries.

The fundamental analysis of profit from the various selling departments would therefore be of gross profit or "mark-up", ie sales value less cost of goods sold. It is likely, however, that some of the fixed costs would be relevant to particular selling departments, particularly the remuneration of sales staff plus possible depreciation and maintenance of display racks, counters and cash registers, special publicity material and identifiable stock loses. It would then be necessary to calculate "net contribution" by department in addition to the gross profit or marginal contribution. The question remains whether:

(a) central warehousing costs;

(b) costs of space occupancy;

(c) other central costs

should be apportioned over the selling departments.

There would not appear to be any benefit from operating a full recovery system, since the basis of apportionment would be to some extent arbitrary. With regard to service department costs, an alternative to apportionment would be the calculation of statistical indicators of:

(a) net contribution per £1 stock held for each department:

(b) net contribution per square metre of floor space occupied.

In judging the relative profitability of the selling departments it would be necessary to take account of:

(a) any policy of selling particular items at a low price (as "loss leaders" to encourage customers to visit the store);

(b) the need to provide a comprehensive range of goods, even though some of them might individually show a low rate of profitability.

2 Delivery service

(a) Annual profit per vehicle under existing conditions

Annual cost per vehicle

	£
Fixed charges	5,400
Drivers' wages	10,260
Running costs, 18,000 × 33p	5,940
	(21,600)

Income

	Ton/miles	£
100 outward journeys = 9,000 miles × 10 tons =	90,000	
Return loads - average journey = 9,000 miles ÷ 100 journeys 400 tons × 90 miles =	36,000	
	126,000 × 24p	30,240
Annual profit per vehicle		8,640

(b) Annual bonus on regular route

		£
5 tons × 9,000	45,000 × 24p	10,800
Bonus at 30%		3,240

(c) Annual bonus on modified route

	£	£
Additional income as above		10,800
Less: 20 miles × 100 trips = 2,000 miles at 33p	660	
Overtime pay 100 trips × £2	200	
		860
Net additional income		9,940
Bonus at 30%		2,982

MULTIPLE CHOICE SOLUTIONS

1 Assignment 652:

	£
Senior consultant - 86 × £20	1,720
Junior consultant - 220 × £15	3,300
Overheads - (86 + 220) × £12.50	3,825
Total cost	8,845
Add 40% profit	3,538
Price	12,383

∴ **Correct answer: D**

2 As hours were in the ratio 1 : 3

Senior hours	=	¼ × 3,000	=	750 hours
Junior hours	=	¾ × 3,000	=	2,250 hours

Total cost:

			£
Senior hours	=	750 × £20	15,000
Junior hours	=	2,250 × £15	33,750
Overheads	=	3,000 × £12.5	37,500
Total cost			86,250

Profit = 40% × 86,250 = £34,500

∴ **Correct answer: A**

3

When consultations	=	4,500
Total cost	=	£269,750
Fixed cost	=	£200,000
Variable cost	=	£69,750

Variable cost per consultation = $\dfrac{69,750}{4,500}$ = £15.50

∴ **Correct answer: A**

Chapter 8 Solutions

1   X plc

Process account

	Ltrs	£		Ltrs	£
Input material	10,000	10,000	Output	8,700	10,092
Labour and overheads	–	800	Normal loss	1,000	360
			Abnormal loss	300	348
	10,000	10,800		10,000	10,800

Output valued at (£10,800 – £360)/9,000 = £1.16 per litre

Normal loss

	Ltrs	£		Ltrs	£
Process	1,000	360	Cash	1,300	468
Bal b/f to abnormal loss	300	108			
	1,300	468		1,300	468

Abnormal loss

	Ltrs	£		Ltrs	£
Process	300	348	Normal loss	300	108
			P&L		240
	300	348		300	348

2   Chemical compound

(a)   **Process A**

	kg	£		kg	£ per kg	£
Direct material	2,000	10,000	Normal loss (W2)	400	0.500	200
Direct labour		7,200	To Process B (W3)	1,400	18.575	26,005
Process costs		8,400	Abnormal loss	200	18.575	3,715
Overhead (W1)		4,320				
	2,000	29,920		2,000		29,920

W1   £6,840 × 7,200/(7,200 + 4,200)

W2   Normal loss = 20% of input = 2,000 × 20% = 400 kg

W3   Value of output = £(29,920 – 200)/(2,000 – 400) = £18.575 per kg

(b) **Process B**

	kg	£		kg	£ per kg	£
From Process A	1,400	26,005	Finished goods (W6)	2,620	21.7516	56,989
Direct material	1,400	16,800	Normal loss (W4)	280	1.825	511
Direct labour		4,200				
Overhead		2,520				
Process costs		5,800				
Total costs		55,325				
Abnormal gain (W5, W6)	100	2,175				
	2,900	57,500		2,900		57,500

W4 Normal loss = 10% × (1,400 + 1,400) = 280

W5 Expected output = 2,800 − 280 = 2,520 units; actual output 2,620; 100 units abnormal gain

W6 Cost per unit = £(55,325 − 511) / (2,800 − 280) = £21.7516 (kept this accurate to avoid rounding errors)

(c) **Normal loss (scrap) account**

	kg	£		kg	£
Process A	400	200	Cash – process A	600	300.00
Process B	280	511	Cash – process B	180	328.50
			Balance – transfer to abnormal loss		82.50
	680	711		680	711.00

(d) **Abnormal loss / gain account**

	£		£
From normal loss a/c	82.50	Process B	2,175.00
Process A	3,715.00	P & L	1,622.50
	3,797.50		3,797.50

(e) **Finished goods**

	kg	£		kg	£
Process B	2,620	56,989			

(f) **P & L**

	£		£
Abnormal loss/gain	1,622.50		

3 Process WIP

Physical flow of units

Opening WIP	Units started	Units completed	Closing WIP
50	+ 300	= 275 (bal fig)	+ 75

Equivalent units of production

Units completed (including OWIP units)	275
Closing WIP (75 × 60%)	45
	320

	£
Total cost	
For March	3,596
B/f	100
	3,696

$$\therefore \text{Cost per unit} = \frac{£3,696}{320} = £11.55$$

Value of finished goods	=	275 × £11.55	= £3,176.25
Value of closing WIP	=	45 × £11.55	= £519.75
			£3,696

4 Cleansing

The physical flow of units:

Opening WIP	Units started	Units completed	Closing WIP
-	+ 11,000 kg	= 8,600 kg	+ 2,400 kg (bal)

The 2,400 kg of CWIP need to be split up into two batches due to the differing degrees of completion:

CWIP batch (1): 25% × 2,400 = 600 kg

CWIP batch (2): 75% × 2,400 = 1,800 kg

The effective units, costs and costs per unit are set out in a table as follows:

	Effective units				Costs	Costs per EU (£)
Input	Completed in period	CWIP batch (1)	CWIP batch (2)	Total EU	Total costs (£)	
Materials	8,600	600 (100%)	1,800 (100%)	11,000	5,500 (W1)	0.50
Conversion	8,600	360 (60%)	450 (25%)	9,410	5,646 (W2)	0.60
					11,146	1.10

WORKINGS

1 $2,000 \times £0.80 + 3,000 \times £0.50 + 6,000 \times £0.40$ = £5,500

2 $150\% \times 941 \text{ hours} \times £4/\text{hour}$ = £5,646

The costs may now be attributed to the categories of output as follows:

				£	£
Completed units:	$8,600 \times £1.10$				9,460
Closing WIP:					
Batch (1)	Materials	$600 \times £0.50$		300	
	Conversion	$360 \times £0.60$		216	
				516	
Batch (2)	Materials	$1,800 \times £0.50$	900		
	Conversion	$450 \times £0.60$	270	1,170	
					1,686
					11,146

The process account would then appear as follows:

Process Account

	kg	£		kg	£
Material A	2,000	1,600	Completed	8,600	9,460
Material B	3,000	1,500	Closing WIP	2,400	1,686
Material C	6,000	2,400			
Labour		3,764			
Overhead		1,882			
	11,000	11,146		11,000	11,146

W1 Total number of kg in closing WIP is input – units completed = 2,000 + 3,000 + 6,000 – 8,600 = 2,400

WIP (1) = 60% complete = ¼ × 2,400 = 600 kg

WIP (2) = 25% complete = ¾ × 2,400 = 1,800 kg

5 **Process X**

The physical flow of units:

Opening WIP	+	Units started	=	Units completed	+	Closing WIP
6,000	+	16,000	=	18,000 (bal)	+	4,000

The effective units, costs and costs per unit are set out in a table as follows. Note that since 'all the material is introduced at the start of Process X', the CWIP must be 100% complete with respect to materials:

Input	Effective units			Costs			Costs per EU (£)
	Completed in period	c/f in CWIP	Total EU	b/f in OWIP	In period	Total costs (£)	
Materials	18,000	4,000 (100%)	22,000	24,000	64,000	88,000	4.00
Conversion	18,000	3,000 (75%)	21,000	15,300	75,000	90,300	4.30
						178,300	8.30

The costs may now be attributed to the categories of output as follows:

			£	£
Completed units:	18,000 × £8.30			149,400
Closing WIP:	Materials	4,000 × £4	16,000	
	Conversion	3,000 × £4.30	12,900	
				28,900
				178,300

The process account will thus appear as follows:

Process X account

	£		£
Material b/f	24,000	Closing WIP	28,900
Conversion b/f	15,300	Completed	149,400
Materials in period	64,000		
Conversion in period	75,000		
	178,300		178,300

6 NH Ltd

Process 1

The physical flow of units:

Opening WIP	+	Units started	=	Units completed	+	Closing WIP
–	+	12,000	=	9,000	+	3,000 (bal)

Input	Effective units			Costs		Costs per EU (£)
	Completed in period	CWIP	Total EU	Total costs (£)	
Materials	9,000	3,000 (100%)	12,000	36,000	3.00
Conversion	9,000	1,500 (50%)	10,500	40,530	3.86
				76,530	6.86

The costs may now be attributed to the categories of output as follows:

			£	£
Completed units	9,000 × £6.86			61,740
Closing WIP:	Materials	3,000 × £3	9,000	
	Conversion	1,500 × £3.86	5,790	
				14,790
				76,530

The process account will thus appear as follows:

Process 1 account

	Units	£		Units	£
Materials	12,000	36,000	Process 2	9,000	61,740
Labour		32,000	Work-in-progress	3,000	14,790
Overheads		8,530			
		76,530			76,530

Process 2

The physical flow of units:

Opening WIP + Units started = Units completed + Normal loss + Closing WIP

    –   +   9,000   =   7,600   +   600   +   800 (bal)

	Effective units			Costs	
Input	Completed in period	CWIP	Total EU	Total costs (£)	Costs per EU (£)
Process 1	7,600	800 (100%)	8,400	61,740	7.35
Conversion	7,600	200 (25%)	7,800	42,510	5.45
				104,250	12.80

The costs may now be attributed to the categories of output as follows:

			£	£
Completed units	7,600 × £12.80			97,280
Closing WIP:	Process 1	800 × £7.35	5,880	
	Conversion	200 × £5.45	1,090	
				6,970
				104,250

The process account will thus appear as follows:

Process 2 account

	No	£		No	£
Materials (process 1)	9,000	61,740	Normal loss	600	0
Labour		28,510	Finished goods	7,600	97,280
Overheads		14,000	Work-in-process	800	6,970
		104,250			104,250

7   Product X

(a) A joint product is a product acknowledged in its own right as a main product by virtue of its saleable value. The joint costs need to be apportioned between the joint products at the split-off point to obtain the cost of each of the products in order to value closing stocks and cost of sales.

A by-product is a product that arises incidentally to the main product and therefore will not have a sufficiently high saleable value in order for it to be treated as a main product. The costs incurred in the process are shared between the joint products alone. The by-products do not pick up a share of the costs. The sales value of the by-product at the split-off point is treated as a *reduction in costs* instead of an income.

(b) Costs to apportion = Joint process costs - Revenue from product C
= £272,926 - (2770 × £0.80)
= £270,710

Market value of output:

Product A - 16,000 × £6.10 = £97,600
Product B - 53,200 × £7.50 = £399,000
£496,600

Apportionment of joint process costs:

Product A = $270{,}710 \times \dfrac{97{,}600}{496{,}600}$ = £53,204

Product B = $270{,}710 \times \dfrac{399{,}000}{496{,}600}$ = £217,506

Cost per kg:

Product A = $\dfrac{53{,}204}{16{,}000}$ = £3.325 per kg

Product B = $\dfrac{217{,}506}{53{,}200}$ = £4.088 per kg

(c) Production costs:

	kilos	£
Material P	3,220	16,100
Material T	6,440	10,304
	9,660	26,404
Conversion costs		23,796
		50,200

Cost per kg of output = $\dfrac{50{,}200}{9{,}660 - 0.05 \times 9{,}660}$ = £5.47 per kg

Chapter 16 Solutions to practice questions

Process Account

	kgs	£		kgs	£
Raw Materials	3,220	26,404	Normal loss	483	0
Conversion costs	6,440	23,796	Finished Goods	9,130	49,943
			Abnormal Loss	47	257
	9,660	50,200		9,660	50,200

MULTIPLE CHOICE SOLUTIONS

1 Abnormal loss or gain is the balancing figure in the process account. Any gain will be a debit entry in the account.

The corresponding credit is in the abnormal gain account.

∴ **Correct answer: A**

2 Equivalent units are "Notional whole units representing uncompleted work".

[CIMA definition]

∴ **Correct answer: A**

3

	Units
Total input	13,500
Output complete	11,750
Closing work-in-progress	1,750

Valuation:

			£
Materials	:	1,750 × (£4.50 + £1.25)	10,062.50
Labour and overheads	:	1,750 × £2.50	4,375.00
			14,437.50

∴ **Correct answer: B**

4 The physical flow of units:

Opening WIP + Units started = Units completed + Losses + Closing WIP

2,000 + 24,000 = 19,500 + 3,500 (bal) + 3,000

Normal loss = 10% × 24,000 = 2,400
⇒ Abnormal loss = 1,100
                    3,500

	Completed in period	CWIP	AL	Total
Materials	19,500	3,000	1,100	23,600
Conversion	19,500	1,350 (45%)	1,100	21,950

∴ **Correct answer: D**

Chapter 9 Solutions

1   A Ltd

(a)

Fixed assets

	£000		£000
Balance b/f	1,000		

Share capital

	£000		£000
		Balance b/f	600

Profit and loss appropriation

	£000		£000
Balance c/f	87	Balance b/f	80
		Net profit (see (b))	7
	87		87
		Balance b/f	87

Provision for depreciation

	£000		£000
Balance c/f	425	Balance b/f	400
		Production overhead	25
	425		425
		Balance b/f	425

Debtors

	£000		£000
Balance b/f	600	Bank	380
Sales	310	Balance c/f	530
	910		910
Balance b/f	530		

Creditors

	£000		£000
Bank	170	Balance b/f	290
Balance c/f	230	Materials	110
	400		400
		Balance b/f	230

Cash

	£000		£000
Balance b/f	5	Bank	13
Sales	10	Balance c/f	2
	15		15
Balance b/f	2		

Bank

	£000		£000
Debtors	380	Balance b/f	300
Cash	13	Creditors	170
Balance c/f	377	Production overhead	60
		Administration overhead	40
		Selling overhead	20
		Bank interest	10
		Creditors for PAYE	60
		Wages control	66
		Wages control	20
		Salaries control	8
		Salaries control	16
	770		770
		Balance b/f	377

Bank interest

	£000		£000
Bank	10	Profit and loss	10

Creditors for PAYE and NICs

	£000		£000
Bank	60	Balance b/f	85
Balance c/f	71	Wages control	20
		Wages control	4
		Salaries control	4
		Salaries control	4
		Production overhead	9
		Administration overhead	3
		Selling overhead	2
	131		131
		Balance b/f	71

Materials

	£000		£000
Balance b/f	100	Work in progress	80
Creditors	110	Production overhead	20
		Balance c/f	110
	210		210
Balance b/f	110		

Work in progress

	£000		£000
Balance b/f	50	Finished goods stock	230
Materials	80	Balance c/f	120
Wages control	88		
Production overhead			
Control (150% of DW)	132		
	350		350
Balance b/f	120		

Chapter 16 Solutions to practice questions

Finished goods stock

	£000		£000
Balance b/f	20	Cost of sales	200
Work in progress	230	Balance c/f	50
	250		250
Balance b/f	50		

Wages control

	£000		£000
Bank - direct wages	66	Balance b/f	20
PAYE and NICs	20	Work in progress (bal fig)	88
Bank - indirect wages	20	Production overhead	24
PAYE and NICs	4		
Balance c/f	22		
	132		132
		Balance b/f	22

Production overhead

	£000		£000
Bank	60	Work in progress (88 × 150%)	132
Provision for depreciation	25	Profit and loss (under-absorption)	6
Materials	20		
National Insurance	9		
Wages control	24		
	138		138

Administration overhead

	£000		£000
Bank	40	Profit and loss	55
Salaries	12		
National Insurance	3		
	55		55

265

Selling overhead

	£000		£000
Bank	20	Profit and loss	42
Salaries	20		
National Insurance	2		
	42		42

Cost of sales

	£000		£000
Finished goods	200	Profit and loss	200

Sales

	£000		£000
Profit and loss	320	Debtors	310
		Cash	10
	320		320

Salaries control

	£000		£000
Bank - admin salaries	8	Admin overhead	12
PAYE and NI - Admin	4	Selling overhead	20
Bank - selling salaries	16		
PAYE and NI - selling	4		
	32		32

(b) **Trading and profit and loss account for October**

	£000		£000
Cost of sales	200	Sales	320
Gross profit c/f	120		
	320		320
Production overhead		Gross profit b/f	120
- under-absorbed	6		
Admin overhead	55		
Bank interest	10		
Selling overhead	42		
Net profit	7		
	120		120

Chapter 16 Solutions to practice questions

(c) **Trial balance as at 31 October**

	£000	£000
Fixed assets	1,000	
Provision for depreciation		425
Materials	110	
Work in progress	120	
Finished goods	50	
Debtors	530	
Creditors		230
Creditors for PAYE and NI		71
Wages control		22
Cash	2	
Bank		377
Share capital		600
Profit and loss appropriation		87
	1,812	1,812

2 Integrated accounts

(a) Integration of cost and financial accounting leads to considerable efficiencies in collection and analysis of information through one system rather than two and also ease of abstraction of information for all purposes. Errors may also be caught at an early stage rather than being found at the reconciliation stage.

(b) Items of costing information which are unlikely to be incorporated into financial accounts might be:

   (i)   rental charges made internally;

   (ii) interest on capital charges made internally;

   (iii) depreciation charges made in the cost records after the plant has been fully written down for financial accounting purposes.

(c) Items of financial information which are unlikely to be incorporated into costing accounts might be:

   (i)   appropriations of profit such as donations, taxation and dividends;

   (ii) capital gains or losses;

   (iii) fines imposed on the company.

(d) One alternative to integrated accounts is an interlocking system of separate cost and financial ledgers. Each of these ledgers contains a control account which represents the accounts held in the other and double entry is carried from one ledger to the other via these control accounts. At any time the "cost ledger control account" in the financial ledger and the "financial ledger control account" in the cost ledger should be mirror images of each other, thus effectively cancelling each other out for reporting purposes.

MULTIPLE CHOICE SOLUTIONS

1

Overhead Control		Work-in-Progress Control	
	Absorbed Overhead X	Absorbed Overhead X	

∴ **Correct answer: A**

2

Stores Control		Work-in-Progress Control	
	Direct Material X	Direct Material X	

∴ **Correct answer: A**

3

Work-In-Progress		Finished Goods	
	Finished Goods X	Work-in-Progress X	

∴ **Correct answer: B**

Chapter 10 Solutions

1 Materials

			£
Material A	100 kg × £5	=	500
Material B	50 kg × £15.50	=	775
	150 kg × £13	=	1,950
Material C	30 kg × £12	=	360
	20 kg × -£3	=	(60)
			3,525

Material A: This is not obsolete, so the stockholding is ignored and all 100 kg are charged at current price.

Material B: 50 kg must be bought so this is charged at market price. The 150 kg obsolete stock is charged at its opportunity cost, the NRV.

Material C: 30 kg must be bought so is charged at market price of £12.00. The 20 kg in stock is shown as a net benefit. This is because by using it the company actually saves the disposal cost of £3 per kg.

2 Labour

		£
Skilled labour		
500 hours × £NIL	=	NIL
2,000 hours × £8	=	16,000
		16,000
Unskilled labour		
550 hours × £5	=	2,750
600 hours × £10	=	6,000
		8,750
Total cost		£24,750

3 Overheads

	£
Variable overhead 1,600 hours × £5	8,000
Step up in fixed costs (two months salary × £1,500)	3,000
Total	11,000

4 Machine

The machine is obsolete. The financial accounting measures are irrelevant as they are sunk. The change brought about by using the machine on the contract is the opportunity cost of lost hire income.

Relevant cost of machine:

Three months × £1,000   =   £3,000

5 Research project

Costs and revenues of proceeding with the project.

	£
Costs to date of £150,000 sunk — ∴ ignore.	—
Materials — purchase price of £60,000 is also sunk. There is an opportunity benefit of the disposal costs saved.	5,000
Labour cost — the direct cost of £40,000 will be incurred regardless of whether the project is undertaken or not — and so is not relevant.	(90,000)
Opportunity cost of lost contribution = 150,000 − (100,000 − 40,000)	
Research staff costs	
Wages for the year	(60,000)
Increase in redundancy pay (35,000 − 15,000)	(20,000)
Equipment	
Deprival value if used in the project = disposal value	(8,000)
Disposal proceeds in one year	6,000
(All book values and depreciation figures are irrelevant)	
General building services	
Apportioned costs — irrelevant	
Opportunity costs of rental forgone	(7,000)
	(174,000)
Sales value of project	300,000
Increased contribution from project	126,000

Advice. Proceed with the project.

6 Finale

REPORT

To   Sales manager

From   Management accountant

Date   10 December 20X1

Subject Proposed supply of 500 units of phell

Introduction

This report deals with the relevant costs associated with the production of 500 phells. It provides calculations (see Appendix) and explanations, and states an absolute minimum selling price for the 500 units.

Relevant cost statement

The Appendix to this report contains a statement of relevant costs for the production of 500 phells. It shows a total figure for relevant costs of £143,940. This is the total of future cash outflows that it is estimated will occur if production goes ahead.

Reasons and bases for items included in relevant cost statement

(a) **Materials**

As the company has more than sufficient supply of Jey in stock for the contract and this stock is not used in normal production, then the relevant cost is its opportunity cost. In this case the best alternative forgone is its alternative use in the business as a substitute for Lig.

Kay is a raw material in regular usage by the company, so its relevant cost is its current replacement cost.

(b) **Labour**

Skilled labour is in short supply, and if used on the production of phells will need to be taken off other work. Its relevant cost is the wages for skilled labour operatives plus the lost contribution (net of skilled labour cost) on other work forgone.

A certain amount of unskilled labour (900 hours) is available at no incremental cost to the company (as it is already being paid and is not fully employed). There is no relevant cost for these hours. The additional hours required, involving overtime payments, have a relevant cost which is included in the statement, as it involves additional expenditure that would not otherwise be incurred by the company.

(c) **Overheads**

Variable overheads are included as relevant costs as they would represent additional cost if production of phells were undertaken. Only the additional fixed costs are included as relevant costs – the existing fixed overhead absorption rate is ignored. The additional costs of hiring special finishing machinery are included as a relevant cost.

(d) **Development costs**

Those costs already incurred are an example of past (sunk) costs and are not relevant. The future development costs involve additional expenditure and are included as relevant costs.

Minimum price

The absolute minimum price that the company should be prepared to accept for the 500 phells is £143,940. In that case cash inflows would just match estimated cash outflows. No profit would be earned but the company would not be out-of-pocket.

Conclusion

This report has concentrated on relevant cost and the calculation of an absolute minimum price. There may be other qualitative factors to be considered, which are difficult to quantify, in the process of making a final decision on whether to go ahead with the production of 500 phells and in the determination of the selling price.

Appendix

Statement of relevant costs for the production and sale of 500 phells

	£
Materials	
Jey (500 × 4) × (9.50 − 1.50)	16,000
Kay (500 × 6) × 14.50 × 1.04	45,240
Labour	
Skilled	
Wages (500 × 5) × 8	20,000
Opportunity cost (500 × 5) × 15	37,500
Unskilled [(500 × 3) − 900] × 6 × 1.5	5,400
Overheads	
Variable (500 × 2) × 8.75	8,750
Fixed	4,000
Machine hire (2 × 2,650)	5,300
Development costs	1,750
Total relevant costs	143,940

WORKING

Calculation of opportunity cost of skilled labour

Skilled labour cost per unit	=	24
∴ Number of hours per unit	=	$\dfrac{24}{8}$
	=	3 hours
∴ Contribution per unit	=	£45
∴ Contribution per skilled labour hour	=	15
∴ Opportunity cost of skilled labour	=	(500 × 5) × £15
	=	£37,500

7 Solution

	A	B	C	D	Total
Materials required	3 × 50,000 = 150,000	1 × 40,000 = 40,000	3 × 60,000 = 180,000	4 × 30,000 = 120,000	= 490,000
Labour hours required	1 × 50,000 = 50,000	1.5 × 40,000 = 60,000	0.5 × 60,000 = 30,000	1.5 × 30,000 = 45,000	= 185,000

Thus, labour hours is the limiting factor.

Calculate contribution per hour and rank:

	A	B	C	D
Price	50	42	45	55
Variable cost	(28)	(24)	(25)	(36)
	22	18	20	19
Labour hours per unit	1	1.5	0.5	1.5
Contribution per hour	£22	£12	£40	£12.67
Rank	2	4	1	3

Production schedule:

Product	Units	Hours used	Hours left	Contribution per unit	Total contribution
C	60,000	30,000	120,000	£20	1,200,000
A	50,000	50,000	70,000	£22	1,100,000
D	30,000	45,000	25,000	£19	570,000
B	16,666	24,999	1	£18	299,988
Total contribution					£3,169,988

8 Components

(a) Ignore fixed overheads as they are assumed to be non-avoidable.

Component	W £	X £	Y £	Z £
Variable cost of internal manufacture	22	33	18	44
External supplier's price	20	36	24	50
Saving on internal manufacture	(2)	3	6	6
Decision	Buy	Make	Make	Make

(b) W will be bought externally as it has already been established that this is the cheaper option. Limiting factor analysis will be used to find the cheapest plan for the remaining components.

	X	Y	Z
Saving on internal manufacture	£3	£6	£6
kgs of material per unit	1½	½	2
Saving per kg	£2	£12	£3
Ranking	3	1	2

Decision		Cost	kgs
1)	Buy 1,000 Ws	£20,000	10,000
2)	Make 7,000 Ys	£126,000	(3,500)
			6,500
3)	Make 3,250 Zs	£143,000	(6,500)
			NIL
4)	Buy 750 Zs	£37,500	
5)	Buy 2,000 Xs	£72,000	
Minimum cost		£398,500	

MULTIPLE CHOICE SOLUTIONS

1 A relevant cost or revenue is a future cash flow arising as a direct consequence of the decision under consideration.

∴ **Correct answer: C**

2 Use only variable cost to decide

	S £	T £	W £
Variable cost to make:	2.50	8.00	5.00
Price to buy:	4.00	7.00	5.50
Cheaper to:	Make	Buy	Make

Buy T only.

∴ **Correct answer: D**

3 If Q Ltd does not use V in the proposed project, it has two alternative uses:

Use 1: Scrap for £1.50 per kg

Use 2: Use for QX

	£
Cost of modification per unit of QX = £1 × 3	(3.00)
Saving per unit of QX = 2 × 4.50	9.00
Total saving	6.00

Saving per kg of V = $\frac{6}{3}$ = £2.00

They are giving up a saving of £2.00 for every kg of V used in the proposed project. This is the relevant cost.

∴ **Correct answer: C**

4 Work on contribution only, which is profit + fixed costs.

	H	J	K
Contribution per unit (£)	30	42	38
Labour cost (£)	10	15	10
Contribution per £ of labour	£3	£2.80	£3.80
Ranking	2	3	1

∴ **Correct answer: A**

Chapter 11 Solutions

1 CVP analysis

(a) Fixed cost = £6 × 20,000 = £120,000

Unit contribution = £20 − £12 = £8

∴ BEP $\dfrac{£120,000}{£8}$ = 15,000 units

(b) Contribution : sales ratio = $\dfrac{£8}{£20}$ = 0.4

∴ BEP (revenue) = $\dfrac{£120,000}{0.4}$ = £300,000 (= 15,000 × £20)

(c) Sales (units) = $\dfrac{£120,000 + £45,000}{£8}$ = 20,625 units

(d) Sales (revenue) = $\dfrac{£120,000 + £45,000}{0.4}$ = £412,500

Budgeted revenue = £20 × 20,000 = £400,000

∴ change = £12,500 = an increase of 3.125% (same as percentage increase in units)

(e) Margin of safety = 20,000 − 15,000 = 5,000 units

Margin of safety ratio = $\dfrac{20,000 - 15,000}{20,000} \times 100\%$ = 25%

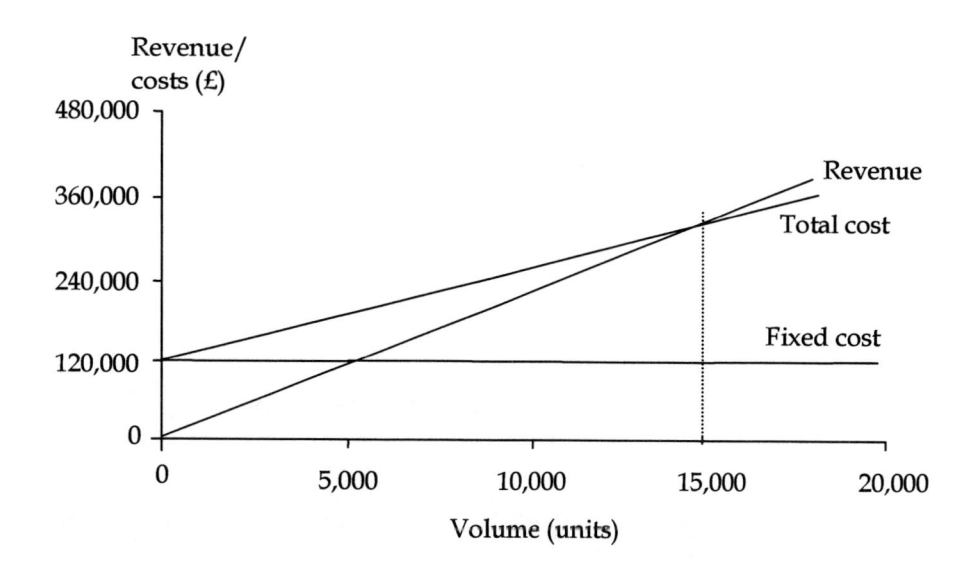

(g)

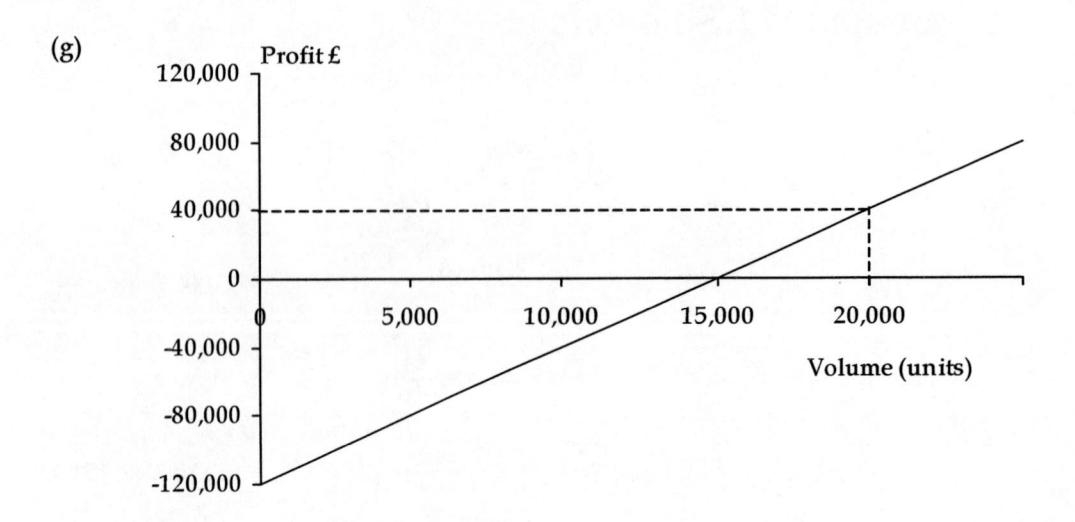

[Profit-volume chart: horizontal axis Volume (units) from 0 to beyond 20,000; vertical axis Profit £ from -120,000 to 120,000. Line crosses zero at 15,000 units, with dashed lines indicating £40,000 profit at 20,000 units.]

(The horizontal axis could show sales revenue.)

2 Polyvinylchloride

Part (a)

Profit figures

Contribution per unit	= £8 - £3.20	= £4.80
Fixed cost	= £47,000 + £25,000	= £72,000
Budgeted profit	= 20,000 × £4.80 - £72,000	= £24,000
Reduced profit (90%)	= 18,000 × £4.80 - £72,000	= £14,400
Increased profit (110%)	= 22,000 × £4.80 - £72,000	= £33,600

Part (b)

Break even point (monthly level)

$$\text{Break even point, BEP} = \frac{\text{Fixed costs}}{\text{Contribution per unit}}$$

$$= \frac{£72,000}{£4.80}$$

$$= 15,000 \text{ units}$$

In revenue terms, BEP = 15,000 × £8

= £120,000

Note: Alternatively this could be found via the C/S ratio.

C/S ratio = Contribution ÷ Sales (often as a percentage)

$$\text{In revenue terms, BEP} = \frac{\text{Fixed costs}}{\text{C/S ratio}}$$

$$= \frac{£72,000}{£4.80 / £8}$$

$$= £120,000$$

Margin of safety (MOS) = Budgeted volume - BEP

$$= 20,000 - 15,000$$

$$= 5,000 \text{ units}$$

$$\text{MOS ratio} = \frac{\text{MOS}}{\text{Budgeted volume}}$$

$$= \frac{5,000}{20,000} \times 100\%$$

$$= 25\%$$

(This shows that the activity level can fall from the original budget of £20,000 by 25% before a loss is made. Other formulae may be used for this ratio, but that shown here is the most appropriate.)

Part (c)

Target profit (monthly level)

$$\text{Required activity level} = \frac{\text{Fixed costs} + \text{Target profit}}{\text{Contribution/unit}}$$

$$= \frac{£72,000 + £20,000}{£4.80}$$

$$= 19,167 \text{ units}$$

Part (d)

Change in cost structure

Fixed costs   = £72,000 + (20,000 × £0.50) = £82,000

Contribution/unit   = £8 - (£1.50 + £1.00 + £0.20) = £5.30

		Revised £	*Original* £
Budgeted profit	= 20,000 × £5.30 - £82,000	24,000	24,000
Reduced profit	= 18,000 × £5.30 - £82,000	13,400	14,400
Increased profit	= 22,000 × £5.30 - £82,000	34,600	33,600

Changing a variable cost into a fixed cost means that if output rises the benefits are enhanced; on the other hand, if output falls the problems are exacerbated.

Break even point $= \dfrac{£82,000}{£5.30}$

$= 15,472$ units $\times £8 = £123,776$ in revenue

Part (e)

Break even charts and P/V charts

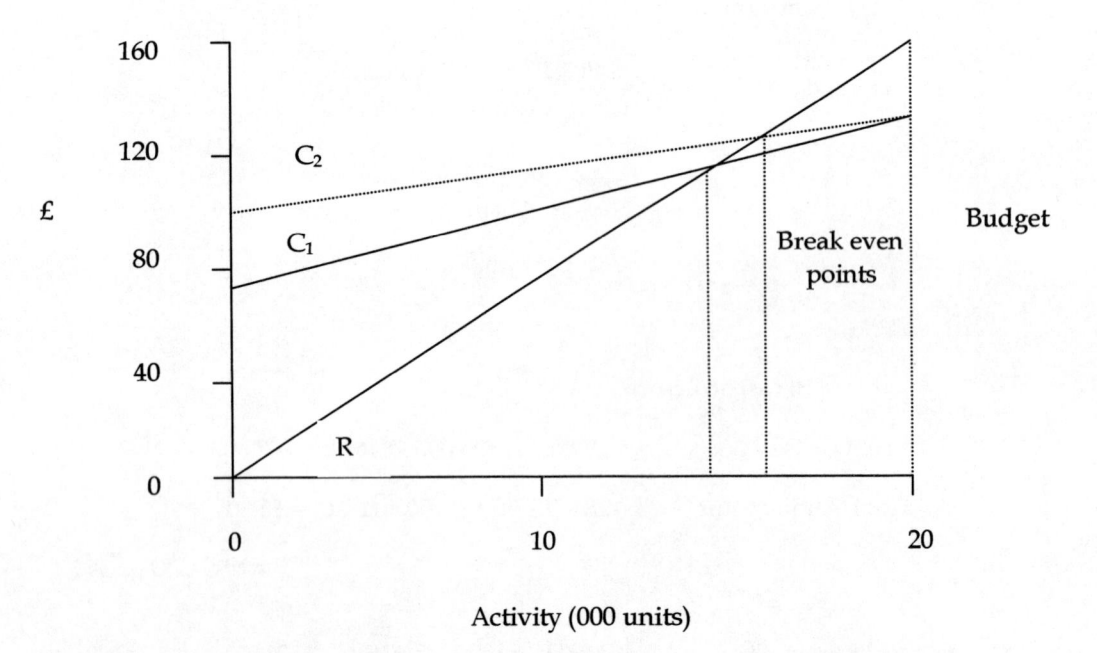

These are graphical representations of flexible budgets as determined in (a) and (d).

To plot these it is useful to find three points: fixed costs; break even points; costs, revenues and profits at budgeted volumes. These are listed or calculated below.

	Revised	*Original*
Fixed costs		72,000
£72,000 + (20,000 × £1.50)	102,000	
Break even point (in units) [102,000 ÷ (8 - 1.70)]	16,190	15,000
(in revenue)	£129,524	£120,000
Budgeted total costs		
£72,000 + (20,000 × £3.20)		£136,000
£102,000 + (20,000 × £1.70)	£136,000	
Budgeted revenue		
20,000 × £8	£160,000	£160,000
Budgeted profit	£24,000	£24,000

Break even chart

Profit volume chart

Profit £000

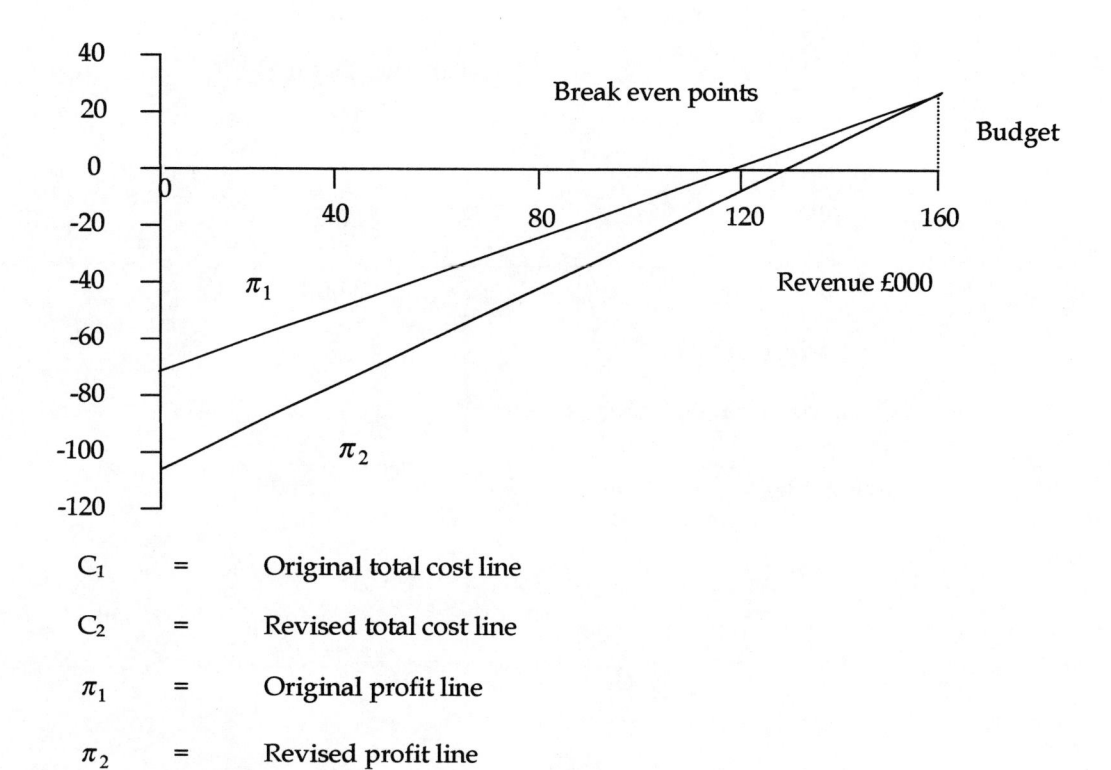

[Profit-volume chart showing two profit lines π_1 and π_2 against Revenue £000 on x-axis (0 to 160), with profit ranging from -120 to 40. π_1 starts at approximately -70 and reaches break even around 120; π_2 starts at approximately -105 and reaches break even around 130. Both lines meet at the Budget point at revenue 160. Break even points and Budget are labelled.]

C_1	=	Original total cost line
C_2	=	Revised total cost line
π_1	=	Original profit line
π_2	=	Revised profit line

MULTIPLE CHOICE SOLUTIONS

1   BEP (in £)   = $\dfrac{\text{Fixed Costs}}{\text{C/S ratio}}$

                    = $\dfrac{60{,}000}{0.4}$

                    =   £150,000

    BEP (in units)   = $\dfrac{£150{,}000}{£20}$

                    =   7,500

∴ **Correct answer: D**

2 BEP (in £) $= \dfrac{48,000}{0.4} = £120,000$

 Margin of safety = Actual sales − BEP

        = £140,000 − £120,000

        = £20,000

 in units, margin of safety $= \dfrac{£20,000}{£10}$

        = 2,000 units

∴ **Correct answer: A**

3 Unit contribution = £50 − £30 = £20

 Unit sales for £5,000 profit $= \dfrac{£25,000 + £5,000}{£20} = 1,500$

∴ **Correct answer: D**

Chapter 12 Solutions

1 Sales budget

Products	Q	R	S	Total
Sales (units)	10,000	8,000	11,000	
Price	£40.00	£36.00	£20.00	
Sales	£400,000	£288,000	£220,000	£908,000

2 Production budget

Products	Q	R	S
Budgeted sales	10,000	8,000	11,000
Opening stock	(5,000)	(3,000)	(6,000)
Closing stocks			
5,000 + (20% × 10,000)	7,000		
3,000 × 80%		2,400	
6,000 − (50% × 11,000)			500
Budgeted production	12,000	7,400	5,500

3 Materials usage budget

Materials		E kg	F kg	G kg	H kg	Total
Used in production of						
Product Q	12,000 × 4	48,000				
	12,000 × 2		24,000			
	12,000 × 1			12,000		
Product R	7,400 × 3½	25,900				
	7,400 × 1		7,400			
	7,400 × 2				14,800	
Product S	5,500 × 4				22,000	
Materials usage		73,900	31,400	12,000	36,800	
Price per kg		£3.00	£2.50	£4.00	£3.00	
Materials usage (£)		£221,700	£78,500	£48,000	£110,400	
Total materials usage						£458,600

4 Materials purchases budget

Materials	E kg	F kg	G kg	H kg	Total
Material usage	73,900	31,400	12,000	36,800	
Opening stock of materials	(20,000)	(18,000)	(6,000)	(4,000)	
Closing stock			6,000		
50% × 20,000	10,000				
20% × 31,400		6,280			
120% × 4,000				4,800	
Material purchases	63,900	19,680	12,000	37,600	
Price per kg	£3.00	£2.50	£4.00	£3.00	
Purchases (£)	£191,700	£49,200	£48,000	£112,800	
Total purchases					£401,700

5 Labour budget

Labour grade		I Hrs	II Hrs	
Worked on production of				
Product Q	1/4 × 12,000	3,000		
	10/60 × 12,000		2,000	
Product R	12/60 × 7,400	1,480		
	24/60 × 7,400		2,960	
Product S	30/60 × 5,500	2,750		
Labour hours		7,230	4,960	
Labour rates		£5.00	£8.00	
Labour costs		36,150	39,680	
Total				75,830

6 Overheads budget

	£
Variable overhead	
Grade I 7,230 hrs × 50p	3,615
Grade II 4,960 hrs × £1.00	4,960
	8,575
Fixed overhead	150,000
Total overhead	158,575

7 Profit and loss account

We begin by valuing stock.

Product Q

		£
Material E	4 kgs × £3.00	12.00
Material F	2 kgs × £2.50	5.00
Material G	1 kg × £4.00	4.00
Grade I Labour	¼ hr × £5.00	1.25
Grade II Labour	⅙ hr × £8.00	1.33
Variable overhead		
I	¼ hr × £0.50	0.13
II	⅙ hr × £1.00	0.17
Stock valuation per unit		23.88

Product R

		£
Material E	3.5 kgs × £3.00	10.50
Material F	1 kg × £2.50	2.50
Material H	2 kg × £3.00	6.00
Grade I Labour	⅕ hr × £5.00	1.00
Grade II Labour	⅖ hr × £8.00	3.20
Variable overhead		
I	⅕ hr × £0.50	0.10
II	⅖ hr × £1.00	0.40
Stock valuation per unit		23.70

Chapter 16 Solutions to practice questions

Product S   £
Material H   4 kgs × £3.00   12.00
Grade I Labour   ½ hr × £5.00   2.50
Variable overhead ½ hr × 50p   0.25

Stock valuation per unit   14.75

Product	Q £	R £	S £	Total £
Opening stocks				
5,000 × £23.88	119,400			
3,000 × £23.70		71,100		
6,000 × £14.75			88,500	279,000
Closing stocks				
7,000 × £23.88	167,160			
2,400 × £23.70		56,880		
500 × £14.75			7,375	231,415

B plc   Budgeted profit and loss account for period 1

	£	£
Sales		908,000
Variable cost of sales		
Opening stock	279,000	
Material usage	458,600	
Labour	75,830	
Variable overhead	8,575	
	822,005	
Less Closing stock	(231,415)	
		590,590
Contribution		317,410
Fixed overheads		(150,000)
Profit		167,410

Note. An alternative presentation could show materials purchases adjusted for opening and closing stocks of raw materials on the face of the profit and loss account.

8 Cash budget

We begin by analysing what cash flows arise from a typical £100 of sales.

	£	%
Cash sales		
10% × £100 × 85%	8.50	8.5
Credit sales		
Within one month £100 × 90% × 40% × 95%	34.20	34.2
Within two months £100 × 90% × 45%	40.50	40.5
Within three months £100 × 90% × 10%	9.00	9.0
Cash received	92.20	92.2
Discounts and bad debts	7.80	7.8
Sales values	100.00	100

Cash flow workings

As K plc is an established business we must take into account cash flows from sales prior to January. These result from debtors on the balance sheet at 1st January.

	Jan £	Feb £	Mar £
Cash received in month			
Jan £15,000 × 8.5%	1,275		
Feb £12,000 × 8.5%		1,020	
Mar £10,000 × 8.5%			850
Cash received one month after month of sale			
Dec £5,000 × 34.2%	1,710		
Jan £15,000 × 34.2%		5,130	
Feb £12,000 × 34.2%			4,104
Cash received two months after month of sale			
Nov £10,000 × 40.5%	4,050		
Dec £5,000 × 40.5%		2,025	
Jan £15,000 × 40.5%			6,075
Cash received three months after month of sale			
Oct £8,000 × 9%	720		
Nov £10,000 × 9%		900	
Dec £5,000 × 9%			450
Total cash flow	7,755	9,075	11,479

9 Cash paid to suppliers

	Sept Units	Oct Units	Nov Units	Dec Units	Jan Units	Feb Units	Mar Units	Apr Units	May Units
Sales	20,000	25,000	22,000	15,000	16,000	20,000	22,000	27,000	30,000
Closing stock	36,000	29,500	23,000	26,000	31,000	35,500	42,000		
Opening stock		(36,000)	(29,500)	(23,000)	(26,000)	(31,000)	(35,500)		
Production		18,500	15,500	18,000	21,000	24,500	28,500		
Material usage (kg)		74,000	62,000	72,000	84,000	98,000	114,000		
Closing stock (kg)		134,000	156,000	182,000	212,000				
Opening stock (kg)			(134,000)	(156,000)	(182,000)				
Purchases (kg)			84,000	98,000	114,000				
Price per kg			£3.00	£3.00	£3.00				
Purchases (£)			£252,000	£294,000	£342,000				
Cashflow					£252,000	£294,000	£342,000		

10 ABC Ltd

(a)

	June £	July £	August £
Material usage	8,000	9,000	10,000
Add closing stock	3,500	6,000	4,000
Less opening stock	(5,000)	(3,500)	(6,000)
Purchases	6,500	11,500	8,000

(b)

Cash Budget: June - August

	June £	July £	August £
Receipts of cash			
Cash sales	4,500	5,000	6,000
Credit sales	29,500	40,500	45,000
	34,000	45,500	51,000

Cash payments			
Wages	12,000	13,000	14,500
Overheads*	6,500	7,000	8,000
Direct materials	6,500	11,500	8,000
Taxation	-	25,000	-
	25,000	56,500	30,500
Net cash flow for month	9,000	(11,000)	20,500
Opening balance	11,750	20,750	9,750
Closing balance	20,750	9,750	30,250

*These figures exclude depreciation, but remember that £6,500 is to be PAID in June, which means that depreciation is already excluded.

(c) The benefit of cash budgets are that they enable management to plan for the future. If the cash budget shows a negative balance at the month end it enables financing to be arranged (eg overdraft), whereas if a high cash balance is forecast then various investment strategies may be investigated.

MULTIPLE CHOICE SOLUTIONS

1   The master budget comprises the budgeted cashflow, budgeted profit and loss account and budgeted balance sheet.

∴ **Correct answer: B**

2   In September, creditors will be paying from June, July and August as follows:

	£
June : 12% × £35,000	4,200
July : 25% × £40,000	10,000
August : 60% × £60,000 × 98%	35,280
	£49,480

∴ **Correct answer: C**

Chapter 13 Solutions

1 Restaurant

We now redraft the operating statement and memo in a form which is more likely to have a positive effect on the performance of the restaurant supervisor.

MEMORANDUM

To: Restaurant supervisor
From: Management accountant
Subject: Performance report
Date: 5 April

I enclose a performance report for your department for the three months to the end of March. The aim of this report is to aid in the efficient use of resources by providing information as to which costs differ from their expected level (the original budget figures) and why.

The original budget figures were based on last year's costs; I would like to meet you next Tuesday to discuss whether these figures are sensible targets for this year. I have tried to make the budget more realistic by adjusting the costs upwards to reflect the increased use of the restaurant (the flexed budget figures). I would welcome any ideas you have as to:

- other adjustments that are necessary to the figures in this report; and
- how the budgets should be established for future periods.

Operating statement

	Note	Fixed budget £	Flexed budget £	Actual £	Variance flexed budget to actual £
No of meals served		32,500	39,000	39,000	
Controllable (variable) costs	3				
Food and other consumables		97,500	117,000	111,540	5,460 F
Labour - hourly paid	2	15,000	18,000	16,500	1,500 F
Power		8,500	10,200	9,250	950 F
Breakages		1,000	1,200	800	400 F
		122,000	146,400	138,090	8,310 F
Allocated (fixed) costs	1				
Overheads		21,000	21,000	24,000	3,000 A
		143,000	167,400	162,090	5,310 F

F = favourable variance

A = adverse variance

The restaurant is evidently being well managed, with many more meals served than in the same period last year, whilst costs have risen by a small proportion. Following our discussion on Tuesday, the performance report, with any agreed amendments, will be reviewed at the meeting of the management committee on 15 April; please ensure you attend to participate in the discussion and explain the reasons for the variances.

Notes to the operating statement:

1. The supervisor is not in a position to influence the level of allocated overhead which is influenced by the chosen method of allocation to each department. These have been separately reported in the operating statement.

2. The supervisor cannot be held responsible for the fact that her own salary differs from the budget. Indeed becoming aware that she has been paid less than anticipated is likely to alienate her from senior management. For this reason, her salary has been excluded from the report.

3. Calculation of the flexed budget:

    All costs other than allocated overheads have been treated as fully variable costs (as there is insufficient information to use the high low method) and calculated as follows:

    $$\text{Cost} \times \frac{39,000}{32,500}$$

    For example: Power costs = $8,500 \times \frac{39,000}{32,500} = 10,200$

MULTIPLE CHOICE SOLUTIONS

1. CIMA definition of a flexible budget:

    "A budget which, by recognising different cost behaviour patterns, is designed to change as volume of activity changes."

    ∴ **Correct answer: C**

2.

	£
Actual expenditure	300,000
less fixed costs	87,000
Actual variable cost	213,000
less overspend	18,000
Budgeted variable cost	195,000

Variable cost per unit = $\frac{195,000}{162,500} = £1.20$

∴ **Correct answer: A**

3.

Overhead	Total Fixed Cost £	Unit Variable Cost £
Direct materials	0	4.00
Direct labour	0	3.50
Production overhead - department 1(W1)	3,600	2.40
Production overhead - department 2 (W2)	4,000	0
	7,600	9.90

∴ **Correct answer: D**

(W1)

			£
At 1,000 units, total overhead	= £6 × 1,000		= 6,000
At 2,000 units, total overhead	= £4.20 × 2,000		= 8,400
Change in overhead			2,400

Change per unit = $\dfrac{£2,400}{1,000}$ = £2.40

At 1,000 units, fixed cost = £6,000 − (1,000 × £2.40) = £3,600

(W2)

		£
At 1,000 units, total overhead	= £4 × 1,000	= 4,000
At 2,000 units, total overhead	= £2 × 2,000	= 4,000

∴ Overhead is a fixed cost.

Chapter 14 Solutions

1   K Ltd

(a)   **Standard Cost Card**

	£
Direct materials 50m^2 @ £3.20	160.00
Direct labour Department A – 24 hrs @ £5.10	122.40
Department B – 18 hrs @ £4.80	86.40
PRIME COST	**368.80**
Variable production overheads:	
Department A – $24 \times \dfrac{45}{30}$	36.00
Department B – $18 \times \dfrac{25}{25}$	18.00
VARIABLE PRODUCTION COST	**422.80**
Fixed Production overheads – $\dfrac{36{,}000}{900}$	40.00
TOTAL PRODUCTION COST	**462.80**
Selling, Distribution and Administration Overheads:	
$\dfrac{27{,}000}{900}$	30.00
TOTAL COST	**492.80**

(b) To calculate the selling price, look at the relationship between price, cost and profit. Remember profit is 20% of price, which means that cost is 80% of price. As cost is £492.80, we have the relationship:

492.80 = 80% of price

$$\therefore \text{price} = \frac{£492.80}{0.80} = £616.00$$

Chapter 15 Solutions

1   Materials costs

	£	£
Actual usage at actual price (actual expenditure)		41,756
Price variance	1,144 F	
Actual usage at standard price		
2,860 litres × £15/litre		42,900
Usage variance	900 A	
Standard wage at standard price		
(Flexed budget expenditure)		
700 × 4 litres × £15/litre (= 700 × £60)		42,000
Total variance	244 F	

Note that the original budgeted production volume of Product A is not used in the calculation of materials variances. This is because we are dealing with a *variable cost* and therefore the budget is flexed to reflect *actual* production volume.

2   Labour costs

	£	£
Actual hours at actual rate (expenditure)		210,000
Rate variance	10,000 A	
Actual hours at standard rate		
40,000 × £5.00		200,000
Efficiency variance	14,000 A	
Flexed budget expenditure		
= Standard hours at standard rate		
6,200 × 6 hrs × £5/hr		186,000
Total variance	24,000 A	

Once again budgeted output is ignored as a variable cost must be flexed.

3   Variable overheads

	£	£
Actual hours at actual rate (expenditure)		107,500
Expenditure variance	9,500 F	
Actual hours at standard absorption rate		
39,000 × £3.00		117,000
Efficiency variance	4,200 A	
Flexed budget expenditure		
9,400 × £12.00		112,800
Total variance	5,300 F	

4 Product D

Materials variances

	£	£
Actual expenditure (given)		136,000
Price variance	11,500 F	
Actual usage × standard price 295,000 × 50p		147,500
Usage variance	8,300 A	
Flexed budget expenditure 23,200 × £6.00		139,200
Labour variances		
Actual expenditure (given)		340,000
Rate variance	18,000 A	
Actual usage × standard rate per hour 46,000 × £7.00		322,000
Efficiency variance	2,800 F	
Flexed budget expenditure 23,200 × £14.00		324,800
Variable overhead variances		
Actual expenditure (given)		75,000
Variance	5,400 A	
Flexed budget expenditure 23,200 × £3.00		69,600

Operating statement

			£
Standard variable cost of actual production (23,200 × £23)			533,600
Variable cost variances			
Materials	F	A	
Price	11,500		
Usage		8,300	
Labour			
Rate		18,000	
Efficiency	2,800		
Variable overhead		5,400	
	14,300	31,700	17,400
Actual variable production cost			551,000
Check on actual costs			
Materials			136,000
Labour			340,000
Variable overhead			75,000
			551,000

5 Fixed

	£	£
Actual expenditure		38,000
Expenditure variance	2,000 A	
Budgeted expenditure 800 × £45		36,000
Volume variance	13,500 A	
Flexed budget expenditure 500 × £45.00		22,500

6 Columbus Ltd

Materials

		£
Actual expenditure		7,700
Price variance	£1,100 F	
Actual usage × standard price 11,000 × $\left(\dfrac{£8,000}{10,000}=80p\right)$		8,800
Usage variance	£400 A	
Flexed budget expenditure $\left(\dfrac{42,000}{40,000}\times £8,000\right)$		8,400

Notes

- The standard price per kg is arrived at from dividing the original budgeted materials cost by the budgeted number of kgs.

- The flexed budget is arrived at by flexing the whole of the original budget onto an actual basis.

Labour

		£
Actual expenditure		10,950
Rate variance	£350 A	
Actual hours × standard rate 530 × $\left(\dfrac{£10,000}{500}=£20\right)$		10,600
Efficiency variance	£100 A	
Flexed budget expenditure $\left(10,000\times\dfrac{42,000}{40,000}\right)$		10,500

Variable overhead

		£
Actual expenditure		5,350
Expenditure variance	£50 A	
Actual hours × standard rate/hour 530 × £10		5,300
Efficiency variance	£50 A	
Flexed budget expenditure 5,000 × $\dfrac{42,000}{40,000}$		5,250

Fixed overhead

Note: The absorption rate is calculated from the original budget $\dfrac{£30,000}{40,000}$ = 75p/unit

		£
Actual expenditure		36,000
Expenditure variance	£6,000 A	
Budgeted expenditure		30,000
Volume variance	£1,500 F	
Actual volume @ standard cost 42,000 × 75p		31,500

Total sales margin variance

	£	£
Budgeted profit from sales		7,000
Actual profit from sales when cost of sales is valued at standard cost:		
Actual sales 42,000 × £1.52	63,840	
Standard cost of sales 42,000 × £1.325 (W)	(55,650)	
		8,190
Sales margin variance		1,190 F

WORKING

Standard cost per unit

$$\frac{£8,000 + £10,000 + £5,000 + £30,000}{40,000} = £1.325/\text{unit}$$

Operating statement

	£
Budgeted profit £(1.50 − 1.325 × 40,000)	7,000
Total sales margin variance	1,190 F
Actual revenue less standard costs	8,190

Cost variances

	F £	A £	
Materials price	1,100		
Materials usage		400	
Labour rate		350	
Labour efficiency		100	
Variable overhead expenditure		50	
Variable overhead efficiency		50	
Fixed overhead expenditure		6,000	
Fixed overhead volume	1,500		
	2,600	6,950	4,350 A
Actual profit			£3,840

7   Flashbulb

Cost variances

Materials

	£	£
Actual expenditure		180,000
Price variance	60,000 F	
Actual usage × standard price 480,000 × £0.50		240,000
Usage variance	14,000 A	
Flexed budget expenditure 452,000 × £0.50		226,000

Chapter 16 Solutions to practice questions

Labour

	£	£
Actual expenditure		550,000
Rate variance	50,000 A	
Actual hours × standard rate 100,000 × £5.00		500,000
Efficiency variance	65,000 F	
Flexed budget expenditure 452,000 × £1.25		565,000

Variable overhead

	£	£
Actual expenditure		120,000
Expenditure variance	20,000 A	
Actual hours × standard rate per hour 100,000 × £1		100,000
Efficiency variance	13,000 F	
Flexed budget expenditure 452,000 × £0.25		113,000

Fixed overhead

	£	£
Actual expenditure		120,000
Expenditure variance	5,000 F	
Budgeted expenditure 500,000 × £0.25		125,000
Volume variance	12,000 A	
Flexed budget overhead 452,000 × £0.025		113,000

Total sales margin variance

Budgeted profit from sales		£125,000
Actual profit from sales when cost of sales is valued at standard cost:		
Actual sales: 452,000 × £3.00 =	£1,356,000	
Standard cost of sales: 452,000 × £2.25 =	£1,017,000	
		£339,000
		£214,000 F

Operating statement

	£
Budgeted profit (£2.50 - £2.25) × 500,000	125,000
Total sales margin variance	214,000 F
Actual revenue less standard costs	339,000

Cost variances

	F	A	
Materials price	60,000		
Materials usage		14,000	
Labour rate		50,000	
Labour efficiency	65,000		
Variable overhead expenditure		20,000	
Variable overhead efficiency	13,000		
Fixed overhead expenditure	5,000		
Fixed overhead volume		12,000	
	143,000	96,000	47,000
Actual profit			386,000

	£
Proof of actual profit	
Revenue (452,000 × £3.00)	1,356,000
Costs (180,000+550,000+120,000+120,000)	(970,000)
Profit	386,000

MULTIPLE CHOICE SOLUTIONS

1 Labour efficiency variance = (Standard hours − Actual hours) × Standard rate

A favourable efficiency variance of £7,800 represents a time saving of $\frac{£7,800}{£6.50}$ = 1,200 hours

Thus standard hours must be 17,500 + 1,200 = 18,700 hours

∴ **Correct answer: D**

2 Material price variance = Actual cost of actual purchases − Standard cost of actual purchases

	£
Actual cost of 6,850 kgs =	21,920
Add: Favourable price variance	1,370
Standard cost of 6,850 kgs	23,290
Thus standard cost = $\frac{23,290}{6,850}$ =	£3.40

∴ **Correct answer: D**

3 Using "grid" layout:

	£	£
Actual hours at actual rate		79,893
Rate variance	807 F	
Actual hours at standard rate 13,450 × £6		80,700
Efficiency variance	300 A	
Standard hours at standard rate 3,350 × 4 × 6		80,400

∴ **Correct answer: D**

4 $\quad$ OAR $= \dfrac{\text{Budgeted Overheads}}{\text{Budgeted Units}} = \dfrac{100{,}000}{20{,}000} =$ £5

Volume variance = Budgeted Overheads − Standard Overheads (for actual output)

$$= £100{,}000 - (19{,}500 \times £5)$$

$$= 100{,}000 - 97{,}500$$

$$= £2{,}500 \text{ A}$$

Note: Adverse because fewer units made to absorb overheads.

∴ **Correct answer: B**

5

	£
Total overheads	8,500
Variable = 800 × £6	4,800
Fixed	3,700

Variances - fixed overheads

		£
Actual expenditure		3,700
Expenditure variance	100 A	
Budgeted expenditure = 900 × 4		3,600
Volume variance	400 A	
Standard expenditure = 800 × 4		3,200

∴ **Correct answer: D**

6

Raw Materials Control	Raw Materials Price Variance
| Adv variance X	Adv Variance X |

Price variance is shown in the materials account, not work-in-progress.

∴ **Correct answer: D**

Index

Abnormal gain	97
Abnormal loss	96
Absorption costing	39
Administrative overheads	116
Attainable standards	200
Attendance	33
Basic standards	200
Batch costing	75
Bin card	13
Bonus payments	34
Breakeven analysis	155
Breakeven chart	156
Breakeven point	155
Budgetary control	189
Budgetary control report	193
Budgeting	168
By-products	109
Cash budgets	179
Contract	76
Contract price	77
Contribution	63
Control cycle	190
Conversion costs	104
Cost behaviour	4
Cost centre	8
Cost classification	3
Cost ledger control account	114
Cost unit	8
Cost volume profit analysis	153
Decision making	134
Defective goods	13
Direct cost	4
Direct expenses	76
EOQ formula	22
Equivalent units	100
Feedback	190
Feedforward	190
FIFO method	24
Fixed and flexible budgets	190
Fixed costs	5, 135
Fixed overhead variances	216
Forseeable losses	80
Functional budgets	172
Goods received note	12
Halsey and Rowan bonus schemes	36
High Low Method	6
Historical cost	135
Holding costs	20
Ideal standards	200
Idle time	34
Incentive schemes	34
Incremental budgeting	171
Incremental cost	136
Indirect costs	4
Indirect materials	12
Integrated accounts	114
Interlocking accounts	114
Internal service activities	88
Inventory	16
Job costing	74
Joint products	109
Labour	31
Labour budget	176
Labour rate variance	211
LIFO method	25
Master budgets	173
Material price variance	208
Material transfers	23
Material usage variance	208
Materials	11
Materials purchases budget	175
Materials usage budget	174
Motivation	169
Normal losses	95
Opportunity cost	135
Ordering costs	20
Overhead Absorption Rate	42
Overheads	40
Overheads budget	177
Overtime	32
Payment	13
Periodic and continuous stock taking	16
Periodic review	18
Planning	168
Pricing issues	24
Prime cost	4
Principal budget factor	172

Process costing 93
Production budget 173
Profit centre... 8
Profit/volume chart.................................. 158
Purchase order.. 12
Purchase requisition 12

Reciprocal servicing.................................. 54
Relevant cost.. 134
Remuneration methods............................ 31
Reorder level system 18
Reorder quantity 19
Retentions... 77

Sales budget... 173
Sales profit (margin) variance 218
Scrap value... 97
Semi-variable cost 5
Service cost centres 52
Service costing.................................... 87, 89
Specific order costing 73
Standard cost 199
Standard cost bookkeeping 221
Standard setting 199
Stepped fixed cost....................................... 6
Stock control card..................................... 14
Stock levels 18
Stock losses.. 17
Stores record card 14
Stores transactions 76
Sunk costs.. 135
Supplier's invoice...................................... 12

Time sheets.. 33

Users of accounting information 2

Variable costs..................................... 5, 135
Variable production overhead cost
    variances.. 212
Variance analysis 205

Weighted average method 26
Work certified.. 77
Work in process....................................... 100
Work in progress control account 115

Zero based budgeting............................. 171

Exam Text Review Form

CIMA PAPER 2 TEXT – MANAGEMENT ACCOUNTING FUNDAMENTALS

We hope that you have found this Text stimulating and useful and that you now feel confident and well-prepared for your examinations.

We would be grateful if you could take a few moments to complete the questionnaire below, so we can assess how well our material meets your needs. There's a prize for four lucky students who fill in one of these forms from across the Syllabus range and are lucky enough to be selected!

	Excellent	*Adequate*	*Poor*
Depth and breadth of technical coverage			
Appropriateness of coverage to examination			
Presentation			
Level of accuracy			

Did you spot any errors or ambiguities? Please let us have the details below.

Page	**Error**

Thank you for your feedback.

Please return this form to:

The Financial Training Company Limited
Unit 22J
Wincombe Business Park
Shaftesbury
Dorset SP7 9QJ

Student's name: ....

Address: ....

....

....